THE WAR OF THE FISTS

D0037398

Anonymous woodcut of the *Guerra dei pugni* with
arms of Giovanni Corner: frontispiece in Basnatio
Sorsi's "Scherzi e Descrittione piacevole della Guerra
dei Pugni tra Nicolotti, e Castellani. Quaderni in
Lingua Venetiana" (Venice, 1663). (Museo Correr,
Archivio Fotografico, M. 7089)

The War
of the Fists

*Popular Culture and Public Violence
in Late Renaissance Venice*

ROBERT C. DAVIS

New York   Oxford
OXFORD UNIVERSITY PRESS
1994

For Donn and Fred

Oxford University Press

Oxford New York Toronto
Delhi Bombay Calcutta Madras Karachi
Kuala Lumpur Singapore Hong Kong Tokyo
Nairobi Dar es Salaam Cape Town
Melbourne Auckland Madrid

and associated companies in
Berlin Ibadan

Copyright © 1994 by Oxford University Press, Inc.

Published by Oxford University Press, Inc.,
200 Madison Avenue, New York, New York 10016

Oxford is a registered trademark of Oxford University Press

All rights reserved. No part of this publication may be reproduced,
stored in a retrieval system, or transmitted, in any form or by any means,
electronic, mechanical, photocopying, recording, or otherwise,
without the prior permission of Oxford University Press.

Library of Congress Cataloging-in-Publication Data
Davis, Robert C. (Robert Charles), 1948–
The war of the fists : popular culture and public violence in late
Renaissance Venice / Robert C. Davis.
p. cm. Includes bibliographical references and index.
ISBN 0-19-508403-9. — ISBN 0-19-508404-7 (pbk.)
1. Venice (Italy)—Social life and customs.
2. Battles—Italy—Venice—History—17th century.
3. Bridges—Italy—Venice—History—17th century. I. Title.
DG675.6.D38 1994
945'.31—dc20 93-20591

2 4 6 8 9 7 5 3 1

Printed in the United States of America
on acid-free paper

ACKNOWLEDGMENTS

A few years ago, shortly after I had discovered the pleasures and challenges of the Chronicle of the *pugni* in Venice's Museo Correr, I mentioned to a more experienced colleague how much I would enjoy the chance to write my own history of the city's *battagliole*. His immediate response was, in so many words: Why? Who would ever want to read about such a tasteless topic? Admittedly, most of those who have approached the *Serenissima* over the years have done so with more decorous themes in mind than this jumbled plebeian world of bridges, brawls, and boozing local heroes: there is after all a persistent reverence that Venetianists generally assume when entering their chosen field. Happily, as I have explored and worked out the principal themes of the *War of the Fists*, I discovered that my colleagues in Venetian history, and indeed in social history generally, were as likely to be as fascinated and attracted as I was by this cult of popular violence and public disorder that flourished for so many centuries in the heart of the world's Most Serene Republic. It is largely due to their constant encouragement, support, and criticism—their understanding of the central role of popular culture in an absolutist society—that this book has been possible.

I would like to thank particularly Theodore K. Rabb, Guido Ruggiero, and Brendan Dooley, who read the preliminary drafts of this work and who offered me the benefit of experiences much wider than my own in a whole range of historical fields. Their taking the time and effort to offer criticism of my ideas and approaches seems to me to reflect modern academic collegiality at its best and most fruitful. I would also like to thank a number of Venetian archivists, without whose generous assistance neither I nor the great majority of visiting foreign scholars would ever have much hope in getting our research done: especially kind to me have been Michela Dal Borgo and Alessandra Sambo at the Archivio di Stato; and Alberto Lo Cascio, Franca Lugato, and Riccardo Monni at the Biblioteca of the Museo Correr. For her continual moral support, her often inspiring ideas, and her artwork, I am also very much in debt to my wife, Cindy: not only has she listened patiently and sympathetically to my constant ramblings about Venetian popular culture, but she has also drawn the maps through which I have attempted to explain it.

I am especially grateful to generous institutional support, without which this work would only have been completed much more slowly and with more difficulty. Florida Atlantic University's College of Humanities not only made available to me extensive microfilm and computer support, but also funded two summers' research in Venice that helped expand the original scope of this project. By offering me a year's resident fellowship, the Institute for Advanced Study helped bring this study to completion and give it its present form. Perhaps no more ideal environment has yet been envisioned for the promotion of free scholarly work and thought than that provided by the Institute; it allowed me to write up my research and meet interested colleagues in a range of allied fields. I would like to express my particular appreciation for having the chance to present early versions of chapters of this work in the medieval seminar, organized and directed by Giles Constable and Walter Simons, at the Institute's School of History. I would also like to thank those fellows of the School who read and offered so much helpful and useful criticism: Hillary Ballon, John Williams, Paul Hyams, Katherine Tachau, Alexander Knysh, and John Beldon Scott.

While at the Institute I was also able to call on Roberto and Maria José Rusconi for their generous advice in translating the Venetian dialect poetry that I have used throughout this work. Thanks to the Rusconis, it has been possible to turn this evocative yet often frustratingly obscure doggerel verse into an English that faithfully follows the original, and sometimes even maintains its rhythmic sense. My thanks, too, to Richard Jackson for freely giving his time in an attempt to make me computer literate; and to Patricia Labalme and Kenneth Setton for their hospitality and devotion to Venetian scholarship. Above all thanks to Gary Macy, whose tireless work and enthusiasm always reminded me that scholarship is a joy and a privilege, and that historians and scholars should ultimately research and write with the goal of making their discoveries available and understandable to all the world.

Columbus, Ohio   R. C. D.
June 1993

CONTENTS

THE WAR OF THE FISTS

INTRODUCTION

The Chronicler's Art

O Marte, O Baco, o fradei zurai!
D'arme e del chiuchio tuti do' paroni. . . .
Donème grazia, cari compagnoni,
Che mi possa cantar le guere, i fati
De Castelani, Canaruoli, e Gnati!

O Mars, O Bacchus, O sworn brothers!
Lords of both arms and of boozing. . . .
Grant me the gift, dear exalted companions,
That I might sing of the war and the deeds
Of the Castellani, Cannaruoli, and Gnatti![1]

Sometime around 1669 or 1670 a Venetian essayist set out to write an account of the festivities that the Republic of Venice had put on in 1574 to honor the visit of the French king Henry III. His identity remains unknown: possibly he was a gentleman, but more likely he made his living as a lawyer, notary, or professional writer.[2] His commemorating an event nearly a century old was not unusual: cultivated men and women of his era were fond of reading and writing such histories, and this royal visit had certainly been ostentatiously splendid enough to tempt a patriotic Venetian to invoke it yet again. What was odd about this anonymous narrator was that he skipped altogether over the events that had fascinated most earlier writers—the sumptuous regattas, floats, masqued balls, and theatrical performances put on for the king's three-day visit—and fixed instead on a single event: the great war with sticks, or *guerra di canne*, staged the final day by two opposing factions of Venetian artisans on a city bridge.[3] It was rough, burlesque entertainment for a king: a mock battle, or *battagliola*, in which mobs of working men, decked out in helmets and shields, pummeled each other with wooden sticks for about two hours in a chaotic brawl. For our narrator, however, this melee represented the high point of the entire celebration, an event "so famous, memorable and without precedent" that it deserved recounting in every detail: not just the clash itself, but also all the elaborate preparations and stratagems necessary for collecting, organizing, and sending to battle the hundreds of combatants. To tell the whole story took him perhaps twenty-five thousand words, crammed (with numerous amendments, additions, and cancellations) into nearly fifty-three quarto pages.[4]

Spilling so much ink over a workers' brawl that had taken place one Monday afternoon ninety-six years earlier may seem a quixotic task even for the often eccentric literary world of late Republican Venice. Yet upon completing his first effort, the author was apparently so satisfied with the results that he promptly decided to undertake a much more ambitious project: that of telling the story of his city's bridge battles from 1574 down to his own day. Wars fought with sticks and shields, it was true, had long since been outlawed and abandoned, but Venetian artisans were still regularly gathering at bridges to battle bare-handed, waging the so-called *guerre dei pugni*, or wars of the fists, with as much enthusiasm as ever. He would, he proclaimed, broadcast, explain, and (if need be) defend "to the curious foreigner" and local residents alike the story of this peculiar and uniquely Venetian entertainment, "so beloved and esteemed by all the Venetian people, as well as by foreigners . . . [and] worthy of being seen by kings, cardinals, and the first knights of Europe."[5]

In planning his project, however, our aspiring Chronicler of the *pugni* (as we might as well call him) realized that writing the history of the wars of the fists would require a different approach than he had used in reconstructing the battle of 1574. King Henry's visit had been enough of an event that within a matter of months a host of eager writers had rushed to publish "sonnets, octaves, popular songs, and madrigals," in both Venetian and macaronic Latin, to commemorate the occasion. This was not exactly the sort of documentation most conscientious historians would find suitable, it is true, but the Chronicler did come across one especially detailed poem written for the occasion by a certain Bortolomeo Malombra, who had earlier made a name for himself by celebrating the battle of Lepanto in verse. Here was the kind of reportage that the Chronicler needed, for (as he observed) Malombra had "sung in ottava rima of all the above-mentioned receptions, celebrations, and honors, but [had] most of all strived to describe the beginning, middle and end of the *battagliola*, with all the names and surnames of the leaders of both factions, along with the preparations, orders, councils, and all the most important happenings that occurred."[6]

But the battle of 1574 was a unique occasion. Later *guerre dei pugni* might attract thousands of fighters and ten of thousands of spectators, but lacking a king in the audience, these encounters did not usually appeal to local poets. The Chronicler evidently realized that he would have to fill the role of Malombra himself, observing and recording as best he could the varying details of each encounter as it happened. Since his desire was to write a genuine history of the *guerre dei pugni*, however, he also needed to provide an account of *battagliole* of the past. To do so, the Chronicler hit upon the expedient of interviewing men who had taken part in earlier encounters; he was apparently able to find plenty of old veterans of the *pugni* still around who were willing to help him with his work. It was a kind of precocious journalism that allowed him to extend his history back four decades or more without the aid of any written records or accounts:

> For having with historical accounts and evidence fully told the true story [about the battle of 1574], one should also, with the same [methods], be able to recount the wars of the fists, which have been carried out down to the present day, after the wars of the sticks had been outlawed ... but because it is not possible to pull from the memories of men or from other accounts what had happened in these [*battagliole*], there having passed ninety-six years from 1574 to 1670, therefore I have determined to write only about those [encounters] that were carried out in our times, after the plague [of 1630– 1631], beginning in 1632 up to the present year 1670, because from these it will be possible to draw [out] the precise truth about everything, as far as will be possible and the memory of the oldest [participant] will permit.[7]

The result of the Chronicler's efforts was an untitled work that survives only in draft form and consists of twenty-three loosely bound bundles. One of these is the original account of the war of the sticks fought in 1574; two others purport to tell about the origins of Venice's factions and the reasons for their antagonisms; a fourth is a lengthy narration of the first four years of the war of Candia (1645–1669); and the remaining nineteen are all devoted to the wars of the fists fought between 1632 and 1673.[8] It is these last nineteen packets that might be called the Chronicle of the *pugni* proper, for each of them tells the story of the *battagliole* fought during a particular year, detailing the preparations beforehand; introducing the major participants; recounting the combat itself in minute detail; and concluding with accounts of the celebrations, vendettas, and police crackdowns that almost inevitably followed. Altogether the nineteen packets amount to almost four hundred manuscript pages, or some quarter-million words: a unique and up to its time arguably the most extensive descriptive account of a popular cultural event ever produced.

Upon opening the Chronicle of the *pugni*, one is soon struck not only by its size and detail—it narrates the story of scores of battles, brawls, and melees waged all over the city by hundreds of individuals—but also by the novel, not to say peculiar, vision it offers of a city and society usually known for very different traits. Not that the Venice of the Chronicle does not retain its canals, gondolas, public squares, and bridges; far from it: all of these were vital and constantly recurring elements in every *battagliola*. Rather, in the Chronicle the city's well-known features take on a different valence, change their names, alter their functions. Ordinary bridges become tournament fields, their central step an arena, or *arengo*; canals change from watery thoroughfares into grandstands for spectators, while balconies and even rooftops end up as crowded as city streets; marketplaces turn into a kind of no-man's-land, and city squares become the sites where artisan armies muster. Moreover, the men who people the Chronicle, while they are still very much Venetians and are still identified as aristocrats, clerics, merchants, craftsmen, and laborers, have somehow slipped out from their recognizable and familiar social places. Instead of ordinary names, they now sport bizarre noms de guerre and have arranged themselves in unfamiliar hierarchies delineated by any number of odd titles, such as "factionaries," "bosses," "godfathers," or "old wise ones." No longer citizens of a common polity, they have become fierce partisans of groups that are intensely tribal to the point of carrying out armed raids on one another's territories. They know themselves no longer just as Venetians but by a variety of strange names: as the Bariotti, Gnesotti, Zuecchini, Rialtini, Cannaruoli, or Gnatti; and above all, as the Castellani and the Nicolotti—the two great factional identities of the Chronicle that color, influence, and direct all the human actions that fill its pages.

It is, in short, a Venice full of unexpected connotations and unforeseen heroes: not very much like the Republic of decorum, hierarchy, profit, and social control that most of the world has known for centuries. A tantalizing and rarely seen vision and one that comes to us with a striking liveliness of detail, character, and color. For the Chronicle is as precise as it is long, with surprisingly little of its quarter-million words given over to rhetorical flourishes, but a great deal to spirited yet workmanlike narrations about the planning, fighting, and celebrating of hundreds of bridges battles and lesser events. While the Chronicler described his work rather modestly as a simple history of Venice's *battagliole*, almost of necessity he also had a lot to say about the artisans and laborers who waged those "little battles." As a descriptive source on this particular aspect of working-class life, the Chronicle is "thick": it tells and retells how these Venetians carried out their wars, until there emerges from its pages a sense of the experience of the *battagliole* from the inside, from the plebeian point of view. We begin to see not only what the protagonists of the *pugni* did, but also why they did it: the interconnection between action, ritual, and expression that provided the dynamic and gave sense to their encounters.

But detailed and extensive though it may be, how far can we actually trust this story, told to us by a nameless *anonimo* about the often outlandish and extravagant deeds of largely unknown men? We would certainly like to believe that this Chronicle is the gold mine of popular culture that it appears to be, but gold mines can be deceptive in their glitter. Not that artisans did not really fight *battagliole* on Venice's bridges in the sixteenth and seventeenth centuries: dozens of poems, etchings, paintings, and even a bronze or two attest to the hard fact of the encounters. Moreover, we can be fairly confident that men organized themselves and fought more or less in the ways the Chronicler said they did: there fortunately survive two lengthy and substantially corroborative descriptions of the *battagliole* written by a pair of Frenchmen who came to Venice in the mid-seventeenth century and who later wrote of the *pugni* and other curiosities of the city in guidebooks they produced for their fellow countrymen.[9]

The problem with a source such as the Chronicle of the *pugni* is not that it was a complete fantasy—an elaborate pastiche, say, composed by a monomaniac—but rather that it purports to portray for us a social and cultural terrain that is for the most part unknown and unverifiable. How much can we believe the Chronicler's promise "to draw [out] the precise truth about everything" concerning the *pugni?* It is a promise that would test not only his journalist's talents at marshaling the particulars about scores of encounters—some witnessed by him personally and others evidently not— but also his historian's skills in telling his narrative with a minimum of stylistic and rhetorical intrusions.

To verify the accuracy of the Chronicle of the *pugni* completely would be an undertaking doomed to frustration from the outset: after all, many of the details in the work are quite unique—mentioned by no other author, corroborated by no other documents. Still, the plebeian world of the bridges did not exist in complete isolation from the rest of Venetian society, and from the historic record it is possible to sift sufficient traces of the *pugni* to allow us to judge just how conscientiously the Chronicler applied himself in his work. He was, for example, fairly meticulous when it came to setting his action: his portrait of Venice is both highly detailed and geographically precise, with all the city's canals, streets, and alleys, down to its most obscure little courtyards, or *campielli*, presented in their proper relationship to one another. As a result, his accounts of complicated battles and skirmishes can be easily traced, while walking the streets of the modern city: whenever this proves difficult, it is because of subsequent changes in the physical layout of the city itself. The Venice of the Chronicle is accurate down to its individual houses, some of which are identified by the names of their occupants: owners and tenants who can also be found in the state's tax rolls.[10]

How accurately the Chronicler recorded his protagonists is more difficult to ascertain, for most of the hundreds of fighters and spectators that he named were artisans, petty merchants, or laborers: in other words, everybody and nobody in an age when men of their class were still generally known only by first name and occupation. Still, a few of them have left some traces in the state archives: a dozen or so, for example, turn up (complete with their noms de guerre: Balloon, Mankiller, Carob, and so forth) in the police records of the Council of Ten; not surprisingly, they were most often charged with unlawfully fomenting riots at public bridges.[11] The Ten's files contain similar indictments against a handful of Venetian nobles, also charged with disobeying the law and causing disorder during the *battagliole*; gratifyingly enough, they are the same patricians who figure prominently in the Chronicle of the *pugni* as factional supporters, fight promoters, and occasionally as simple rioters. Finally, the Chronicler was accurate in naming the police themselves: most of the dozen or so Captains of the Council of Ten, whose often somewhat theatrical activities he records, also turn up in the public record, in the surviving pay rosters of the Ten.[12]

Yet if the Chronicler scrupulously noted down individuals and settings, he was often less than punctilious at keeping his dates straight; sometimes he missed by as much as a year or two the occasions when notable visitors came to the city and were treated to the spectacle of a *battagliola*. Although the events of the twenty-five year War of Candia loom large across his narrative, the Chronicler repeatedly managed to confuse the timing of events in that conflict, along with their resulting impact back in Venice. His weakness with dates is especially evident in events at the beginning of the Chronicle, to the extent that he asserted that the first *battagliola* of his narrative was put on in the fall of 1632, specifically "to celebrate the liberation of the afflicted Venice from the prison of untimely death [of the plague]," when, according to the records of the Council of Ten, this celebration was in fact staged almost a year earlier.[13]

Such difficulties in matters of dating certain events are curious in light of the Chronicler's usual meticulousness in other details. Very likely, at the distance of nearly four decades, memory—either his own or those of the "oldest ones" whom he consulted—had become selective. Looking back as they were at the 1630s and 1640s from the early 1670s, and accustomed to thinking in terms that were still more verbal than literate, the Chronicler and his informants working together were evidently quite agile at recalling memorable individuals and events. What they seem to have found more difficult, however—working as they were without ready access to such written records as newspapers, journals, or official files—was the task of placing these high points into their proper context, dating them with respect to each other or outside events.

Perhaps well aware of the difficulties in reporting such minutiae from almost half a century earlier, the Chronicler evidently tried to cover up or fill in the various gaps and uncertainties in his narrative by falling back on what writer's arts he possessed: borrowing, for example, a combat scene from Tasso or setting prebattle orations in the manner of Thucydides.[14] How much the intrusion of such literary techniques, with their elitist "great culture" implications, serves to separate the recounting of these earlier years from the actual course of events is difficult to say. Classical and literary allusions, that special language of the educated in early modern society, would seem to have had no place at the bridges: the seventeenth-century artisans who staged the *battagliole* would not have been readers of the classics (or probably much of anything else) and would have therefore missed the heroic, ironic, or sporting connotations of such references. On the other hand, even simple, brawling laborers and sailors would probably have known what the Chronicler meant when he called his protagonists "a Samson," "a true Hercules," "another Achilles," or "a new Mars," and such seemingly classical expressions may actually have been in common use among those who frequented the bridges.[15] Likewise, Venetians of all classes would have recognized—and no doubt have enjoyed—the burlesque scenes that especially abound in these early years of the Chronicle.

Sometimes they are tales that seem too bizarre or comic to have actually happened—as though the Chronicler or his informants had confused events they had witnessed at the bridges with half-remembered scenes from the commedia dell'arte. Yet the collective memories of those who followed the *pugni* were in fact fairly reliable, at least in the general outline of such anecdotes, if not in their precise dating: some of the most particularly outlandish stories told in this first part of the Chronicle can actually be verified by reference to other sources.[16]

In any case, the Chronicler's reliance on memory (supplemented by the occasional literary device) has the effect of dividing his narrative into two dissimilar halves: the work's first twelve bundles, which run year by year without a break from 1632 to 1643, then skip forward to include 1649; and a later group of seven bundles, which cover the *battagliole* of the years 1665 through 1671, along with an encounter that was planned (but never held) in 1673 to honor the visiting Cardinal Chigi.[17] Those of the first group are for the most part much shorter than those of the second, averaging around four to six thousand words, or about ten manuscript pages each (both verso and recto of each sheet are numbered). While not exactly sketchy, these first packets have some of the flavor of a storyteller's accounts, their narrations distilled by memory, shaped and moved forward by the striking incidents or anecdotes they contain. Each year seems in its own way to follow a story line, offering miniature dramas of memorable events and individuals, with one or two distinctive and remarkable battles arranged, joined, won or lost, and celebrated in some fashion.

By contrast, the second group is far less tidy; rather, each year is so exhaustively recounted and filled with the minutiae of the *pugni* that even the briefest of them amounts to well over ten thousand words, and the longest—that for 1667—runs to no less than thirty-four thousand words. In these later years, the particulars seem at times to overwhelm the narrative itself: protagonists fairly tumble past, doing much but seemingly accomplishing little, embroiled in ultimately inconclusive activities that refuse to fit into any sort of recognizable story line. As a result, the encounters of these years do not seem to come to especially satisfying resolutions: men are forever arranging *battagliole*, but they rarely seem to get around to actually fighting them. Perhaps this jumbled narrative can be blamed on the Chronicler's attempt to shift from the role of historian—which had served him well enough in the earlier years—to the rather more uncertain role of journalist. While he had personally witnessed the events of these years, if anything he seems to have remembered them all too well; he evidently made a point of attending every *battagliola* he possibly could and may well have passed his time among the spectators busily taking down notes about everything he saw, perhaps with the idea already in mind of later producing his Chronicle. Some of these scraps of paper still survive, tightly folded up and stuck in the binding of the manuscript; a few appear to be notes jotted down on the spot—occasional bits of verse, for example, copied off a placard—while others may have been afterthoughts the Chronicler intended to work into a second draft that was never accomplished.[18]

The Chronicle of the *pugni* could thus be said to narrate the same events in two different fashions, each owing a great deal to the different and contrasting methods he used: an historical/literary approach for the years 1632–1649, and a more purely journalistic technique for the years 1665–1673. Should one half be considered more reliable (and thus more useful) than the other? Both parts certainly have their flaws: descriptions of encounters in the earlier years are perhaps overly polished, given more sense of drama and direction than they may have actually possessed at the time; the later years are if anything reported from too close to the action, presenting events that appear chaotic and evidently without much design or purpose. Neither, it must be admitted, can really serve the historian as that transparent "window" that would yield a truly clear and undistorted view into the *battagliole* "as they really were": after all, no written account could ever hope to encompass the myriad points of view that these thousands of participants—fighters, spectators, touts, foreigners, and policemen—would have brought to a world as complex and confused as that of the *pugni*.[19]

Yet if both these approaches turn out to be less than ideal in conveying to us the particulars of the *battagliole*, taken together they might be said to offer a perhaps unexpectedly accurate account of the experience of the *pugni*, both as a cultural expression and as popular entertainment. The more immediate, if also more chaotic, later years of the Chronicle, capture just how tenuous and uncertain the structure, honors, and outcome of this world actually were for the protagonists of the *pugni*. At the same time they bring to life the sheer excitement of the encounters, while conveying a sense of amazement that such outrageous displays of purely plebeian energy could succeed at all in the rigidly hierarchical and controlled world of late Renaissance Venice. Moreover, as we have already seen, it is from these later years—where the same sorts of events, activities, and practices are told and retold scores of times, until their minute variations of detail become clear—that we can hope to extract a "thick" description of the *battagliole*. It will be a process that resembles the work of an ethnographer in the field, as he or she draws an account of a tribal culture not from a single informant but from dozens, often finding the valance and the meaning of actions and expressions as much in the discrepancies as in the agreements of what is reported. From the wealth of detail contained in the reports for the years 1665–1673 we may occasionally find it difficult to puzzle out exactly what the workers of Venice were doing at the bridges, but we can at least sometimes manage to discover what they were saying in these violent encounters, about themselves, their communities, and their lives.[20]

At the same time, the earlier years of the Chronicle provide the chance to "read" what the rituals of the *pugni* might have meant to Venetian workers in cultural terms. If the Chronicler and his informants suffered from a certain amount of historical myopia in reconstructing the events that took place three or four decades in the past, there is little reason to believe that this account would have rung false to contemporaries. Indeed, no teller of tales, as Natalie Davis has argued, would want to recount his or her story in baldly neutral terms, for narrator and audience always make their way together over a shared terrain of values and symbols that shape and color the terms (if not the ends) of their discourse.[21] In a worker society still largely attached to the immediacy of nonliterate communication, the passage of time would operate selectively on the collective memory: as individual *battagliole* receded into the past, the more tangled or uncertain encounters would tend to be discarded and forgotten in favor of those remembered as particularly decisive or exceptional. The accounts of the 1630s and 40's, shaped and edited by the limitations of memory though they may have been, were still more or less true in terms of how these events would have been recalled by the great majority of those who had actually participated in them: their anecdotes and encounters were already well on their way to building the mythic and collective past of the *pugni*, forming in the process that community sense of what was proper and what was illicit at the bridges.

The Chronicle of the *pugni* is above all a narrative. Its author was interested in telling his story, not in interpreting it. Even telling his readers why the *battagliole* were important seemed to have been beyond his analytic powers (enough to note that "they are enjoyed by kings, princes, cardinals, and other powerful ones").[22] Although I have felt some reluctance at subjecting this rather freewheeling work to too much interpretive intrusion of my own, it still seems that the world of the *pugni*, as presented in the Chronicle, more or less naturally invites several avenues of analysis: approaches that are reflected in the chapters that follow. The first of these will offer a social geography of the *pugni*, based in large part on the Chronicler's own careful descriptions of how and where the *battagliole* transpired. The second will attempt a "reading" of the battles themselves, in the sense of a step-by-step exploration of just what men did at fighting bridges in Venice and (as this seems a related question) what sort of men they were. There then follows a chapter offering an ethnography of the *pugni*, exploring the systems of honor, identity, and celebration that were generated by faction and the *battagliole*. The final chapter is devoted to the *pugni* as they were perceived, followed, and (frequently) manipulated from the outside: by the more privileged classes of the city and by the state itself, through the agency of its police. In so far as each section represents a different approach to the story of the *battagliole*, each offers its own set of conclusions, about what its particular view of this complex topic can tell us about Venice, its people, and their values.

But if telling the story of the Venetian *pugni* has made a certain amount of analytic framework inevitable, I have tried to keep the intrusions of theory and conjecture to a minimum. In the end, we still know too little about the cultural world of early modern artisans and workers to support great theoretical towers or to explain satisfactorily the workings of minds that were so different from our own. Under the circumstances, it seems enough just to better understand something of the madness and the fervor that made otherwise ordinary men fight and sometimes die to capture ordinary canal bridges: to make some sense of what it was that drove the workers and artisans of Venice to "extravagances so memorable that they truly make the battles of the fists . . . not lowly affairs but events of the highest consideration, unique and without equal in all the world."[23]

1

Why Bridges?

Ghe xè i Ponti de piera, e là s'aspetta
L'union, la calca, che fa sto zioghetto....
La s'una piazza se vede la morte
Speso, senza la morte, trionfar.

There are the bridges of stone and there awaits
The gathered crowd that plays this little game....
There, on a piazza, *one often sees*
The triumph of death without the dying.[1]

Throughout the sixteenth and seventeenth centuries, often several times a year, Venetian workers and tradesmen would gather on a Sunday or holiday afternoon to battle with their fists or with sticks for possession of a bridge. These encounters were known as the *battagliole sui ponti*, the "little battles on the bridges," and they could take several forms: from individual boxing duels and small-scale brawls held to amuse a few hundred or perhaps a thousand onlookers, to enormous, prearranged wars, prepared for days in advance and battled out for hours before tens of thousands of spectators. Those who competed at Venice's bridges did so as members of the city's two great geographic factions, known as the Castellani and the Nicolotti. Such were the passions that their factional loyalties could arouse that men were routinely injured and maimed in the fighting; some would almost inevitably be killed as well: trampled by the crowd, punched to death, drowned in the muddy waters under the bridge, or brained by flying rocks or roof tiles. When the passion for the *battagliole* swept the city, all other popular interests and concerns vanished, until it seemed that "the be-all and end-all of these people is nothing more than for each side to crush the other . . . just so they can possess the two paces of paving stone that are [known as] the Crown of the Bridge [*Piazza del Ponte*]."[2]

Such antagonism and passion might not have been altogether surprising if prompted by desire for a great prize, such as the monumental Rialto

13

Bridge that linked the two halves of Venice over the Grand Canal; thus did the massive Ponte di Mezzo over the Arno River for centuries serve the men of Pisa as an appropriately imposing tournament field for deciding their own factional battles. Yet the *battagliole* of Venice did not contest such a prize as the Rialto, but only seemingly ordinary neighborhood bridges tucked away in back corners of the city, and often no more than four or five yards wide. What was the attraction of such bridges, that artisans—praised in other circumstances as "wise and sober"—would repeatedly court maiming or even death for the sake of "two paces of paving stone"?[3]

Bridges are of course an essential part of Venice's special topography— just like its waterways, islands, and public squares, or *campi*. Something like 450 were to be found in the 1570s, and about as many survive in the city today.[4] Yet if they seem to be everywhere in modern Venice, bridges were actually a somewhat late addition to the city's geography. What little documentation we possess indicates that for the Republic's first half millennium—perhaps until the era of the First Crusade—bridges were almost unknown, since most of the channels that separated the islands clustering around *Rivo Alto* were still too wide to be spanned. In any case, early Venetians were more at home in their boats than on land, accustomed to going about the city by water and not on the few rudimentary streets. Houses were built to face on the canals, and the vacant lands behind them were called *campi* because they were quite literally fields, suitable for gardens, storing water, keeping animals, and dumping rubbish. Only as the original channels were narrowed over time by the encroachment of new or larger palaces, storehouses, workshops, and homes, could they be spanned by bridges, linking these neglected back lots and alleys into a second, terrestrial network that lay somewhat haphazardly superimposed on top of the city's original maze of canals and waterways.[5]

Factionalism in Venice evidently long predated the bridges that would eventually become its focus. Renaissance historians of the city traced these factional rivalries back to the original settlement of the Rialtine islands, to immigrants who kept alive earlier territorial hostilities. Reports survived from the time of Doge Beato (ca. 810) that spoke of pretend battles between the two factions, waged by every sort of citizen ("but for the most part *civili*") armed with sharpened sticks (*canne d'india*).[6] Since the archipelago of islands that constituted early medieval Venice could hardly have boasted a bridge worthy of the name until the late twelfth century— by which time the first pontoon structure at the Rialto and a few stone bridges had appeared—these factional encounters would certainly have been held on land: on marshy banks, or—more likely—on the grass *campi* in the center of most islands.[7] As such, the sort of quasi-ritual brawls for neighborhood supremacy that were mounted by these early Venetians would have closely resembled those held in many other Italian communes, where since at least the tenth century rival bands of youths had battled for supremacy in open fields with fists, or stones, or wooden swords and shields: the only significant difference would have been that warring factions in Venice traveled to their battlefield by boat.[8]

The first surviving official notice of these *battagliole* dates from 1369, when the city's Great Council (*Maggior Consiglio*) issued an edict encouraging citizens to engage in both the regatta and the *battaglia universale* on the first day of each new year—evidently in the hope of developing martial skills among the populace. Yet even at this relatively late date there is no indication that the encounters were actually held on bridges. No allusion to a genuine bridge battle occurs until 1421, when a verse recalls a battle with sticks staged that year on the Ponte dei Servi.[9] Throughout the fifteenth century bridges seemed to vie with the public *campi* as the preferred sites for such clashes; as late as 1509 Marino Sanudo could still write about "a grand battle of boys and grown men" taking place in the *campo* of Santa Margherita.[10] Nevertheless, by Sanudo's day the ascendancy of bridges was already becoming evident: the public appeal of these encounters had proven so strong that the state itself started arranging bridge battles to amuse visiting dignitaries with this uniquely Venetian pastime. The Chronicler of the *pugni* noted that *battagliole* were being staged as early as 1493, when one was put on at the Ponte di Santa Fosca for the duke and duchess of Ferrara. Soon, it would seem, everyone wanted to "get upon the bridges" *(montar sui ponti)*, to the extent that by 1505 the Council of Ten had to intervene in the name of public order to punish those who "dare assemble or make war at the bridges."[11]

Quite possibly this newfound enthusiasm for fighting on canal bridges was a product of the changing Venetian topography itself, for it was in these same years that the city began a drive to convert its wooden bridges to structures of brick and stone. For generations Venetian pedestrians had gotten about on narrow, flat bridges built of planks with railings, sometimes erected on pilings, sometimes simply nailed down to lashed-together boat hulls. Such bridges were no doubt the scenes of many fights—their narrowness would have ensured endless arguments over right of way—but they would also have been much too restrictive to invite any sort of large-scale *battagliola*. Furthermore, not even the largest wooden structure was completely secure under the weight of a great crowd, as was made graphically clear when one of the earlier versions of the Rialto Bridge collapsed in 1444, caving in under the weight of the mob of spectators who had come to watch a naval procession honoring the marquis of Ferrara.[12]

Although Venice's first stone bridges date from the twelfth century and one of the most famous fighting sites in the city—the Ponte dei Pugni at San Barnabà—was rebuilt in stone in 1337, the city's great era of converting bridges from wood to stone and brick was 1450–1600, culminating with the monumental Rialto Bridge built of Istrian marble in 1591.[13] Sansovino believed that the decision to switch from wooden to stone bridges was spurred on by the need to allow the passage of the gondola topped with a cabin, or *felce*, an increasingly popular mode of transportation that could not pass under the older bridges. Giacomo de' Barbari's

detailed view of Venice in 1500 offers something of a snapshot of this
process when it was halfway completed, with many canals still spanned by
flat wooden bridges, while others show the distinctive hump of stone
arches. By the 1520s Marin Sanudo was able to note that "the oldfashioned
bridges of wood are all being renovated in stone," and at end of the century the conversion program was essentially completed, such that the city
of Sansovino's day could boast "450 and more bridges of *pietra viva.*"[14]

There seems to be little doubt that the very existence of these new stone
structures acted as a stimulus for the *battagliole*: already by the mid-1500s
there are reports of such battles being held at bridges all over the city.[15]
Yet the mere availability of arched stone bridges cannot fully explain why
they were singled out as the staging grounds for factional combat. Other
popular festive events, such as bull runnings (*cacce di toro*), bearbaitings,
outdoor feasts, and organized ball games, were generally held in the neighborhood *campo*, the area that had been the wasteland of each island in
Venice's earlier days but which over the centuries had become the center
of many of these communities, often ringed with palaces and shops.[16] By
late medieval times the local *campo* had also become the staging ground
for religious activities and processions, as parish churches began to take
advantage of the open space on their inland side. It could thus be said that
both sacred and profane celebrations were held in the heart of the neighborhood space, where the parish population might most easily gather and
best share a sense of community.[17]

Considering that the parish *campo* was the normal space for virtually
all other local celebrations, why was this convenient staging ground abandoned for the *battagliole*? By the mid-1500s, it indeed seemed that no
one in Venice ever thought to stage such mock battles except on this rather
cramped and restricted surface that, at an average of only around fifteen
by fifty feet, offered only a fraction of the space available in the larger *campi*.
By the seventeenth century bridges had come to be regarded as so ideally
suited for factional combat that on the rare occasions that Venetians decided
to wage a *battagliola* on land, they felt it necessary to erect a kind of temporary bridge/platform on which to stage it. When the residents of Sant'
Angelo parish wished to celebrate their election of a new priest (*parroco*)
in 1668, they naturally held the revelries—the usual festive dancing and bull
runnings—at the *campo* at their parish center. In the middle of the *campo*
they also put up a plank bridge (*ponte di Tavole,*) however, so that in the
midst of these other festivities local youths could fight each other and all
comers, entertaining themselves and the assembled parish gentry with "the
war so esteemed and desired by all the Venetian people."[18]

It would seem, in fact, that bridges' apparent limitations were actually
factors that made them into especially attractive sites for factional confrontations. Accessible only from their two ends, bridges naturally channeled
factional "armies" in a comparatively orderly fashion toward the central
fighting arena, known as the *arengo*, at the crown of the bridge. *Campi*
were by contrast entered by *calli* from many sides and obstructed by vari-

ous trees, stalls, and wellheads; any *battagliole* held in such space ran the real risk of turning into open-ended brawls that produced neither factional honor nor public entertainment.[19] In the same manner, the Venetian canal bridge also provided a clear and well-defined battlefield, for its arch was not described by small, continuous steps (as it is today), but by broad, slightly tilting *piazze,* two or sometimes three of them rising on each side and a humped *piazza di mezo* at the center. Moreover, the stone bridges were open on their sides, in most cases without any sort of protective parapets. When a fighter (or an entire squad) went over the side and tumbled into the water below, he was defeated, and was effectively removed from the scene—perhaps humiliated by a dunking, but probably uninjured—to make way for the next eager participants.[20]

Their structure also gave bridges a psychological role in factional battles. Arched and open, they lifted up those who occupied them, granting an especially advantageous perspective of the surrounding area. From such a vantage point it was possible to observe the flow of the city, to spy out friends, to mock rivals, and if need be to see approaching patrols of police *sbirri* in good time to make off safely. At the same time, bridges could function as stages, providing a public platform for men well known for their vocal capacities and contentious desires to assert their own superiority at the expense of their opponents (Figure 1.1). When on 23 October 1639 a large number of Nicolotti found themselves in possession of the Ponte dei Pugni at San Barnabà, they knew how to take advantage of their commanding position: "Shouting 'Viva, Viva Nicolotti!' they . . . took up positions on the bridge of San Barnabà. Then with whistles and inducements, with their voices and gestures full of scorn . . . they called and challenged the Castellani crowd to battle."[21]

At the same time, bridges also occupied a particular social place in the Venetian popular world. It seems that in the haziest beginnings of the Republic, when each individual island was the cradle of a separate, self-conscious community, the canals running between these settlements were as much boundaries and barriers as they were channels of communication. As these communities evolved by degrees into parishes, or *contrade,* each with its own church and *campo,* canals may have diminished in size, but many still retained something of their original function as the dividing line between neighborhood groups: parishioners were accustomed to use the term *entro i ponti,* or "inside the bridges," when speaking of the physical territory of their own *contrada.* Bridges that crossed these old boundaries were for the most part places of transit, the more so since their abutments were typically used as dumping places for garbage awaiting the occasional scows that came to haul it off. A kind of social no-man's-land that was neither land nor water, not clearly belonging to one parish or the other, on such bridges encounters were likely to be fleeting, or even violent, as passersby knocked into one another while hurrying on their way.[22]

If such bridge space was marginal to local communities, it also tended to attract marginal individuals. Those who lingered there were altogether

Figure 1.1 Bridges provided natural stages for Venetians; Palazzo Zenobio, with its quay and bridges, on the Rio dei Carmini. (Museo Correr, Archivio Fotographico, M. 7089)

a different sort than the "frugal and wise" Venetians so often praised by foreign visitors. Some were petty vendors; selling matches, trinkets, and the like, often little more than vagabonds offering a few paltry goods in competition with the more established merchants situated around the *campo* at the parish center.[23] Hanging about with them were idle and often aggressive young men: unemployed journeymen or *bravi* armed with daggers or other cutting weapons, ready for amusement's sake to pick a fight with passersby or the *sbirri* of the police. Easily moved to violence at all times, their tempers were still more easily set off in the hot days of July and August, "when the sun usually heats the blood."[24]

For those looking for a fight, bridges were convenient gathering points not only for shouting insults at those across the canal but also for making up bawdy songs and dancing the provocative *moresca*.[25] Bridges situated at parish boundaries were the natural salient for aggressive displays by one neighborhood group against another. Such provocations might be the result of parish festivals, where long bouts of feasting and drinking could end with belligerent crowds moving off to gather at these boundary bridges to shout insults at their neighbors of the adjoining parish. The bridges also served as staging bases for noisy raids, or *scorrerie*, across the canal. These burlesques of the military sortie were launched with the intent of racing to the heart of the adjoining neighborhood: to its parish church or *campo*, if possible. Running through the narrow alleys, occasionally armed with stones, young men sought to surprise and frighten residents as much as possible, before returning to the bridge's highly visible platform to jeer and await some retaliatory response from their youthful rivals on the other side.[26]

Castellani and Nicolotti

Youthful clashes on parish bridges probably often arose spontaneously, for aggressive impulses and personal animosities were never far from the surface among such idlers. But as likely as not, when fights did break out among these young men, they would quickly take on a factional coloring. Factionalism appears to have been one of the key organizing principals of Venetian society, less formal perhaps, but no less ubiquitous than the city's parish structure or the official tripartite division of its population into nobles, citizens, and plebs. Faction in Venice was geographically based and traced its origins back to the earliest days of the city. Legends that were already well established by the sixteenth century held that the city had always been polarized, by virtue of its being settled by peoples of two different and contrasting backgrounds. The Rialtine islands that would eventually become Venice were, according to these myths, first peopled by the *gente da terra*, refugees from the mainland, and especially from the Byzantine city of Heraclea, whence they were also known as the Eracleani; and by the *gente da mar*, immigrants who had come from the islands around the Venetian Lagoon and who were therefore sometimes called the Isolani. By around the year 800 these two somewhat antagonistic groups had supposedly established themselves on those parts of Venice closest to their origins; with the Eracleani on the landward area, and the Isolani on the islands facing the sea. Soon thereafter, there were reports of stick battles raging between them.[27]

Whatever the actual origins of these two factions, tradition did not assign them any specific territorial domain within the still-forming city until late in the twelfth century. In the year 1171 Venetian authorities decided to clump together the city's seventy or so parishes into six administrative districts. The three *sestieri* of San Marco, Castello, and Cannareggio were laid out on the right bank of the Grand Canal, while the *sestieri* of San Polo, Santa Croce, and Dorsoduro were established on the left bank. No doubt it was a decision motivated strictly by a desire for more efficient policing and tax collection, for the benefit of Venice's nascent bureaucracy; still, this repartitioning of the city may well have also acted as a stimulus for factional self-consciousness. Those who made their homes within the three *sestieri* closest to the mainland—that is, in Cannareggio, San Polo, or Santa Croce—retained (or perhaps developed anew) something of a common identification as *gente da terra*; by the late thirteenth century they seemed to have dropped their old factional name of Eracleani and were calling themselves instead the Cannaruoli, after the dock workers and cattle butchers (*becheri*) of Cannareggio, who originally were the most coherent and aggressive contingent of the faction. Those living in the three seaward *sestieri*—of San Marco, Castello, and Dorsoduro—kept up their traditional identification as sea peoples, continuing to be known as Isolani, or (increasingly often) as Castellani, after that *sestiere* where there clustered the better part of Venice's tough and contentious shipbuilders and sailors.[28]

There is no way to know whether the Venetian authorities who divided the city into sixths were taking into account these factional loyalties when they set up the *sestieri*. It is worth noting, however, that although the state had assigned three *sestieri* to each side of the Grand Canal, this most obvious dividing line in Venice was not in the end the polarizing axis for factionalism in the city. Instead, the factional boundary ran more or less at right angles to the Grand Canal, for the most part along a series of minor canals, bridges, and alleys (Map 1). Such a division might be taken as an indication that the two factions did indeed represent an echo of an early and long-vanished seaward/landward split in Venetian society. Certainly, the psychological effect of having the two rival factions in close contact with each other, rather than separated by the wide Grand Canal, would be of particular importance in shaping and intensifying their deep antagonisms.[29]

So ran one account of the origins of Venetian factionalism, linking the hostilities between the two sides of the city to immigrant animosities and neighborhood loyalties. Like so many other ritual observances and celebrations in the Republic, however, the battles of the bridges traced their mythic descent from more than one traditional source.[30] Onto this original tale

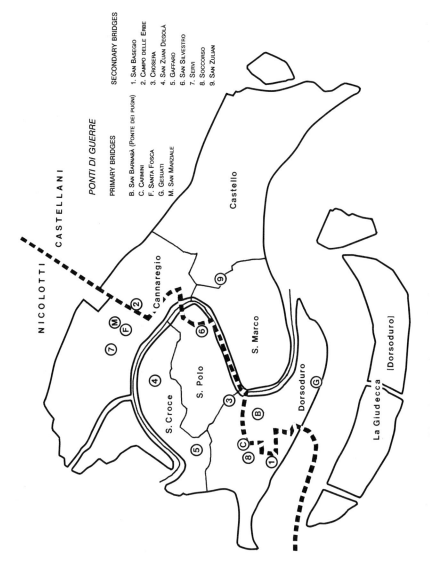

NICOLOTTI

CASTELLANI

PONTI DI GUERRE

PRIMARY BRIDGES

B. San Barnaba (Ponte dei Pugni)
C. Carmini
F. Santa Fosca
G. Gesuati
M. San Marziale

SECONDARY BRIDGES

1. San Basegio
2. Campo delle Erbe
3. Croisera
4. San Zuan Degolà
5. Gaffaro
6. San Silvestro
7. Servi
8. Soccorso
9. San Zulian

Cannaregio

Castello

S. Polo

S. Marco

S. Croce

Dorsoduro

La Giudecca

[Dorsoduro]

Map 1. Venetian factional geography and the fighting bridges.

of the Eracleani and Isolani there was in time grafted a new story, one which served not only to explain subsequent changes in the factional geography but also to give greater emotional depth to the hostilities that lay at the heart of the bridge battles.

The story, which seems to have been pieced together from a tangle of Old Testament and classical themes of favoritism, treachery, rebellion, and exile, was set in the last quarter of the thirteen century, when Bortolomeo Querini was made the bishop of Venice. As a gesture—either of gratitude or of patronage—Querini chose to reward his home parish of San Pantalon, in the *sestiere* of Dorsoduro, by exempting its residents from the obligation of paying him the Church's inheritance tax (the *decima dei morti*). Before long, however, those who lived nearby began to copy the favored residents of San Pantalon, apparently convincing themselves that merely living in the same *sestiere* gave them an excuse to dodge their taxes. The result (so the story goes) was that by the time Querini's successor, a Bolognese named Ramberto Polo, was chosen as bishop of the city in the early fourteenth century, the residents of no fewer than five of the eleven parishes of the *sestiere*—that is, San Nicolò dei Mendicoli, Angelo Raffaele, Santa Margherita, San Basegio, and San Pantalon—were all acting as if this concession was their special and perpetual right. As an outsider who had little sympathy with localism and special privileges in his diocese, Polo promptly challenged this exemption, and when the parish priests of the five *contrade* still refused to pay their *decima*, he resolved to force the issue by demanding payment in person. It was an unfortunate and unpolitic decision, for when Polo tried to enter the rebellious district he was met by an angry mob, led by none other than the parish priest of San Pantalon himself, one Bartolomeo Dandolo. The argument that ensued between the bishop and his flock soon led to violence, and while trying to flee, Polo was set upon by the enraged mob and torn to pieces at a remote, dismal canal that would subsequently be given the name of *Malcanton*.

According to some, it was this "enormous crime" that raised the long-standing factional antipathies of Venice to a permanent and implacable hostility. The problem was that Polo, though an outsider to the city, was by virtue of his residence also held to be a member of the Castellani faction: his cathedral, after all, was located at San Pietro di Castello, on the far eastern end of Venice. Those who killed him, as residents of the *sestiere* of Dorsoduro, were also Castellani, and therefore murderers of a leader in both the spiritual and factional sense. Naturally, the guilty were punished. The Church excommunicated the five rebellious parish priests and presumably the state itself managed to hunt down at least some of the killers. Apparently, there was also a general sense that something should be done against those who lived in this part of the city, on the far western edge of Venice, for having behaved so disrespectfully toward their bishop. Since, according to another parallel myth, it was the fishermen of San Nicolò parish who had been the most "tumultously" involved in the crime, their community would bear the brunt of a ritual punishment: henceforth their *gastaldo*, or community leader, known as the Doge of the Nicolotti, would be required to wear red robes of office "in perpetual memory of the blood spilled by the bishop."

Such punishment evidently seemed too limited and perhaps too ritualistic to satisfy the outrage of others of the Castellani faction, however. These partisans proceeded to carry out a kind of secular excommunication of their own against everyone who lived in these five infamous parishes, "declaring that they would not accept them any longer at their gatherings . . . and that this would last without any hope of remission at any time, regardless of the remonstrations that may be offered." According to tradition, the Castellani stuck to their threat, refusing to have anything to do with the banished parishes, until finally, *molto irritati*, the fishermen of San Nicolò in particular decided to turn away from their old faction. Leading the other renegade parishes, they asked to join up with the Cannaruoli, who—evidently less disturbed than the Castellani about associating with clericides—willingly took them in.[31]

The bloody legend of Bishop Polo may have provided a convenient mythical framework for explaining the unrelenting hostility between factional partisans in Venice, but there may well have also been more prosaic causes for this rift within the Castellani faction and the enduring antagonisms that continued centuries later. Certainly, economic and status competition may have played a role in turning half of the parishes of Dorsoduro against their fellows. The deep-sea fishing community, which was centered in San Nicolò and Angelo Raffaele parishes, was noted for its strong sense of professional solidarity, and the fishermen who overwhelmingly made their homes there were known not to be especially sympathetic with the eel-fishers and other small-boat Lagoon fishermen of neighboring Sant' Angese and San Trovaso parishes. When the split came, these latter two parishes remained with the Castellani, expressing a particular dislike for the men of San Nicolò and Raffaele who were otherwise among their closest neighbors.[32]

It is also quite likely that these deep-sea fishermen found themselves cast out of the Castellani because over the centuries they had succeeded all too well as a self-conscious and growing community of fighters. As such, their continued presence within the faction would have constituted a threat to the traditional leaders of the Castellani: the sailors and the state shipbuilders of the Venetian Arsenal (the *arsenalotti*). Certainly, there was a traditional antipathy between fishermen and shipbuilders in Venice, and it is open to question whether there was room in one faction for two such large, self-confident, and aggressive communities of disciplined fighters. In any case, it is clear that after the split occurred the fishermen of San Nicolò and Angelo Raffaele soon became the dominant group in their new faction, while the *arsenalotti* maintained their traditional role as "the head and the principal nerve of all the Castellani sect."[33]

Quite possibly the supposed expulsion of the five renegade parishes by the Castellani should be seen as part of a general shifting of factional allegiances, an indication that at least until the sixteenth century factional identities were less fixed in terms of social geography than they would eventually become. This fluidity was also reflected by changing loyalties in the island community of Murano, which lies about a mile off the north coast of Venice proper, and which (according to some commentators) considered for a time setting itself up as a third faction, independent from the other two and going by the name of Gnatti (the Dolts). Discovering by the mid-1500's that they were in fact too few to compete on their own effectively, however, the Muranese supposedly decided to throw in their lot with the Castellani. Likewise, the sparsely populated islands of the Giudecca (Sant' Eufemia parish) seemingly wavered in their loyalty until around the 1520s, before finally joining up with the Castellani. There seems to have been a consensus that such late additions to the Castellani side were allowable, if not indeed quite appropriate, since they had the effect of making up for the fighting strength lost when the five Dorsoduro parishes left the faction.[34]

Shifting factional allegiances thus did not always respect the state's somewhat arbitrary divisions of the city into *sestieri*, even if these large administrative zones may have given a general overall shape to the factions' territories. Along the factional boundary that ran between the *sestieri* of Castello and Cannaregio, factional loyalties seem to have been determined as much by occupation as by residence. At many battles there were often to be found groups of men from the eastern end of Cannaregio fighting on the side of the Castellani: these were primarily the *specchieri*, or mirror makers and mirror sellers, of San Canciano parish—who regularly sent a contingent of fifty or sixty men—along with smaller squads from other neighborhoods located still more deeply within Cannaregio.[35] Another pro-Castellani enclave within a Nicolotto *sestiere* was to be found at the Rialto, the only point of direct factional contact along the whole swing of the Grand Canal. A squad of so-called Rialtini—evidently from the San Polo *contrada* of San Giovanni di Rialto—occasionally showed up on the Castellani side, and men from around the nearby parish church of San Silvestro would sometimes join them in fighting against their Nicolotti neighbors.[36] In the absence of any popular traditions to explain them, how can these apparent deviations from the expected coincidence of faction and *sestieri* be reconciled? With the *specchieri* of San Canciano, at least, such anomalous loyalties may be a sign of how artisan groups shifted about the city, in a sort of internal migration. The mirror makers were engaged in a comparatively new profession (they did not set up a guild until 1564), and it was said that "the greater part of them are foreigners or from Friuli." New to the city, it is likely that many *specchieri* made their first stop in the glass-making center of Murano, where they not only picked up their training and connections in glass work but acquired their Castellani loyalties as well.[37]

It remained only to formalize the names of the factions, and this was finally settled on 11 October 1548, in a memorable encounter that in its way could be said to contribute yet a third foundation myth to the history of the *battagliole*. Supposedly still smarting from the humiliation of their expulsion of nearly 250 years earlier, the fishermen of San Nicolò and the other renegade parishes challenged the Castellani, on behalf of all the Cannaruoli faction, to a battle with sticks and shields that was to settle this dishonor once and for all. Confident that they would win, the men of San Nicolò attached conditions to their challenge: the Castellani, if they lost, would have to abandon their factional name, and instead call themselves the apparently derisory term of Bragolini; in addition they would have to duel with the Cannaruoli wherever and whenever the latter wished, in effect placing themselves at the beck and call of their old enemies. Such stipulations were apparently considered so demeaning that the implication seemed to be that, should the Castellani actually lose, they would be so humiliated that they would effectively cease to exist as a faction altogether.[38]

Despite this apparent risk to both their honor and their identity, the Castellani accepted the challenge of the Cannaruoli and indeed countered with their own set of conditions. If the Cannaruoli lost, they would have to abandon *their* name, and accepting the dishonor of the renegade parishes, henceforth would all be known as the Nicolotti. Moreover, the five renegade parishes were to stop once and for all their demands that they be readmitted to the Castellani: the split between the two factions was to be complete and immutable. When the day of battle came the Castellani attacked their opponents "with the cruelest of cudgelings," and eventually managed to win the day. As a result, the five renegade parishes were banished for good, and with the rest of the Cannaruoli faction took on what had been the somewhat shameful name of Nicolotti. But the men of San Nicolò soon begin to treat this apparent dishonor as a matter of pride, to the extent that they imitated the ritual penance of their *gastaldo* and all started wearing red caps to the bridges, in memory of the blood of Ramberto Polo.[39]

By the mid-1500s, the once-shifting factional landscape in Venice had became fairly fixed and would remain essentially stable for the next two hundred years. The Castellani and Nicolotti divided the city between them, with the boundary running roughly between the *sestieri* of Castello and Cannaregio, following the Grand Canal from above the Rialto Bridge to around Ca' Foscari, and then continuing west to cut the *sestiere* of Dorsoduro in half (Map 1). It was a highly polarized world in which little could be called truly neutral territory. There were, to be sure, areas in the city that were so public that neither faction could really claim them: in particular, the commercial and ceremonial centers of Venice at the Rialto and Piazza San Marco, as well as the luxurious Mercerie that connected them; likewise, the Grand Canal and the Canal of the Giudecca were understood to be shared by all. Yet at the same time these apparently free and public areas in the city could easily turn into a kind of no-man's-land. Places where everyone had to go for business or pleasure were all the more likely

to be the scene of factional arguments and disputes. The result, with factional enemies sure to be placed in close contact with each other, was that
these geographic and social centers of the city were, if anything, the most
likely locations for factional brawls. The city's two fish markets (*pescarie*)
at San Marco and the Rialto, especially became the scene of almost continuous violence between Castellani and Nicolotti partisans.[40]

A somewhat more ambiguous zone of the city, in factional terms, was
its Jewish quarter, the three Ghettos known as Vecchio, Nuovo, and
Nuovissimo. Certainly the Jewish merchants who were required to live and
keep shop in the area had no love of brawls of any kind in their midst,
and on the occasion when a running factional street fight spilled into the
campo of the Ghetto Nuovo, they were quite as ready as their Christian
counterparts in the Mercerie to rush to the scene with "swords, bars, and
clubs" in hand to separate the brawlers.[41] Yet by virtue of their place of
residence deep in the *sestiere* of Cannareggio, at least some Jews also appear
to have considered themselves loyal Nicolotti. Certainly, when local festivals were held to celebrate a Nicolotti victory on the nearby Fondamenta
dei Ormesini, the Jewish community took part as well: decorating with
showy and costly draperies the windows of the high Ghetto buildings facing the Fondamenta, so that the women of the Ghetto—"enrapturing all
who looked at them"—would have an appropriate and ornate vantage point
from which they could watch the festivities and wave to the revelers down
below.[42] Some Jews also seem to have been active fighters for the Nicolotti
in the bridge battles themselves. One of them, called Samuel the Jew, got
himself into serious trouble at a *battagliola* in 1637, when he got carried
away by the excitement of the moment and punched a police captain in
the face.[43]

The factional partition of the city gave certain bridges a new importance that made them the central focus of what might be termed an entire
cult of the *pugni*. Whereas in earlier days bridges all over the city had been
tried out as sites for the *battagliole*, after the 1540s many of these would
be discarded in the light of a more clearly defined factional world. Since
Venice's bridges came in every shape, size, and situation, some potential
battle sites, having been tested, were eventually abandoned simply because
they were too narrow, twisted, or inaccessible for the ever-larger crowds
of fighters and onlookers who sought to be present at the *battagliole*.[44]
Others were given up because of their location relative to the factional
boundaries, for when a bridge was too clearly situated in the home territory (*in casa propria*) of one of the factions, its role as a staging ground
for *battagliole* changed significantly. Sometimes it was a simple question
of the danger involved: certain otherwise popular bridges were so deep in
one faction's territory that even to get to them exposed opposition squads
to the real risk of attack. This was especially true for the Ponte dei Gesuati,
since most Nicolotti who wished to reach this bridge by land had to pass
through Sant' Angese parish. Here the residents—known as the Gnesotti—
were such hostile and volatile partisans for their faction that they were quite

likely to throw stones and chairs or dump boiling water on any opposition squads that dared to cross their territory on the way to the battle site.[45]

Yet staging *battagliole* on bridges located deep in one or the other faction's home grounds could have other, more subtle effects on the course of an encounter. When factional members fought on bridges *in casa propria*, it was generally held that they were entering the combat with considerable advantage, with their wives and relatives close at hand to shout encouragement and with easy access not only to food and wine but also to fresh clothing and weapons. And while they themselves would enjoy every sort of support from their own nearby houses and taverns, their opponents, having made the potentially disheartening trip through hostile parishes, were forced to fight in unfamiliar and unhelpful surroundings.[46] Although it might seem logical that both factions would try to arrange battles on bridges *in casa propria*, this was in fact rarely the case. Instead, equations of honor and shame figured so strongly in the *battagliole* that such a territorial advantage was generally considered unfair, and as a rule factional partisans tried to avoid fighting if at all possible deep in their own territory. Although sometimes sham offers to do so were made, the Castellani and Nicolotti were much more likely to issue a challenge to fight in their opponent's backyard.[47] The reason was fairly simple: should a faction start with such an advantage, it was widely understood that a victory would somehow count for less than had they fought outside their home territory.[48] Even worse was the possibility that a faction might fight *in casa propria* and actually lose. In that case the shame would be infinitely greater: to avoid such an outcome, it was generally understood that fighters faced with defeat on their home bridge could be expected to resort to the most extreme measures—which might include attacking their opponents with stones, roof tiles, and knives—even though this was itself a somewhat shameful response.[49] Aware of the extent to which a faction would go to win *in casa propria*, opponents knew how to turn the question of honor on its head, making public (though perhaps not especially sincere) offers to fight deep in the other side's territory as a open sign of their contempt for their enemies' ability to defend themselves, even when at home.[50] The Castellani clearly knew what they were doing when, having already trounced the Nicolotti once,

> as the superior and the victors, they showed such confidence, [as if] they thought nothing of their rivals; indeed, they freely said that they would even go [to fight again] at the Ponte dei Carmini, which is *in casa propria* of the Nicolotti. This proposal . . . disturbed the Nicolotti people greatly, making them feel even more despised and scorned, that they could be threatened with the battle coming to their own territory . . . and after a long confusion, many wanted to accept the challenge and others no; it seemed to some the height of cowardice [that they should] abandon their own advantage, but it was the opinion of many that the great courage of the Castellano had discouraged the Nicolotto's bravery. The Nicolotti [themselves] were convinced that there had been some damage to their reputation.[51]

Such considerations of honor and tactics meant that most bridges of the city would automatically be out of bounds as sites for the *battagliole*. Few were willing to risk the physical dangers of traveling deep into enemy territory, and the prospects of winning unfairly or (worse yet) losing outright on a home bridge were even more unpleasant. In the end, only four or five bridges in all Venice seem to have enjoyed the proper location, size, and situation to qualify them in the popular mind as true *ponti di guerre*. In a very real sense these particular bridges were not only the focus of the *battagliole*, but of all Venetian factionalism: the central *piazze di mezo* at their crowns was in fact the true no-man's-land that defined the boundary line between the two sides.[52]

These few bridges were found in two widely separated parts of the city, with one group located at the eastern end of the *sestiere* of Cannareggio, and the other along the factional border that split the *sestiere* of Dorsoduro. In Cannareggio the two most popular bridges were those of San Marziale and Santa Fosca, attractive to the factions because they were large and easily accessible from nearby *campi* and *fondamenta*, or quays (Figure 1.2). That of San Marziale, in particular, was considered "privileged beyond all the others to host those especially celebrated and notable wars [that are] put on for [visiting] Princes, Cardinals, and Great Lords of Italy, due to its location, beauty, convenience and size" (it measured a good seventeen by fifty feet, according to de Ville).[53] Both bridges—situated less than a hundred yards apart—were located well inside the *sestiere* of Cannareggio, but since they were easily accessible through the territory of the pro-Castellani mirror makers of San Canciano parish, they were seen as lying within the factional border zone and thus considered as true *ponti di guerra* (unlike, for example, the Ponte dei Servi, which was only slightly further along but still was treated as definitely in the Nicolotti *casa propria*). The bulk of the Castellani army apparently preferred to come to these bridges by boat in any case, bypassing the tangled city and its potentially hostile enclaves and traveling by open water to the Sacca della Misericordia, thence to the wide Canale della Misericordia, and finally covering the short distance to the fighting bridges on foot.[54]

The other three key bridges in the world of the *battagliole* lay in Dorsoduro. Of these, the Ponte dei Pugni at San Barnabà was certainly the most important, rivaled only by the bridge at San Marziale as Venice's quintessential *ponte di guerra* (Figure 1.3) Although just thirteen feet in width, and therefore considered by some to be rather narrow, the Ponte dei Pugni gained its battle stature thanks to its ideal location. Balanced just on the factional border between the opposing *contrade* of San Barnabà and Santa Margherita, the bridge connected two long and ample *fondamenta* running along the Rio di San Barnabà: these in turn provided easy access to the battle site from the staging grounds of each faction, the Castellani in the Campo of San Barnabà and the Nicolotti in the Corte di Tagliapietra, near Campo di Santa Margherita. So regularly were *battagliole* staged at the Ponte dei Pugni that the bridge could be said to have shaped

Figure 1.2 *Battagliola* on the Ponte di Santa Fosca; from Gabriel Bella (1780s). (Museo Correr, Archivio Fotografico, *varie* 20165)

Figure 1.3 *Guerra dei pugni* at the Ponte dei Pugni at San Barnabà; from D. Lovisa, *Il Gran Teatro di Venezia* (1720). (Museo Correr, Archivio Fotografico, M. 33646)

and altered the surrounding cityscape, as passages were bored through adjoining walls, doorways were widened or fortified, and nearby houses were modified to accommodate the movement of the fighting squads or the comfort of spectators.[55]

By the late seventeenth century the Ponte dei Pugni at San Barnabà had won another distinction that it shared only with the Ponte di San Marziale. Enthusiasts of the *pugni* arranged to have a marble footprint implanted in each of the four corners of the *piazza di mezo*, at the crown of the bridge. These *impronte* (or *stalfini*, in popular jargon) were intended to provide a scratch mark for contestants and their referees during individual matches; they also had the effect of putting the two bridges that they adorned into a class by themselves as *ponti di guerra*, making them the "dominant and reigning bridges" in the city.[56]

The other two principal *ponti di guerra* in Dorsoduro were the bridges of the Carmini and the Gesuati, although as already noted, both were considered as lying *in casa propria* of one or the other faction. Nevertheless, because of their unusual size both bridges continued to serve as the site for *battagliole*, especially when battles were prearranged and therefore larger affairs. The Ponte dei Carmini was nearly as wide as San Marziale, and the Gesuati was famed as "bigger than any other on which wars are fought, with three wide and spacious *piazze* on each side; such that to occupy this site twice as many people are needed as on any other bridge."[57] Furthermore, each site enjoyed a special fame. The Carmini had the distinction of having once served as the site for the most memorable *battagliola* of all: that staged with *canne d'india* in 1574 for the visiting French king Henry III. The Gesuati was known for its capacity to accommodate vast audiences, for its position on the Zattere meant there was virtually no limit to the number of spectators that could come to the encounter in their boats and clog the wide Canale della Giudecca from one bank to the other. When a *battagliola* was held there in 1639, a good thirty thousand onlookers were said to be present:

> and the innumerable voices, the whistling, and the beating of oars on the boats made a noise in the air that resembled thunder, that when it begins from one pole to another continually roars and reverberates; such was this booming and pounding, that it was heard as far away as Fusina [on the mainland] and beyond the Lido, for some distance out to sea.[58]

Aware of how important their favorite bridges were for the *battagliole*, factional partisans made sure that not only the spans themselves but also the nearby *fondamenta* were sufficiently well maintained to stand up under the weight and abuse of thousands of fighters and spectators.[59] Then as now, the decay of the Venetian infrastructure was a constant problem, although in earlier times stonework and foundations were more likely to be weakened or destroyed by severe cold than by the *acque alte* of today. In the mid-seventeenth century especially, "the cruel colds and freezes attacked the *fondamenta* already consumed by age, weak and with little

substance, [causing them] to fall easily into the canal." State authorities seem
to have always been behind in keeping up with such repairs about the city,
and at least sometimes it was not until a bridge actually collapsed—as with
the Ponte di San Marziale, which "disintegrated and fell into the canal from
one end to the other"—that the appropriate magistrate would finally decide
to rebuild the structure entirely.[60] As a result, favorite *ponti di guerra* might
well be crumbling to the point of being too dangerous for a *battagliola*,
though not collapsed enough to attract the attention of the authorities. In
such circumstances, factional partisans might decide to do some provisional
repairs themselves; if the work called for additional building materials, they
were perfectly willing to commandeer whatever they needed from nearby
structures or warehouses.[61]

A World of Faction

Their ability to give focus and expression to the city's factional life gave
these few bridges their special importance. Factionalism was universal among
Venetians in these centuries: artisans, *cittadini*, and nobles; men, women,
and children; even priests, monks, nuns, and Jews—all can be found taking part.[62] Yet whether one considered himself or herself a Castellano or
a Nicolotto was not a matter of choice, but simply a question of accident,
for Venetians were born into their faction and generally kept their loyalties for life.[63] Factional allegiance was just as arbitrary for those who moved
to the city: new immigrants were expected to automatically assume the
loyalties of their first *contrada* of residence, which stayed with them thereafter. Guests in the city usually ended up taking the side of their host,
although some of the more important visitors could find themselves actively
courted by the nobility of one side or another.[64] Long-term visitors to
the city might develop multiple attachments to their adopted faction, much
in the manner of the marquis di Fluentes, ambassador of Spain, who
"favored the Nicolotti faction from personal inclination, and also because
. . . his royal palace is located among the most esteemed Nicolotti of
Cannareggio, and then because he had [rowing] in his gondola the
[renowned Nicolotti fighters] Moro at the helm and Piero Palladin at the
center."[65]

Factional loyalties were so strong that the Castellani and Nicolotti could
claim the support of men who lived far outside the actual confines of the
city, but who would still respond to the traditional call. To maximize their
army's strength, the Nicolotti would summon fighters from such nearby
areas as Malamocco, Mestre, and Fusina, and would also send recruiters
up the Brenta, to Dolo and Stra, and "even as far as Monselice, Padova,
and Este," a seventy-kilometer journey that would have taken several days.
The Castellani would typically prepare for a grand battle by

> sending their supporters with boats loaded with provisions of war, that is with
> [money], placards, corselets, [boxing] gloves, and Dalmatian caps, to . . . the

places of their allies beyond the city, that is, to Murano, Burano, Mazzorbo, Torcello, the Lido, the Vignole, and other islets, to make a general roundup of their people.[66] (See Map 2.)

Although factional membership in Venice was both universal and arbitrary, the result was not one of casual or wavering loyalty to the group. Artisans who moved out of their native factional territory to opposing *contrade* in order to open shops or set up new households were aware of the hostility and provocations they were likely to face if they were to express their original loyalties too publicly.[67] Nevertheless, many continued to flaunt their enthusiasms, no doubt out of a sense of factional dedication and personal honor. Such hardy souls, if they did not know when to hold their tongues, ran the risk of becoming the target of vigilante action, of the sort that once nearly caught up with the butcher known as the Sponzeretto, who lived in Santa Marina parish in Castello, but who kept a stall in the Beccaria, deep in the Nicolotti territory. Well known as a factional leader at the bridges and by no means shy about his own prowess or opinions, the Sponzeretto was once cutting meat and discussing the previous *battagliole* with his fellow—mostly Nicolotti—butchers, when their friendly arguing suddenly flared into open dispute. With everyone already conveniently supplied with large choppers and himself heavily outnumbered by hostile co-workers, the Sponzeretto could easily have been cut to pieces had it not been for the timely intervention of some fellow Castellani butchers and fishmongers. Likewise, although the Nicolotti merchants who did business on the Mercerie—which ran through the Castellani *sestiere* of San Marco—may have been more cultivated than butchers, they too had to watch themselves if they wished to avoid getting dragged into brawls like the one that erupted in 1635, stretching along "the whole Mercerie, from the Ponte dei Baretteri as far as [Piazza] San Marco."[68]

The loyalties of factional partisans were evidently dogged enough to influence the flow of social interactions between families, neighbors, and communities. The French writer Alexandre Saint Disdier, in his 1679 guidebook to Venice, noted that "one finds among the populace certain leaders of these factions who have so thoroughly persuaded themselves one cannot be an honorable man while following the opposite faction that they would prefer to deny one of their daughters a goodly fortune rather than let her marry a man who was of the other side." In the highly polarized world of the *pugni* questions of faction were never far from the surface, and matrimony between Castellani and Nicolotti families meant establishing amicable ties where there should only be rivalry. Far better to make the basic, socially defining choice of a spouse from among those of one's own side, the more so since a factional mésalliance could leave a fighter caught between his old factional comrades and his new in-laws, fully trusted by neither side.[69]

The factional imperatives of the *pugni* thus tended to shape the social geography of Venice, just as it did the city's physical topography. The fac-

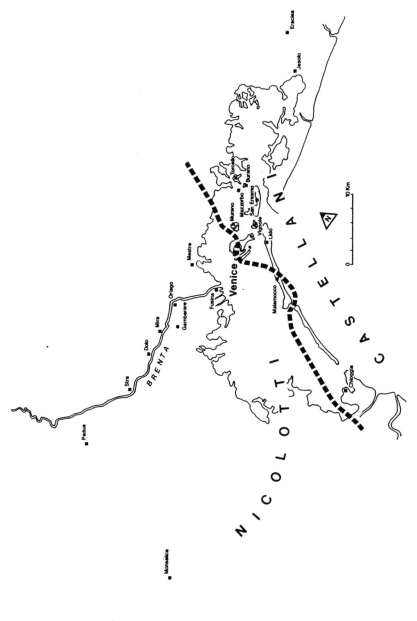

Map 2. Larger factional loyalties: the Lagoon and the *terraferma*.

Este

Monselice

Padua

Stra

Dolo

Mira

BRENTA

Gambarare

Oriago

Fusina

Mestre

Venice

Murano

Mazzorbo

Torcello

Burano

San Erasmo

Vignole

Lido

Malamocco

Chioggia

NICOLOTTI

CASTELLANI

Jesolo

Eraclea

10 Km

0

N

tional boundary line cut across the worker districts of the city like an invisible force field, altering and impeding what would have otherwise been the natural formation of social ties and networks. Residents who lived nearest to this boundary line seem to have been among the most implacably loyal to their respective faction and the most intensely hostile to their neighbors on the other side of the border, even though their proximity often meant that these were workmen engaged in similar trades, who by rights should have been the most inclined to socialize and intermarry. And so, when it came to picking a spouse for their children or a bride for themselves, these factionally conscious men were distinctly more inclined to do their choosing from among those of their own side rather than from those across the border. The tenacity of such prejudices is amply borne out in a survey of the parish records of the mid-seventeenth century. The two neighboring *contrade* of San Basegio and San Trovaso were separated by the factional boundary as it wound through the *sestiere* of Dorsoduro, and residents of both parishes were around 75 percent more likely to marry someone on their own side of the Nicolotti–Castellani line than to cross over the border to find a spouse. Some of this factional disparity was due to parish endogamy, which was quite strong among Venetian artisans, but it is still true that when the Trovasini did choose to marry outside their own parish, they would do so far more often with residents of fellow Castellani parishes, just as the Basegiotti would find their spouses from among Nicolotti allies.[70]

This sort of factionally influenced endogamy was also reflected among those seeking to establish the other fundamental form of familial ties, that of godparenting. Such relationships appear to have held real weight at the bridges, and, as far as it is possible to arrange a prosopography of the *pugni*, it seems clear that in the thick of combat, co-parents (*compari*) showed much the same tendency to fight together and aid one another as did real brothers and other near blood relatives. Therefore, it is hardly surprising that fathers of newborns who were initiating these bonds of artificial kinship with another man were 70 percent more likely to choose their child's godfather from their own side than from the enemy side of the factional boundary. For most Venetian artisans baptism, like marriage, was a ceremony that celebrated not only the family and its new connections, but also the neighborhood. As such, these rites centered on the parish church and *campo*, commemorating the community and the familiar in ways that turned inward, sometimes in a calculated snub to those living nearby, on the other side of the factional frontier. Indeed, after the sacred observances and the feasting were over, it was not unknown on such occasions for groups of drunken youths to move as a mass to their parish boundary, shouting "Viva Castellani" or "Viva Nicolotti," in the hope of provoking their neighbors into some kind of violent reaction.[71]

That factional adherence was taken so seriously in a city as cosmopolitan as early modern Venice might at first sight seem surprising. Indeed, even some contemporary observers assumed that such strong allegiances could only be explained by some ancient political origin—the continuing influence of half-forgotten animosities between Guelph and Ghibelline was suggested—but there is little to imply that the two factions ever stood for any position beyond simple opposition to one another.[72] The factional loyalties conferred on a Venetian by his place of birth stayed with him throughout his life, and changing sides was no casual matter: Casoni asserted that such a conversion could only be accomplished by a kind of baptism that was "a profane imitation of the sacred ceremony."[73]

Certainly, some were tempted to desert one side for the other, for membership in one's faction had to coexist with all the other social obligations of this closely knit city. Yet those who gave in to the blandishments of relatives or powerful patrons to switch sides, or those who deserted in anger after a quarrel with their cofactionalists, had to be quite careful if they intended to remain active at the bridges. Should such a *renegado* suddenly turn up at a *battagliola* fighting with the other faction and be recognized by his old comrades, he would certainly find himself the target of a concerted and consciously vicious attack, for "if it is suspected that someone in these wars more favors the opposing side than his own, not only will they kick him out of their company, but sometimes they will even kill him."[74]

Considered still worse, however, were those who betrayed their faction for a price: should even the suspicion of such treachery attach itself to a factional leader, it could prove fatal. When the word began to spread through the city in late December 1635 that the Nicolotti leader Iseppo Cenerin had surrendered the Ponte di Santa Fosca somewhat too quickly because he had been bribed by a wealthy Castellano partisan, Cenerin soon learned that his old comrades were plotting to kill him:

> [So] he resolved to flee the dangers and to protect his life by leaving the city and hiding away for the course of a year, so that the souls of the Nicolotti could quiet down. . . . But it would have been much better for him if he had stayed away forever, because soon after returning, he was wretchedly murdered in the Spadaria at San Marco, skewered in the back from one side to the other with a sword . . . without ever knowing who had done it.[75]

Such seemingly brutal enforcement of factional loyalties was not only justified as appropriate for group honor but was moreover seen as proof that the *battagliole* and the world of the *pugni* were not "a simple curiosity or a vulgar recreation" but the embodiment of ideals fitting for a militaristic and honor-conscious age. Contemporaries reached for the military metaphor to describe and explain to themselves the demands of duty and loyalty which the *battagliole* made on every factional "soldier," and could treat the factions themselves as a kind of mobilized citizenry—two republics, as it were, that existed in the bravura of their armies. The Chronicler of the *pugni* certainly saw the murder of the hapless Cenerin in these terms, as proof that the Battles of the *Pugni* . . . are not lowly things of little importance, but of the highest consideration . . . the more so because [the factions] observe the use, the rigors, the laws, and the punishments practiced in the armies of the great princes: [when] some soldier or captain is revealed to the prince—sometimes with little proof—as suspected of treason or of little faith, these men pay the ultimate penalty with their head, or before the firing squad."[76]

Yet if factional partisans often expressed their passions for the *pugni* in these extreme terms, it must also be remembered that the *battagliole* were primarily festive events, where the quest for personal honor and factional supremacy were blended with raucous enjoyment and social amusement. The tensions that naturally resulted between these two imperatives of militant honor and convivial brawling would seem to have been at least partly worked out at the social base of the factions, through the squads that did most of the actual fighting. In truth the Castellani and the Nicolotti were neither monolithic hordes nor disciplined armies but were more loose conglomerations of disparate small groups, in which face-to-face contact between highly social individuals was essential and neighborhood intimacy was taken for granted. Even though men fought each other as Nicolotti against Castellani at the *battagliole*, they came to the bridges as members of these local squads—particularist groups whose structure helped produce the special blend of burlesque and bellicosity that distinguished the *pugni*.[77]

Fighting squads at the *battagliole* were typically composed of forty or fifty men, whose association was generally based on their living in close proximity to one another. Sometimes shared occupation also played a role in shaping the squads, for in the *battagliole*, as indeed in so much of early modern Venetian popular society, the guild or the looser *universitas* was a central factor in shaping a working man's public associations.[78] Was occupation or residence the more fundamental organizing principal in forming fighting groups at the bridges? Both work and neighborhood were clearly essential in bringing men together, and sometimes squads were drawn from both at the same time; as with the company made up of the *sportelle* (food porters), who were all neighbors in San Pantalon parish.[79] Still, in the end it would seem that in the world of the *pugni*, fighting squads tended to be based more often on residence than on the workplace. Nowhere is this better demonstrated than in the drunken arguments that would occasionally erupt over factional matters between Castellani and Nicolotti workers of the same trade who had gathered socially—at a preferred *tavern* perhaps, or at the guild *scuola*, or even on a group outing:

> Twelve or sixteen cobblers . . . part masters and part journeymen . . . decided to go see the festival that the Muranesi usually hold in August when they rebuild their [glass] furnaces, and, being together at an Inn, since they were not in agreement over their support of the factions, they got into the hottest dispute, to the extent that one of the most ardent among them (maybe also incited by the anger of Bacchus) punched a companion in the face. Another, seeing his friend offended, knocked [the attacker] off his bench onto the

ground. . . . [A]nother pulled out one of the wide knives [that] they carry, cutting in a blow two fingers off [that one's] left hand . . . until [finally] everyone had pulled out daggers, knives, cleavers, swords, boathooks, harpoons, and [even] skewers from the kitchen . . . thinking nothing of being knocked down, disembowelled, or killed.[80]

Nevertheless, there were still two especially coherent occupational groups prominent at the bridges: the fishing community that led the Nicolotti and the shipbuilders of the Arsenal (the *arsenalotti*) who headed the Castellani.[81] Each, as we have seen, dominated their respective factions, but it was a dominance derived not simply from the large number of fighters each community could send to the *battagliole*. Equally important was the special kind of men these were, shaped and disciplined by the particular and highly organized nature of their usual labors. For the fishing community this especially meant the demands imposed on these men by making their living sailing with Venice's deep-sea fleet. These hundred or so fishing boats—popularly known as the "Boats of Miracles" (*Barche dei Miracoli*)— made monthly forays out into the upper Adriatic in search of sardines and similar fish: each boat carried on board "three or four men of great force and great valor," robust fighters called the Paluani, who formed the core of the three hundred-strong contingent that the parish of San Nicolò regularly sent to the bridges. "Everybody knows," the Chronicler of the *pugni* once said, "that lacking these men, there is no hope of seeing a battle," and indeed, their impact on the *battagliole* was such that the encounters themselves tended to synchronize around their presence, running on a monthly schedule that coincided with the periodic returns of the boats to port to refit and renew their crews.[82]

The Paluani seem to have made some effort to set themselves apart as fighting companies. They arrived at the bridges in their squads of forty or fifty in "truly military order, all dressed in uniform, with berets, overshirts, and breeches of red wool." They marched to the battle site by twos, in a long procession with each fighter placing his hands on the shoulders of his companion.[83] So important were the Paluani for the *battagliole* that when, in April 1637, the state wished to stage a *guerra ordinata* at the request of Cardinal de Leon, their absence away at sea threw the success of the entire program in doubt. Eventually, a group of Nicolotti partisans took four longboats (*peote*) and chased after them, catching up with the fleet just off Caorle, but not before they had already cast out their trawling nets:

[Thus] it was not possible to persuade these people to return to Venice, least they prejudice their fishing and their interests. Seeing that it was a desperate situation, these people being so hard and stubborn, [the partisans] . . . therefore cleverly decided to spread out with two of their boats and cut the outstretched nets, which they did. These [Paluani], seeing that they had lost the hope of fishing any more, calmed themselves down, the more so since it was promised them to make up with money all their losses; furthermore, there were among them many youths eager to do battle.[84]

During the *battagliole*, the Paluani habitually sought out the workers of the state Arsenal as their most worthy opponents.[85] The *arsenalotti* had the particular advantage over other resident workers of the city of having a certain amount of military training: skills in group discipline acquired from their service with the naval galleys, which they were able to turn to good account when at the bridges.[86] On more than one occasion a squad of *arsenalotti* was kept in reserve until the *battagliola* reached a crucial point. Then, "with the sounding of a [military] fife, there emerged like famished lions sixty fresh soldiers from the Arsenal . . . skilled and courageous."[87] The men of the Arsenal, along with whatever groups of sailors and soldiers from Dalmatia who happened to be in port, habitually traveled to the battle site by boat, often assembling a virtual flotilla of workboats and naval cutters. Their nautical processions to San Barnabà traveled along the Bacino di San Marco and up the Grand Canal, with banners waving and "accompanied by the sound of drums, trumpets, flutes, and castanets [*gnacchere di gallia*]" and could bring out the entire city to watch.[88] Sending upward of four hundred fighters to the bridges, the *arsenalotti* were so numerous that occasionally they would further subdivide themselves, according to profession, into single squads of caulkers and sawyers (*calafati* and *segatti*).[89] They were at least as essential to the *battagliole* as the Paluani, to the extent that when the War of Candia broke out in 1645 and many of the shipbuilders were sent off with the fleet, all large-scale fistfights were suspended for several years. A nearly unbroken string of Nicolotti victories later in the century would be ascribed by contemporaries less to their own prowess than to the high toll the war had taken among the *arsenalotti* and their sailor allies.[90]

Shared work and special discipline were certainly important in forming the fighters of each of these principal contingents. Yet their special employment should not obscure the fact that these men also had a strong sense of themselves as members of close-knit and geographically defined communities. Venetian fishermen were overwhelmingly concentrated in the city's two westernmost parishes of San Nicolò and Angelo Raffaele, while shipbuilders filled the four parishes surrounding the state Arsenal at the east end of the city (but most particularly the *contrada* of San Pietro di Castello). As a result, fishermen and shipbuilders came to the bridges both as companions of work and as neighbors; if anything, the two relationships only served to reinforce one another. On most other occasions when the Chronicler of the *pugni* identified squads by occupation, this same sense of geographic community was also present. The *farinati*, for example—those stevadors who specialized in unloading flour and who fought for the Nicolotti "all dressed in a uniform of white canvas"—all lived and worked together in the baking center of the city, near the Rialto.[91] The *scortegadori*, or cattle slaughterers, also fought as a Nicolotti squad and had their work and homes together out on the far end of the Cannareggio, where their dirty occupation would least offend their fellow citizens.[92]

The importance of residence in making up these fighting squads can hardly be doubted: most of them were certainly recruited primarily as neighborhood rather than as workplace groups (Map 3). The largest of these squads were identified with particular parishes, and some had a reputation for group spirit and ferocity equaling that of the fishing and shipbuilding contingents. First among these were probably the Gnesotti of Sant' Agnese parish: several hundred formidable fighters (also known to dress themselves all in white) who nurtured a traditional hostility toward the men of San Nicolò, to whom many were connected by ties of both blood and occupation.[93] "Always daring, audacious, and courageous," and among the most dogged fighters in Dorsoduro—their ambushes of passing Nicolotti squads have already been noted—the Gnesotti assumed tacit leadership of the other principal Castellani squads from their *sestiere*: the Zuecchini from the Giudecca, the Gregoriani from San Gregorio, and the Barnabotti from San Barnabà. Other Castellani squads came from parishes on the opposite side of the Grand Canal: the Formosani, from Santa Maria Formosa, the men from the *contrada* of San Luca, and those Rialtini, *specchieri* and others who lived on the margins of Nicolotti territory.[94]

Key Nicolotti contingents were likewise identified with certain parishes within the factional territory. First among these were the Cannareggio *contrade*—San Gerolamo, which might send a hundred fighters, and Sant' Alvise—but almost as important were the Santa Croce *contrade* of San Simeon Piccolo and San Simeon Grande, along with Santa Margherita in Dorsoduro.[95] Yet some of the more important squads belonging to both factions were not from parishes at all, but from much smaller areas: neighborhoods, secondary *campi*, or even single streets. From Castellani territory there always came one or two squads from the Campo delle Gatte, a small neighborhood on the border of Sant' Antonin and Santa Ternità parishes, and sometimes fighters from the Fondamenta Nova—both in the *sestiere* of Castello. A number of Nicolotti neighborhoods likewise sent their own contingents to the bridges. Among these were Santa Marta, Fosse Capera, and the Arzere—each amounting to little more than a few streets or a single quay in the *contrada* of San Nicolò—and those of the Gaffaro, in the *sestiere* of Santa Croce.[96] The most important of these fighting neighborhoods, however, was that of the Bariotti, the residents of the Lista dei Bari, which ran along the border between the parishes of San Giacomo dell'Orio and San Simeon Grande. Thought by some to have taken the name of immigrants from the south Italian town of Bari, the district was especially associated with the cloth and the weaving trades; the Bariotti regularly sent two or three squads of prime fighters to the bridges.[97]

Certainly the size and therefore the relative importance of any one of these contingents varied widely from encounter to encounter. On the occasion of the *battagliola* held at San Barnabà on 16 October 1667, however, the Chronicler of the *pugni* managed to get access to a rough roster of those taking part on each side. From it, a sense emerges of how the different groups might have measured up against one another, at least

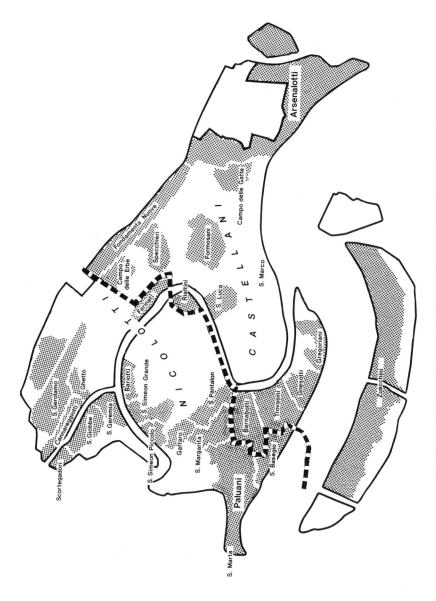

Map 3. Leading parishes and neighborhoods in the world of the *pugni*.

in general terms. Clearly the dominant contingents in each of their factions, the shipbuilders and fishermen still in fact represented fewer than half the fighters of either side:

> The Nicolotti, then, more goaded and provoked than ever, made every effort to round up a large army. The *capi* of San Nicolò let it be known that they had 300 young followers; [those] of Cannareggio, 200; of San Gerolamo, 100; the Bariotti, 150; and those of other parishes and unattached [*fra terra*], 300; then [there were] other companies of the boatmen of the boats from Padua and from Mestre and Malamocco. To the encounter the Castellani gave more than 400 combatants from the House of the Arsenal, including sailors and [those from] the Campo delle Gatte; the Gnesotti and Zuecchini supplied 200; those *fra terra*, 300; and those from Murano, Burano and Torcello, 200.[98]

Coming to battle from every corner of the city and its surrounding islands, these parish and neighborhood contingents turned the monolithic factional armies into a patchwork of individual companies. Like the fishermen and the *farinati*, some of these squads sought to distinguish themselves as a group by wearing matching uniforms, or at least hats.[99] When traveling to the battle site by boat, squads of both factions (but especially those of the Castellani) would also carry their own provisions on board— wine and musical instruments for staging festivities, and whatever weapons might be judged necessary. After a battle was over, the celebration of victory (or, sometimes, the vindication of defeat) would be very much the prerogative of these local groups—of the many parishes and neighborhoods that competed with one another in noise, display, and pride.[100]

The scheduling of the larger, prearranged bridge battles—the so-called *guerre ordinate*—was generally up to the top leaders of each faction, acting in concert with a few patrician and merchant *parteggiani* of the *pugni*. But no leader, patrician or plebeian, had enough prestige to commit his entire faction without first checking with local squad leaders.[101] These neighborhood heroes esteemed themselves highly and, backed up by the groups that they led, were as likely to get into fights and disputes with each other as with their opponents of the other faction: an indication of just how much the "armies" of the Castellani and Nicolotti were really little more than two loose confederations. Sometimes these internal arguments were sharp enough to bring a prearranged *battagliola* to a complete halt, as happened in 1634, when the fishermen of San Nicolò had an angry falling out with some of their oldest allies, the cattle butchers of Cannareggio. The dispute actually had nothing to with the bridges—the fishermen felt that earlier they had been shorted on some bulls they had ordered for a running in their parish—but it so irritated the men of San Nicolò that although they showed up at the bridge, they refused to fight. Instead, they kept their overcoats on and simply stood by in contempt, with their arms crossed, quite pleased to watch the Cannareggiotti take a drubbing at the hands of the *arsenalotti*.[102] Another time the dispute was between the *arsenalotti* themselves and their allied squads of Gnesotti and Zuecchini, about which squads should take the blame for having lost the previous *battagliola*. The scornful accusations that flew between the three groups reached such an intensity that for a few days the entire faction was in danger of coming apart, much to the delight of the Nicolotti.[103]

Significantly, the fighting squads that came to the bridges turn out to have virtually all been from the outskirts of the city. Only a few of the smaller groups—the Rialtini and those of San Luca parish—came from Venice's densely populated center, stretching between the *sestieri* of San Marco and San Polo. Those most heavily involved in the *battagliole* and the cult of the *pugni* were therefore also those most likely to live in the city's peripheral parishes and neighborhoods. There, life was poorer than in the mercantile and ceremonial center, with fewer noble or *cittadini* palaces or the luxurious shops that catered to them. But it was also (as it is today) more open, with smaller, simpler houses, more gardens, numerous *fondamenta*, and the wide lagoon always near at hand. They were neighborhoods that encouraged sociability, and the Paluani, the *arsenalotti*, the Zuecchini, and the Gnesotti owed much of their squads' fighting spirit to the intimate and personal contacts fostered by their tight communities.[104]

Not only were those who came to the *battagliole* generally from Venice's outskirts but the bridges on which they fought were themselves on the edge of the city. The world of the *pugni* was essentially one of movement from neighborhood to fighting bridges that played itself out in the back streets and more remote corners of town. Yet this festive world could also exert a tremendous attraction over the sophisticated center of Venice, and was quite literally able to pull the city's patriciate away from its normal occupations of governing and making money, to bring it hurrying to the peripheral world of fighting bridges and factions. Once, while on its way to battle at San Barnabà, an enormous Castellani flotilla sailed past the Ducal Palace, with banners flying; such was the excitement this vision created among the aristocrats assembled at the Palace for the weekly *broglio* and sitting of the Great Council, that the younger nobles "sped off, racing each other in their gondolas or on land . . . in order to be first to find a good place to see everything." So many charged off to San Barnabà that those few who were left behind had to adjourn the Council for lack of a quorum.[105] Likewise, just the rumor that the factions had decided to schedule a *battagliola* on a workday instead of the usual Sunday could practically clear the marketplaces and commercial centers of their merchants:

> Seeing other people running to San Barnabà, a vast [number] of shopkeepers in the Rialto [would] leave their shops and personal concerns and follow them, without their cloaks . . . just as they found themselves, in their caps and aprons, as furiously as if they were running to put out a fire at home or as if they had been robbed of their goods and property.[106]

Endowed with neither political power nor social prestige, the working classes of Venice—the *popolani*—nevertheless created through the *battagliole* a cultural world particularly their own in the midst of one of the most tightly controlled states in early modern Europe. They did not choose to express this vision of themselves within the primary ritual landscape of the city— on the Grand Canal or along the ceremonial axes that defined the state's heart around San Marco and the Rialto. These were the preserves of the ducal government, realm of the autocratic, hierarchical, processional, and predictable. Some (but certainly not all) Venetian workers and artisans would take part in the manifestations of official culture that flowed along these prescribed routes: their appearance as loyal guildsmen in ducal processions and banquets provided some popular presence in an otherwise strictly patrician occasion. Yet there can be little doubt that such elaborately staged state ceremonials, although they certainly could draw an audience, took a definite second place in the popular mind to the *battagliola*, which was, after all, "the most famous and sought-after recreation of the Venetian people."[107] Unfortunately for the Venetian state's program of civic observances, the principal days set aside for sacred and secular celebrations—All Saints, Santa Giustina (for the battle of Lepanto), Christmas, Santo Steffano, and Candlemas, among others—were also the days that most often lent themselves to the *pugni*. It is true that the glitter and pomp of official ducal processions on such occasions would have attracted many to Piazza San Marco or other appropriate shrines. At the same time, however, the fishing fleet was often in port on these days and the *arsenalotti* would have been given the day off. Knowing as they did that formal state processions would require the police to stick close to the city center, in attendance on the doge, idle workers saw such holidays primarily as occasions for the liberation of the bridges from state control, when *battagliole* staged on the city's periphery could take place free from police meddling.[108] Taking full advantage of the moment, thousands of workers were apparently quite happy to leave Venice's ceremonial center to its patriciate, making off to the bridges to pursue their own violent celebrations. Even on Christmas itself—"the day that for the solemn festival of Our Lord should truly be more devout than licentious"—enormous crowds of fighters and their partisans would gather for a *battagliole*, racing out of church as soon as mass was over and showing, in their dash for a good vantage point at the bridge, as little regard for the solemnity of the occasion as would modern sports fans.[109]

   On those public feast days that occurred during the fall *battagliole* season two different sets of ritual activities could thus be found taking place in Venice. Those in the city center—following the state's ceremonial agenda—stressed above all order, wealth, decorum, and power; they were the Venetian patriciate's formalized representations of the res publica, both to itself and to outside observers.[110] But what, then, were the *battagliole*— contrasting and even competing ritual events—saying in their turn? Quite clearly, of course, they were an expression of disorder, the exaltation of violence over civic peace. Representing the world of the patrician ceremonial turned upside-down, a full-fledged *battagliola* was probably as close to complete plebeian chaos as anything this social environment could tolerate, closer even than the reckless excesses of *giovedì grasso* that concluded the Carnival. It was the complete disregard for the principals of civic order implicit to the *battagliole* that would continually provoke the Venetian state to bring the event under some kind of control.[111]

The *battagliole* were also celebrations of personal honor. Fighting in pairs or in large mobs on a public stage, men sought to excel and gain a name, both among their peers and with whatever distinguished spectators might be present. When high nobility was known to be in the audience, fighters went to every extreme in the hope of being noticed and talked about "even in the most distant foreign lands."[112] The cult of the *pugni* was thus a vehicle for stressing the value of the individual: his prowess, his aggressiveness, his sense of proper conduct. In its emphasis on personal virtue, the world of the bridges formed a counterpole from that of San Marco, the state's formal landscape of position and rank, of processions composed in effect of so many empty robes, filled by and granting status to the holders of the offices they represented.

But as much as celebrating violence or the individual, the ritual of the *battagliole* was about faction. The world of the *pugni* underscores the continuing self-conscious parochialism of Venetian artisans and workers, in the face of a dominate patrician center. Many studies in recent years have charted the movement of northern Italian urban elites away from parish or family centers of power: the formation of more cosmopolitan and citywide networks was in many ways essential for the foundation of a patrician ruling class, as medieval communes evolved into capitals or regional centers. But it would be a mistake to assume too hastily that the urban lower classes, which could expect no similar political or social benefits, would be as ready to abandon their familiar, if peripheral, neighborhood territories. Popular behavior in the context of the *battagliole* gives us a strong indication that at least in the minds of many workers, Venice was still much the same cluster of independent-minded island communities that it had been before the first wooden bridges were erected.[113]

It is quite reasonable to suspect that for many Venetian workers the world of the *pugni* represented a popular answer to the centralizing encroachment of the patrician state. At the same time (indeed, often at the same moment) that the rulers of the Republic—the doge, the *Signoria*, the Senators, Grand chancellor, and representatives of the *scuole grande*—gathered in San Marco in the ritual expression of the hierarchical rigidity, civic harmony, and political unity that made the continuation of Venice possible, thousands of ordinary citizens (and a good many patricians as well) were deserting the city center for outlying bridges, where they demonstrated precisely the opposite spirit. Venetian factionalism found its cultural justification in terms that were agonistic, localist, and plebeian; as a popular cult, the *pugni* served in a sense as an antimyth to the patrician and humanist Myth of Venice. As such, it portrayed a people founded in division, deriving their strength not from any shared sense of order and harmony, but from the assertion and expression of many group identities in the name of factional interests. In its way, the cult of the *pugni* represented the glorification of the fractious spirit of free confederation over a centralizing order imposed by a divinely supported hierarchy; of competition over submission; and of the familiar community over the more distant court of the prince. Such counterurges in the Venetian *popolani* refused to disappear in the post-Renaissance city; indeed, they may have intensified in the face of centuries of increasing social rigidification and centralization.[114]

Venetian factionalism thus extended beyond the single polarity of the Castellani and Nicolotti to encompass a range of popular factional identities that included not only occupation and parish but *campo* and street as well. For thousands of ordinary Venetians aggressive impulses were expressed factionally, in an aggregate of identities, all somehow coexisting within the harmonious embrace of the Republic. These antagonisms and loyalties that divided the city found their mythical expression in a series of foundation legends about the *pugni*: interwoven tales of immigrant rivals, assassinated bishops, public honor and shame, and neighborhood self-consciousness. Together they made up an antimyth of Venice that gave form and identity to this plebeian vision of itself, rationalizing the intensity of the passions aroused at the *battagliole*. Yet the true genius of Venice's artisans and workers was not so much that they produced this myth of faction—the formal expression of which fell, in any case, more naturally to literate and cultured spectators like the Chronicler of the *pugni*—but that they managed to make cultural sense out of this confused social amalgam by means of an ordinary feature of their own neighborhoods turned into a ritual stage. On the marginal space of local bridges they found the setting to enact for themselves their own disorderly drama, that working out of individual ambitions and factional conflict that had no place in the hierarchically ordered world of San Marco or the Rialto.

2

Horatius on the Bridge

E in quello su la piazza per sta giostra
Se vede un Zovenon con un passo avanti
Co la man sotto 'l fianco, e co i so vanti
Conzao per scomenzar la prima mostra

And there on the piazza for this joust,
One sees a grand youth with one foot forward,
With his hand at his side and with his gloves
Ready to begin the first mostra.[1]

On 21 July 1574, after having watched the Castellani and Nicolotti battle over the Ponte dei Carmini for nearly three hours, the French king Henry III made a sign from his balcony to halt the match. For Henry, the combat—enthusiastically waged by six hundred Venetian artisans armed with helmets, shields, and *canne d'India*—had been entertaining, but in the end he reportedly complained that the event "was too small to be a real war and too cruel to be a game."[2] Henry was probably simply expressing his own royal taste in amusements, but he was right in his observation that the *battagliole* were neither exactly sport nor all-out war: they were little battles held on a stage, a drama put on by ordinary artisans who were at the same time both warriors and actors, common rioters and sports heroes. While some saw the battles as expressions of organization and skill that were "among the most pleasing amusements in the city of Venice," others considered them little more than popular riots, "harmful, hateful, and conducive to thousands of scandalous deeds."[3] This essential ambiguity of the *battagliole* seemed to appeal to the artisans of the city, who apparently had no desire to define these encounters with the same sort of formal rules that would circumscribe Siena's race for the Palio or Pisa's *Giuoco del Ponte*. If, in Venetian factional warfare, the object was the conquest of a city bridge, the proper means for accomplishing this end would never be explicitly defined: anyone who attempted to regulate matters at the bridges could well expect to be met with the ironic demand "to know where these obligations are found in the rule book?"[4]

As far as we know, the Venetian *battagliole* were staged and fought without any formal or written regulations—none have survived (as they have from Pisa), nor were any ever mentioned in the various accounts of the event.[5] To many observers—especially visiting foreigners unfamiliar with Venetian amusements—these battles for bridges must have made very little sense. Some encounters—which were commonly referred to as "prearranged wars" or *guerre ordinate*—were put on with elaborate orchestration, requiring days of preparation and involving the efforts not only of thousands of local artisans but also of much of Venice's nobility and merchant class, and sometimes the highest authorities of the state. But the great majority of the bridge battles were much more spontaneous affairs, swirling apparently out of nowhere from the tranquil streets and *campi* of the city and magically materializing into sudden, roaring brawls, complete with thousands of spectators. In either case, there was never much certainty as to how the encounter would proceed. Battle programs might be agreed to ahead of time by factional leaders, but plans could be easily abandoned (often by those same leaders) as the tempers of fighters and the public changed, such that the encounters could transform themselves from individual boxing matches to mass battles to shoving contests to stonings and back again to boxing matches—all with dizzying rapidity.

Considering the irregular and often extemporaneous manner in which Venetian workers approached this, "their most preferred and sought-after amusement," it would be nearly impossible to arrive at any clear idea of what actually went on at the *battagliole* without the help of a source such as the Chronicle of the *pugni*. There are, it is true, a few descriptions of the event written for their contemporaries by foreign observers: that provided by the Frenchman Alexandre Toussaint Limojon de Saint Disdier, in his guidebook *Le Ville et la République de Venise*, is especially detailed and informative.[6] Yet in dealing with an event as vast, chaotic, and spontaneous as the *guerre dei pugni*, such essentially thumbnail descriptions, like the many paintings, etchings, and bronzes of the *battagliole*, necessarily stress only certain (generally the most vivid or bizarre) aspects of the encounters, while almost inevitably falling short of capturing the full range of what the fighters themselves intended or experienced. It is only thanks to the Chronicle of the *pugni*—a work as sprawling and sometimes incoherent as the battles themselves—that it is possible to even attempt to understand what was going on on these Venetian bridges. In the hundreds of individual one-on-one matches and dozens of full-scale battles that the Chronicler describes, there emerges from his many superficially identical accounts something of the range of events and behavior that one could expect to see at the *battagliole*. Moreover, his habit of frequently labeling the acts of individuals and indeed of squads and entire factions as "discreet and honorable," "failing to win admiration," "customary and appropriate," or "dishonest and not practiced at the bridges," makes it plain that there was a system of worker values directing behavior at the bridges. With the Chronicle as a guide, the modern reader can at least reconstruct these behavioral boundaries of the *battagliole*: what were in essense the unwritten cultural "rules" of the *pugni* that gave the complex event a coherency even without the kind of formal *capitolari* that distinguished the Palio of Siena or the *Giuoco del Ponte* of Pisa.[7]

The Art of the Pugni

In its original form Venetian factional combat was expressed in battles waged either with sharpened sticks or robust cane from the lagoon, the latter known as *canne d'India* (Figure 2.1). Such were the first, semimythical confrontations supposedly staged in Venice, and in following this violent medieval pastime residents of the city were by no means unusual. Pretend wars between fighters who wielded sticks and rocks, and who protected themselves with shields, helmets, and body armor, were a regular occurrence in Italian cities during the communal era. Some towns—in particular Pisa, with its *Giuoco del Ponte*—kept up the custom into modern times. The sticks were typically employed as much for thrusting as for beating; in Venice at least it was customary to harden the point at one end by soaking it repeatedly in boiling oil. A well-aimed jab even with such a simple weapon could easily prove fatal, so Venetian artisans went to the bridges thoroughly protected in the age of the *guerre di canne*. Their defensive equipment featured most prominently an iron helmet, or *celada*, that was cruder but virtually as robust as those used in knightly tournaments. Fighters also decked themselves out with some kind of covering for the torso; a few sported a full-fledged iron and leather cuirass, but most were content with the less showy and unobstructive *zacco*, or body mail, that was worn under the shirt. High-quality (and expensive) *zacco* could be counted on to stop the thrust of even a metal-tipped pike, while not inhibiting movement in the manner of a bulky cuirass. Since it was worn in a way that was not readily visible, true partisans of the bridges might also wear their *zacco* while going about the streets on regular business or to their local tavern, on the off chance that they might get involved in a factional brawl.[8] To further ward off the lunges of enemy sticks in the *guerre di canne* combatants also equipped themselves with a leather or wooden shield, called a *targa* or *rodella*. In a pinch, however, men could defend themselves almost as well with the adroit use of their cloak, which might be carried into battle wrapped around the left arm (Figure 2.2).[9]

The *battagliola* witnessed by Henry III at the Ponte dei Carmini in 1574 was one of the last in Venice to be waged with sticks and shields. By the end of the century the venerable pastime of the *guerre di canne* had been completely replaced by the somewhat less bloody but equally exciting *guerre di pugni*. The demise of stick warfare in the city has generally been credited to the Venetian state's increasing opposition to such disorderly and "popular" pastimes. It is a tradition in Venetian social history

Figure 2.1   The sixteenth-century *guerre di canne*; woodcut
accompanying Alessandro Caravia's "La verra antiga dei
Castellani, Canaruoli, e Gnatti, con la morte de Giurco e
Gnagni, in lengua brava" (Venice, 1550). (Museo Correr,
Archivio Fotografico, M. 33644)

that dates back at least to the mid-nineteenth century, when Alessandro
Zanotti praised the Council of Ten—the Republic's primary policing magistracy and an adversary of civic mayhem generally—for its eventual suppression of the "detestable practices" of the *guerre di canne*.[10] Yet the Ten's
decisiveness in this matter seems to have been more apparent than real, as
was so often the case in the tacit and constant interchange between the
city's patrician rulers and its ordinary citizens. Although stick fights in the
city were indeed officially outlawed by the Ten the very day of King Henry's
departure (an edict that would be issued again a year later), it is also clear
that Venetian workers had no intention of throwing away their sticks, helmets, and shields.[11] It appears that despite the ban a few optimistic and

faithful Nicolotti followers decided to hide away several boatloads of surplus *canne* in anticipation of the day when they would be able to return to the bridges. They got their opportunity when the government decided to arrange at least two further (if somewhat reduced) stick wars for state occasions: one at Santa Fosca in 1582 for the representative of the Turkish sultan Murad III and another for the ambassadors from Japan in 1585, at the Ponte dei Servi.[12]

The fact that ordinary Venetians were both willing and perfectly able to hang on to these and other implements for waging the *guerre di canne* (men were still coming to the battles in *celade e curasse* in the 1640s) suggests that not all workers in the city were intimidated by the Ten.[13] This may account for the existence of a kind of antimyth about this transition from sticks to fists, a story that the Chronicler repeated many years after the event and that gives most of the credit for the change to the good sense of the fighters themselves rather than to the repressive force of the Ten and its police. According to this version, it so happened during the

Figure 2.2 Fighter dressed in armor for the *guerre di canne*; Jan Grevembroch in *Varie venete, curiosità sacre e profane* (1755–1765). (MCAF, M. 24061)

battagliole staged in 1585 for the Japanese ambassadors that the Castellani fighters ran out of sticks before the Nicolotti did—having broken or lost all of theirs in the water, while their opponents, as already noted, had been farsighted enough to bring the extra *canne* they had hidden away years earlier. Although the Castellani were at an apparent disadvantage, far from losing heart a squad of *arsenalotti* had a positive inspiration:

> They agreed to throw away the rest of the sticks that they were carrying, along with their shields, their cloaks [*gabani*], and outer clothing, and meet the Nicolotti squads with fists. They were not injured by the sticks of the enemy, who could no longer stab nor beat with them, for the Castellani would punch them in the face or the chest. [Thus] they advanced up the bridge with few casualties. . . . The men of San Nicolò, seeing that these injuries from fists were inevitable, and what was more important, highly damaging . . . resolved that they too should cast aside their sticks, shields, and cloaks, and meet the Castellani as equals. This new mode of combating caused great curiosity and wonder in everyone.[14]

Quite possibly this story is apocryphal: at the very least it seems unlikely that unarmed men would fare so well against such heavily armored adversaries. In any case, a host of more mundane causes may also have contributed to the decline of the *guerre di canne*, not the least of which might have been the simple expense of maintaining the armor, a cost largely supported by noble partisans. Unquestionably, men lumbering about the city outfitted in helmets and breastplates would also have been far more conspicuous than simple pugilists, and thus much more likely to have attracted the unwanted attentions of the *sbirri* of the Ten.

Yet the version reported by the Chronicler does make several important assertions about Venetian factional combat. One of these is that at the bridges there was room for only one form of fighting, and for whatever reasons, once the *guerre di canne* had begun to fall from popular favor, it could not coexist alongside the *pugni*: the two styles of fighting were just too different. The story had a symbolic import as well, in asserting that the fast-moving boxer, armed only with his fists and skills, won out over the more stolid stick wielder at the bridges not because the state had so commanded but because he was an innately superior fighter. That an essentially naked man should triumph over a heavily armored adversary was itself—in an age dominated by professional soldiers, hierarchical armies, and not a few remnants of chivalric ideals—a seeming paradox highly charged with republican and egalitarian overtones. The boxer's victory was one of pragmatism rather than of patrician law, the result of an intrinsically plebeian decision as to what worked best at the bridges.

The egalitarian implications of this change from sticks to fists at the bridges rested in its turn on a still more significant popular assumption: that there was indeed an art to the *pugni*. The pugilist was able to triumph over the clumsy stick wielder because he was more skillful at his craft, in particular, he knew how to throw a punch (*tirar un pugno*) under the guard of his adversary. Enthusiasts of the *pugni* believed that these skills were particularly Venetian, developed and perfected by the *popolani* of the city.[15] Although the wide diffusion of boxing in subsequent centuries may lead many modern readers to assume that throwing a straight punch is a perfectly natural act, there is every indication that in the days when men were primarily accustomed to express their aggressions by means of implements—swords for patricians, and knives or a staff (*legno*) for commoners— such skills were by no means universal. Newcomers to the *battagliole*, such as the soldiers from Dalmatia (*Schiavoni*) who regularly passed through the city, soon gave away their ignorance of the art of the *pugni* by swinging their arms about wildly as if they still had sabers in their hands. The Nicolotti who fought against them knew how to make short work of such novices, for:

> [A]lthough these [Slavs] were accustomed to sorties and raids, to musket and harquebus fire, and to coming to the clinch with sharp steel, nevertheless battling with fists above a narrow bridge was much different from their training and courage, and therefore most of them were thrown down from the bridge into the water by the Nicolotto skill."[16]

The fame of Venetian pugilists was such that by the end of the seventeenth century they were in demand to give demonstrations of their skills in other cities—as in 1670, when the Bolognese decided to stage a *battagliola* on one of their own bridges as part of their celebrations for San Bartolomeo's Day. A number of Venetian exiles (*banditi*) and merchants who were in Bologna and nearby Ferrara were requested by the festival organizers to fight against a squad of local men. Although the Bolognese were provided with some Venetian leaders, they were completely overwhelmed by their opponents,

> who with hostility were only waiting to give pitiless punches to the Bolognese, who did not even know how to throw a punch trained, I would say, for the Venetian *battagliola*, but rather [they fought] in the manner of the Dalmatians, who never lead with the point of the fist, but only as if they were chopping wood with an axe. The Bolognese for the most part threw themselves voluntarily into the water, since they could not tolerate the violence of the Venetian Fist.[17]

Thus by 1600 bridge fighting in Venice had passed entirely from *canne* to *pugni*.[18] Only the remnants of the earlier sport survived: in the habit of some die-hards to keep on bringing their *targhe* to the bridges, and in the Chronicler's continuing reference to one-on-one boxing matches as *steccadi*—an old expression for stick fights.[19] By the 1660s helmets had disappeared from the scene, and *zacco* had become a fairly rare sight—no doubt in good part because those who wore the heavy metal mesh knew that it greatly increased their chances of drowning should they be knocked off the bridge into the water.[20]

In contrast to the stick fighters, who in preparation for battle dressed themselves in elaborate equipment, participants essentially undressed them-

selves for the *guerre di pugni*. Indeed, the sudden appearance of disrobed
men (*spogliati*) among the Sunday crowds that gathered in the *campi* or
near the bridges was a visual and psychological sign that a battle was
imminent. This stripping consisted first of all of the removing of one's
overcloak, or *ferrariolo*, a garment of dark blue or black wool that was
commonly worn during the cold fall months of the *battagliole* season.[21]
As long as a participant continued to wear his *ferrariolo*, he was clearly
not in the mood for combat; factional leaders generally did not mount
the bridge to serve as referees without leaving their cloaks behind with
friends beforehand, not only to gain more ease of movement but also, quite
simply, to avoid ruining a rather costly piece of clothing that could easily
fall into the water during a fight.[22] Too expensive to be worn by the meaner
sorts of workers—porters, some boatmen, and those who would instead
wear the shorter *gabbano*—the *ferrariolo* also carried with it something of
the implication of gentility, a badge of *signori honorati e molto commodi*
(Figure 2.3).[23] Perhaps because he had this in mind, the Chronicler of
the *pugni* habitually referred to the audience crowding around the *battagliole* as the *gente dei ferrarioli*, a somewhat wry metonym to indicate
the superior station and generally noncombatant status of these onlookers,
"who came more to look at the war than to make it."[24]

With the *genti dei ferrarioli* providing a uniform if somewhat somber
backdrop, those who intended to take part in the fighting went through
the rituals of undressing. It could be a time-consuming process, as men
took off their shirts or their *gabbani* and wound them into rolls which they
then wrapped around their waists in a *fascia*, to protect the kidneys from
blows. Fighters also needed some time to get their long hair (*zazzara*)
secured in place under their rimless fighting caps, known as *capelli alla
schiavona*.[25] They would then don felt shoes (*scalfarotti di feltrone*) to
protect against the slipperiness of the muddy bridge surface, and take off
their rings, so their punches might not cut unfairly.[26]

It was evidently cutomary to fight bare-chested in the one-on-one
boxing matches (the *mostre*) that often preceded the general assault on the
bridge (the *frotte*): fighters who availed themselves of the protection of a
leather or cardboard chest cover (once commonplace in the *guerre di canne*
and known in their various forms as *corsaletti, cassi, pettorali,* or *busti*) might
be tempted to cheat by putting on several more layers of padding underneath. Some sort of corselet was, it is true, commonly worn by those taking part in the *frotte*, although considering that these coverings were often
made of shiny silver cardboard, they may have been intended as much for
decorative as for protective purposes. This consciousness of cutting a fine
figure was if anything more evident during individual combat than in the
melee of the *frotte*. The fishermen from San Nicolò—known after all as
the *gente delle camisole*—certainly kept on their red overshirts while fighting at the *mostre*, as did certain factional leaders, who might sport gold
embroidered caps.[27] Some individual fighters might also come to the bridge
wearing the livery of an aristocratic patron or master—decked out in sat-

Figure 2.3 Gentlemen wearing a tabarro
(*ferrariolo*); Grevembroch. (Museo Correr, Archivio
Fotografico, M. 23784)

ins, for example, with specially colored hose or *braghese*—although apparently not as many as might be expected, considering the extensive patronage ties that existed between patricians and pugilists during these years. There seems to have been a sense of limits to this sort of personal embellishment going into combat, evidently reflecting a feeling that the fighting arena of a bridge was a serious place, one of comparative simplicity, where frivolous or strange costumes were inappropriate or disturbing. Thus, when it was rumored that the Castello fighter Stramatel (meaning "Completely Crazy") would be appearing dressed in the apricot-colored silk hose supplied to him by an admiring patron, he was jeered by the Nicolotti crowd: "Stramatel, where are you? Show us your silken socks!" When the Nicolotto goldsmith Bonhomo insisted on presenting himself at the *mostra* not only fully dressed, but outfitted in a mourning cape with a bizarre hat, the Castellani were at first afraid to send a champion against him, considering it unlucky that someone should come to the bridges "in lugubrious clothes that one only wears in a funeral cortege."[28]

Fighters also equipped themselves with gloves, or *guanti*. These were not the padded sort—the protective "mufflers" that would be first introduced in British boxing circles during the eighteenth century—but were made of simple leather, closely fitted and designed to protect the fighters' hand while also "giving them a firmer punch." Customarily, each participant would wear just a single glove, on his right hand—unless he were *zanco*, or left-handed.[29] Originally, fighters did not appear to treat their glove as anything more than just another piece of boxing equipment. Indeed, the recruiting parties sent to outlying communities before a *guerra ordinata* routinely loaded their boats with *cassi, corsaletti,* and *guanti* to give to all the new fighters they managed to enroll.[30] By the later seventeenth century, however, the more renowned duelists began to sport two gloves, often with a more distinctive and personalized look: sometimes made out of hard leather, sometimes extending halfway up the forearm or even to the elbow (in which case they were called *manopoli*). As with dress in general at the bridges, however, simplicity with gloves was considered by many to be a virtue, especially after one fighter tried to get away with wearing a glove especially sewn with extra stitchings of lute strings, designed to rapidly bloody his opponent's face. If someone were suspected of attempting to use such a *guanto avantaggioso*, two identical new gloves might be thrown into the center of the bridge instead, and each faction's leaders could choose which one their man would use.[31]

Once he had completed his preparations, a fighter was said to be *in arnese*, or outfitted for war. If he were as redoubtable as the famed duelist Mazzagatte ("Cat Killer"), he was no doubt an impressive sight: "[S]purring everyone to admire him, [with] his naked chest, [waist] girdled with a red sash, with his right hand at his side, armed with a glove to the elbow and with single-soled shoes, he made himself known as a true Warrior."[32]

Yet before Mazzagatte or any other warrior could be expected to present himself on the bridge to do combat, the battle site first had to be prepared, both physically and psychologically. When the factions had prearranged their battles beforehand, in the so-called *guerre ordinate*, they would typically give themselves at least two or three days to make some rudimentary repairs on the often decayed bridge surface. Furthermore, to reduce the risk of injuries to participants, fans and followers of the *pugni*—referred to by the Chronicler as *parteggiani* or *fattionari*—might also see to it that the canal beneath the bridge was cleared of floating rubbish and submerged obstacles, that sawdust was sprinkled on the bridge surface to reduce its slipperiness, and that bundles of straw (*stramazzi*) were placed around the *fondamenta* and bridge abutments to cushion those who might fall off the bridge backward. Such straw padding seems to have made the battles even more spectacular: when fighters felt less afraid of tumbling down on the stone of the quays, they were willing to positively fling themselves at the enemy ranks. The squads themselves might also take a hand at setting up barricades of beams and planks in adjoining *campi* and *calle*, with the aim of regulating the flow of fighters to the bridge and keeping the ever-present *gente dei ferrarioli* at a safe distance.[33] Sometimes this enthusiasm for altering the surrounding cityscape to suit the needs of the *battagliole* could get out of hand: more than once factional partisans took it in their minds to actually break holes in existing walls in order to gain easier access to the bridge; they were usually opposed, though not always stopped.[34]

At the same time, a host of petty entrepreneurs also descended on the site, in hopes of profiting from the spectacle. Food hawkers—some perhaps servants on their afternoon off—would set up business, ready to offer the crowds "dumplings and chestnuts: *gnochi e maroni*". Whether the encounters were to be large-scale battles arranged days in advance or only a series of duels between individual champions, energetic builders would soon cover the adjoining quays with benches and bleachers, or *palchi*, for paying spectators. Flimsy affairs made of barrels and planks and prone to collapse under the weight of an enthusiastic audience, *palchi* still attracted hundreds of customers, who were willing to pay a few shillings (*soldi*) apiece for a good view of the conflict.[35] Those fortunate few who held leases on the houses near the bridge could expect to realize far greater profits, for Venetian and foreign patricians would pay them ten *scudi* or more (a hundred times the cost of a spot on the *palchi*) for a well-placed window seat.[36] Spectators would also crowd the rooftops of these houses during the *battagliole*, and presumably they had to pay for the privilege (Figure 2.4). Because they were altogether a more fractious crowd than those on the balconies and bleachers below, those who precariously perched on these rooftops high above the battle site could also prove extremely costly for the enterprising landlords who rented them their spots: in their enthusiasm such spectators could often start tearing off the roof tiles from around where they sat, launching them in showers at the fighters and onlookers below until "the houses [on which they sat] were left stripped to their roofbeams."[37]

Meanwhile, the Venetians themselves would have to be brought to the proper frame of mind—the fever pitch of factional antagonism that was necessary if a successful *battagliola* were to take place. The customary season of the *pugni* was the fall—roughly from between the feast of the Assumption (August 15) until Epiphany—but the activity of stirring up tensions could easily begin as early as June. This was accomplished in particular by teenaged boys, for whom "in the season in which the weather generally boils . . . there also began to boil and arise their ardor and their fights, to the point that they would have nothing else in mind."[38] As already noted, youths, *bravi*, and other idlers tended to hang about on or near the bridges all over the city, but in the summer months especially these youth groups took on a factional coloring, as young men identifying themselves as either Castellani or Nicolotti began to coalesce at opposite sides of the preferred *ponti di guerre* to taunt and provoke each other.[39]

Although sometimes older partisans seeking to hasten the *battagliole* season tried to heat up factional tensions by goading their own or their neighbors' sons to attack opponents on the other side, usually no such prodding was necessary to induce local youths to brawl with one another.[40]

Figure 2.4 During the *battagliole* spectators filled nearby rooftops. (Museo Correr, Archivio Fotografico, M. 3992)

As Saint Disdier observed; "The little children that meet in the streets will argue over their [favorite] champions, and if they are of contrary factions, they will never separate without coming to blows." Eager to emulate the renowned fighters among their elders, even boys *di prima scuola* were fond of aggressive display for its own sake, putting on *mostre* in the quite literal sense of the word, as a showing of oneself. To a large extent, simply appearing on the bridge *in arnese*—that is, stripped down and ready to fight—was enough to provoke youths on the other side to respond in kind. If this failed to get a reaction, jumping and leaping—*saltando in faccia l'inimico*—were also effective, especially if accompanied by an array of verbal insults and challenges.[41]

The presence of youth groups from both factions hanging about the bridge abutments or adjoining *fondamenta* appears to have greatly increased and intensified the territorial and boundary significance of the bridge itself. At such moments youths became acutely sensitive to the provocation and challenge implicit in setting foot into each other's domain, and naturally made much of leaping up on to the bridge's central *piazza di mezzo*—the essence of a factional no-man's-land—to drive home their displays and exchanges of insults.[42] If one side were slow to respond to such challenges, the more ambitious boys from the other side might well dash across the bridge as a group to carry their provocation bodily onto enemy territory. Should, as sometimes happened, such bold youths arrive at the *ponte di guerra* and find no significant opposition on hand, they might be rash enough to try a full-fledged *scorreria*, a sort of raid into opposition territory. Shouting insults, running along the streets, and perhaps arriving as far as the doors of their enemies' parish church, they sought as noisily as possible to provoke outrage and indigation.[43] More often, however, there already were a good many young men hanging about on the other side, and so such incursions would barely get beyond the edge of the bridge before meeting stalwart opposition. Thereupon, spirited fighting would generally ensue, involving anywhere from a few dozen to upward of a hundred youthful antagonists.

The Chronicler of the *pugni* sometimes referred to such brawls as *scaramuccie*, or skirmishes, perhaps to underscore both their preliminary nature and their identity as factional frays rather than casual melees. For those older men who liked to observe such fracases between neighborhood youths, there were certain tacitly agreed-upon elements that made for a good *scaramuccia*. The fighting should be limited to punching, wrestling, and shoving, without the use of any daggers or knives. Moreover, the encounter should be open and spontaneous, with the youth of the two factions all mixed together, engaged on all the seven *piazze* of the bridge—if not on the *fondamenta* on either side. Typically, such youthful encounters were short-lived, however, with one side quickly routing the other either because they were older or more numerous or because they came to the bridge armed with pockets full of stones (*sassi* or *cuogoli*).[44]

The continuous sight of youth groups showing off and fighting around one of the *ponti di guerra* over a succession of summer feast days would in time leave the two factions "pregnant with war" (*gravido di guerra*).[45] As the season wore on, more experienced fighters would be galvanized into action, either annoyed by the taunts thrown at them by enemy youths or simply drawn by the love of combat into abandoning their places on the sidelines. Sometimes an escalating series of clashes and encounters would follow, as increasing crowds of passersby stopped to watch and ever-larger and more mature groups of fighters would capture the bridge from younger, weaker groups, only to be expelled in their turn. Such a succession would usually culminate with the arrival of a few squads of one of the more disciplined neighborhood contingents, quickly assembled from nearby *campi* or taverns and marched in haste to the contested bridge. When the battle site was the Ponte di Pugni at San Barnabà, this usually meant a gang of the aggressive Gnesotti from Sant' Agnese parish, or a few columns of the *gente delle camisole* of San Nicolò; at the Ponti di Santa Fosca or San Marziale, the Cannareggiotti could be expected.[46]

The mustering of such squads was the responsibility of local fighters of repute, whom the Chronicler of the *pugni* referred to as *capi, capi di companie*, or sometimes *caporioni*.[47] These men, as the latter term makes explicit, were neighborhood leaders: they not only rounded up the fighters of their district when a *battagliola* seemed imminent, but they also formed them up into disciplined columns (that is, *rolar le fille*) when it was time to attack the bridge itself. At any one time, there appear to have been a dozen or so active *capi* on each side, ordinary artisans who were sufficiently devoted to the values and antagonisms of factional competition that they would work ceaselessly to promote the cult of the *pugni* in their own neighborhood. Some maintained their leadership in the *pugni* for years, springing as they did from lineages of fighters whose local dominence spanned entire generations.[48] Indeed, the splintered nature of the Castellani and Nicolotti factions, with their many parish and local contingents, was quite likely produced by of these neighborhood *capi* and their recruiting activities. The fifty or so fighters in each local squad probably represented about the maximum number of men that any one *capo* could be expected to control, whether at the neighborhood tavern or in the thick of the *battagliole*; they were likewise the limit he could expect to round up by "beating on the doors of friends or relatives." The names by which these squads came to be known—the Barnabotti, the Rialtini, the scortegadori—may well have said as much about the range of the personal influence and recruiting enthusiasm of individual *capi* as they did about fighters' geographic or workplace solidarity.[49]

The relationship between a *capo* and the fighters of his neighborhood was one of mutual support. Each conscientious *capo* made a point of keeping an eye on the upcoming youths of his district, taking pains to recruit and train those that seemed to offer the most promise as future fighters.[50] Before a battle he went to "the most frequented places of recreation" and saw to it that his men got as much as possible of the fighting gear, food, wine, or money being disbursed by his faction's wealthy *protettori*. Some *capi* were so dedicated to the *pugni* that they would "maintain their companies at their own expense, both at their private houses and at the taverns and wineshops, abandoning their own interests and duties [in the process]." The fighters repaid this support with loyalty to their *capo*; they were more than willing to leave their daily work several days before an encounter to help him arrange a *guerra ordinata* and to be his most enthusiastic boosters should he decide to offer himself in the single combat of the *mostra*.[51] In a sense, the *capi* and their squads could be said to have defined each other. Each renowned leader's reputation grew together with the quality and fame of the fighters he trained and commanded in combat. In turn, a squad found its coherence in its *capo*, rallying to the standard (*insegna*) that he carried, willing to follow him into thick of the fight, and taking it especially hard if he were badly or unfairly injured—to the extent of either leaving the bridge in despair or renewing its attack with an increased desire for vengeance.[52]

As newly arrived squads swelled the ranks of fighters on both sides of the bridge, the crowd of onlookers rapidly increased as well. Even for the fairly spontaneous clashes initiated by youthful gangs, an audience of several thousand could materialize in less than a half hour, as the word of an impeding encounter flashed through nearby *campi* and shops. When battles were arranged several days in advance, the numbers that turned out could be truly staggering: the Chronicler wrote of gatherings ranging from ten thousand "between fighters and the surrounding crowd" to "more than thirty thousand, every one of them shouting." Though his figures should be treated cautiously, all contemporary accounts of the *battagliole* stress the event's enormous drawing power among Venetian men and women of all classes and occupations. They also make it clear that huge numbers of enthusiasts were perfectly willing to cram themselves into any available space around the designated bridge whenever they had hope of witnessing a battle. Besides filling every balcony, window, and rooftop that provided any kind of view of the scene, they also packed the *fondamente* leading to the bridge, as well as other bridges further up or down the canal. Those who had boats rowed them frantically as soon as word of a *battagliola* began to spread, in the hope of mooring as close to the bridge as possible; by the time the fighters had actually started to contest the bridge, the canal underneath was packed with *barche*, *gondole*, and *peote* for hundreds of yards in either direction, "as if it were land and not water."[53]

In all this crush there was bound to be a good deal of discord—especially as patricians seeking a better view tried to force their way through the crowd at sword point—and the violence within the audience often attained a level not much lower than that on the bridge itself. Spectators were also prone to panic: a few rocks thrown into the crowd or even the glimpse of a drawn pistol could easily trigger a stampede in which dozens might be trampled or shoved into the water. That this mob was able to stabilize itself at all in these circumstances was largely due to the topography inherent in the battle site: the canal under the bridge provided a fairly effective barrier between the supporters of the two sides, defining the circle of onlookers as two coherent halves that could freely applaud their factional champions yet still not so easily get at each other to turn the bridge battle into a public riot. This physical separation of the two sides set the larger, factional stage that was so essential to the *battagliole*.[54] In this arena, the two noisy, distinct, and competing hoards of dedicated Nicolotti and Castellani partisans vied with one another—by means of shouts, whistling, and above all, by the beating of oars on gondolas or sticks on the shutters (*scuri*) of nearby houses—to magnify the successes of their own champions and the failures of the enemy's.[55]

So high did passions run during the battles that should any members of one army find themselves accidently caught on the wrong side—that is, if they were *trapassati* by overrunning the bridge during a charge—they risked a serious beating that sometimes proved fatal. To avoid such dangers while still keeping themselves informed of enemy squad movements and tactical maneuvers, factional leaders resorted to the typically Venetian solution of infiltrating the opponent's principal gathering places with spies (*spie*; also called *esploratori* or *confidanti*). Apparently these agents were able to move about in the opponent's territory while the battle was underway and factional tensions were at a flash point because they were not recognized for what they were: some perhaps because they were not native-born Venetians, others evidently because they were factional turncoats. The best of them were able to insinuate themselves right among the enemy leadership councils, bringing back detailed reports of troop numbers and future battle plans.[56]

After organized fighting squads appeared on the scene, with factional passions already running high, the *battagliola* could develop in any of several directions. Abruptly, and often with no warning whatsoever, the two sides might simply attack each other en masse, both charging toward the center of the bridge in a concerted effort to punch (or push) the other off into the water or back onto its own *fondamenta*.[57] This was the *frotta* at its most spontaneous, begun without any particular planning and often with too much haste for any factional leaders to step forward and direct the fighters. Often, like the preliminary *scaramuccie* of youth groups, these impulsive clashes were of short duration; still, their open and undisciplined nature caused them to be much appreciated by onlookers:

> The brawl was marvelously convoluted, as there was fighting on all the *piazze*, but hardly had one squad taken over one *piazza* than immediately it lost another. The bridge was always in litigation, because now the Castellani were expelled to the foot [of the bridge] and now they . . . chased the Nicolotti as far as their own territories; but because the factions grew ever larger, the fight grew equally more contentious.[58]

More frequently, however, the factions would halt just short of an open attack and instead mass on their respective sides of the canal to threaten and shout insults at each other. The failure of the two groups to realize a *frotta* straight away was usually because the leaders of one side were afraid that their fighters were either outmanned or too inexperienced to have a good chance of winning. If their opponents did indeed feel be superior in strength or numbers, they would have all the more reason to try to provoke their enemy into an ill-considered attack, taunting them with shouts that they had weak bowels and were fit only to fight with children.[59] As well as calling out "arrogant and most insulting words," those of the superior side might also *festeggiare* with more explicit gestures: occupying part, half, or (more rarely) all of the *ponte di guerra*. There they would jump about and dance the aggressive *moresca*, and sometimes they might drape the bridge in mourning—which could even include lugging a black gondola cabin (called a *felce*) up to the *piazza di mezo*—while "shouting that the bridge wept in sadness, for the death of [their opponent's] bravery."[60]

Sometimes such direct or symbolic acts were enough to goad the enemy into plunging into a full-scale *frotta*. More often, however, recognized factional leaders had by this time begun to assert some control over the ranks of both sides, making it at least as likely that cooler heads would prevail. Recognizing that they would be entering combat at a disadvantage, leaders on the weaker side would seek to restrain (by force if necessary) their more excited fighters and would propose instead to stage some number of *mostre*. Often their request would be accompanied by the promise to stage a *frotta* at some later time—either at the end of the series of *mostre* or on the next available feast day.[61] Since the leaders of the stronger faction were well aware that this was little more than a ploy to salvage a bit of honor out of an otherwise embarassing situation, they might be tempted to refuse or—especially if their fighters were already occupying the bridge—they would agree to clear the bridge only under certain conditions. These might include requiring their opponents to shame themselves first by admitting they had been beaten or setting up some complex procedure for staging the *mostre* to prevent any later reneging on a promised *frotta*.[62]

The term *mostra* means a display or exhibition, and certainly a fighter's showing off was an essential part of single combat on the *ponte di guerra*. Although the actual fighting itself was more properly called a *cimento* or *steccado*, the Chronicler of the *pugni*, Saint Disdier (with the French cognate *montre*), and other contemporary commentators on the *battagliole* often used the term *mostra* to refer to the one-on-one boxing match in its entirety.[63] There was some sense to this, for from the moment he first presented himself as a contestant in the center of the bridge, through successive rounds of boxing, to his moment of celebrating victory (or conceding defeat), the fighter, or *duelista*, was constantly showing himself, acting out on a public stage his personal claims for honor and reputation. It was essential that each combatant who came to the fighting arena should "show himself well" (*mostrarsi bene*), for display was a vital element in the art of the *pugni*. If, thanks to his past notoriety or swaggering conduct, a duelist issued his challenge and no opponent came forward to face him, he effectively won a default victory that was no less honorable than one achieved by hard boxing. Not surprisingly, the best fighters made an art of coming onto the bridge scowling, shouting threats, and flexing their muscles before the enemy crowd; "using every skill and effort to be acclaimed."[64]

Despite its obvious importance for determining both a fighter's reputation and the course of the *battagliole* overall, this showing-off period was not organized in any clearly defined way. Most typically, aspiring duelists would simply put themselves forward on their own; either advancing to the center of the bridge and calling out the name of a specific opponent they wished to fight, or just standing silently before the opposing faction, essentially offering an open challenge to anyone who dared to come forth. Occasionally, however, duelists would be nominated by their factional companions—either by a few leaders, by enthusiasts in the audience, or by the entire factional army acting together. Those who had received the challenge on the other side were usually quick to come forward in reply; especially if singled out by name, they would have had a hard time avoiding a summons to come up and fight, although some did beg off without complete loss of honor.[65] Apparently all but the fiercest champions who offered an open challenge to the enemy could expect to be quickly answered, although if the challenger were well known it might take ten or fifteen minutes for the young men on the other side to decide (often by fighting among themselves) who would have the right to meet him.[66] Once they had both come to the middle of the bridge, the two duelists would seek to project their self-confidence and prowess by scowling, gesturing aggressively, and leaping about. Such swaggering around on the relatively restricted area of the *piazza di mezzo* was important for establishing the right atmosphere for the match to follow, but since there were often dozens of *mostre* to be fought in a single afternoon, too much of this posturing and strutting about could also be taken as a sign of being "vain, ambitious, and capricious."[67]

Holding *mostre* significantly (although often only temporarily) changed the direction of the *battagliole*, away from the sort of free-form brawls that typified the youthful *scaramuccie* to a more focused and more "adult" type of contest. The task of ensuring some form of order in these bouts was up to those factional leaders known as *padrini*, whose arrival at the center of the bridge was usually a sign that such matches were about to begin. Normally meaning "godfather," *padrino* was also the term used for the seconds in duels of honor between gentlemen. In the context of the *pugni*, the *padrini* would seem to have combined elements from both these roles: they were referees during the one-on-one *mostre* and often as not also the commanders and leaders of their respective factions.[68] Not only did they supervise individual boxing bouts on the bridges, deciding the winners and keeping an eye out for unfair combat, but they also controlled the strategic placement of the fighting squads during the *frotte* (often leading their charges as well) and were ultimately responsible for announcing—and enforcing—their faction's surrender in the case of defeat. At the same time, many a *padrino* kept up an active place among the first ranks of individual boxers, presenting himself in the *mostre* to seek both individual and factional honor.[69]

Despite the undoubted power they wielded over those who came to the bridges, there is no indication that the selection of *padrini* was any more carefully regulated than any other aspect of the *battagliole*. Often, especially when the whole encounter was rather spontaneous, one or more *padrini* quite literally "made themselves" on each side, coming forth to take a leadership role completely on their own (in which case, however, they might be referred to only as *mezi padrini*). Yet for *padrini* to be effective leaders and referees, they at least had to be certain of commanding the general respect of both sides. As a result, most of them were chosen by the consensus of their factions; anyone presenting himself who was commonly considered too "quibbling and peculiar" (*cavilloso e bizarro*) risked finding that no one else was willing to serve with him. Since authority at the bridges depended primarily on having the fighting reputation necessary to back up orders, the most acceptable *padrini* were mature *capi*, men perhaps somewhat past their prime, but still not to be trifled with by the aggressive young beginners of either faction. When especially well-known fighters were expected to appear in *mostra*, equally renowned *padrini*—often two for each combatant—were considered necessary to supervise them, both as a question of honor and because they were the only individuals available with enough authority to keep such proud duelists under a minimum of control.[70]

Since *padrini* were chosen from among the most experienced, partisan followers of each faction, no one expected them to be impartial when they served as referees at the *mostre*; some in fact were relatives of the duelist they were meant to supervise.[71] Indeed, fighters trusted that their *padrini* would particularly try to dupe or cheat their enemy on every occasion possible. Yet such was the reputation of these men as factional leaders that without them *mostre* seemed to amount to rather paltry affairs, and the fighting contingents, "left at liberty to themselves [were] without orders, without leadership, and without law." When, on the other hand, two or more recognized *padrini* were present, one of the most necessary conditions for proper combat had been achieved. It was in fact only after they had shown themselves that the *battagliola* could be said to be truly underway. From this point on in describing an encounter the Chronicler of the *pugni* typically began to call the *piazza di mezo* at the center of the bridge by with the name that characterized it for the duration of the *mostre*: the *arengo*, that is, the ritual fighting arena of the *pugni*.[72]

Once the initial showing-off period ended, the two fighters and their two *padrini* would prepare themselves to box. A primary responsibility of the *padrini* was to see that the *arengo* remained clear, and that the fighters who occupied it were unharrassed by the partisans on either side. Even so much as a toe protruding over the top step into this protected space was seen as an unwarranted intrusion—cause for noisy protests and possible retaliation.[73] Indeed, if they thought it at all possible, the *padrini* might try to clear their respective troops off the bridge altogether, so that the duelists could go about their fight free from the threat of great crowds looming nearby; as a rule, however, factional passions produced a crush up the first steps of the span that not even the most aggressive *padrino* could completely drive off.

Even if the *battagliole* were generally rather spontaneous and improvisational affairs, some *padrini* knew how to give an appropriately dignified air to the first *mostre* that began the afternoon. The two principal points of negotiation between factional leaders, the number of matches to be held and the roster of participants, were certainly open to their own ceremonial embellishments:

> Thereupon, the Castellani, having conferred together, proposed to hold *mostre*, and as a result, there came two *padrini* onto the bridge, that is Galletto and Zighignola, dressed in black with their hats and *ferarrioli*. They were immediately met by two other *padrini* of the Nicolotti, dressed in the same manner, that is, Billora and Zotto the goldsmith. There passed between them the salutations and regards required and appropriate to their function and position, [and] . . . having exchanged kisses and embraces . . . they stripped off their *ferrarioli* and hats, retaining [only] caps on their heads, and agreed to allow *mostre* at the pleasure [of the fighters].[74]

The fighting itself would not begin until the fighters had ended their posturing and retired to diagonally opposite corners of the *arengo*. At this point the *padrino* of each faction would begin adjusting the position of his duelist, a procedure that in itself could assume a highly ceremonial air. Generally fighters did not start their match at close quarters, as modern boxers do, but rather on a signal would charge at each other from out of their corners "like bulls," evidently hoping to do as much damage from their impact as from their punches.[75] The *arengo* was not large (that of the good-sized Ponte di San Marziale measured about seventeen feet square, that of San Barnabà about fourteen), but it did curve down on either side from the middle of the bridge. As a result of its size and shape, the duelist who arrived at the center of the fighting arena would have the advantage. Therefore, the *padrini* of each side situated their men with the greatest care, making a good deal of show over their efforts to start the match from a position of complete equality ("measuring the *piazza* to within a hair," as the Chronicler put it), while at the same time doing their best to gain any clandestine advantage they could for their own fighter.[76]

The actual fights, or *cimenti*, were divided into a number of rounds, between which the duelists were given a short rest before returning to their corners to start over again. Rounds were known, somewhat interchangeably, as either *salti* (jumps, or dances) or *assalti* (assaults)—terms which taken together nicely describe the actual dynamic of the combat. Often the *padrini* from both sides would agree beforehand to stage bouts of three rounds each, although on occasion the fighters themselves would ask for extra rounds, either as a precondition to their match or after concluding three *salti* without a clear winner. It remains unclear just how long a *salto* lasted, but considering that sometimes dozens or as many as a hundred *mostre* might be staged in a single afternoon, each round could not have taken more than a minute or two.[77] Certainly, fighters and spectators alike considered a willingness to endure five, seven, or ten *salti* as a sign of genuine manhood; conversely, any duelist who settled too readily for only three might be condemned as rather timid.[78]

Saint Disdier observed that, besides a simple default, there were two principal ways to win in the *mostre*: either by leaving an opponent bloodied (*rotto*) or by forcing him to fall into the canal. To these might be added two rather less common ways to claim a victory: with a knockout (either directly, with a punch, or indirectly, by causing an opponent to fall and hit his head) or forcing a rival to give up and abandon the *arengo*.[79] But, curiously enough for such an honor-conscious assembly, winning was not everything in the *mostre*. Although some duelists insisted that they be allowed to keep on fighting until one of them was *rotto*, many others seemed perfectly willing to end their match in a draw. If no great grudge prompted the duelists' encounter (or if many others were eager for their own turn in the *arengo*), the usual custom was to have *tre salti, rotti o non rotti*, that is, a limit of three rounds whether or not someone was bloodied. If both participants completed their rounds apparently unscathed, the *padrini* would end the *mostra* and declare a draw: such an outcome evidently did not carry special dishonor for either antagonist, as long as they had been well matched. As a result, fighters became skilled at getting through their three *salti* without showing visible signs of blood, protecting the delicate parts of their faces from punches or perhaps simply refusing to open their mouths so that opposing *padrini* could not inspect their gums and teeth to see if they were *rotti*.[80]

Boxing in *mostre* was mainly a one-handed affair: using their left forearm to cover the face, fighters punched at each other with repeated rights (Figure 2.5).[81] Since it was easiest to draw blood by punching an opponent in the face, fighters mostly aimed at the nose and mouth, the cheeks or above the eye. This tactic found its place in the jargon of the bridges, in which "to bust the mustache" (*romper il mustaccio*) meant to bloody, and thus defeat, an opponent. Punches to the chin or to the side

Figure 2.5 In the *mostra* fighters met one-on-one;
Grevembroch. (Museo Correr, Archivio Fotografico,
M. 24235)

of the head were correspondingly less common: the former could result in a quick knockout and victory, but they could also injure the attacker's hand. Some fighters might also try to give an adversary a body blow (a *fiancon*)—especially on the first charge—in the hopes of bowling him over. As long as he fell straight backward, down the steps of the bridge, such a fall was unlikely to do much damage to a fighter, however: he was not considered defeated, and indeed would very likely be caught by those on his own side waiting below and pushed back into the *arengo*. There was, it seems, no particular stigma attached to falling or being knocked down inside the *arengo* itself, as long as the duelist was willing to get back up and finish the *salto* (although if he fell back into the crowd on the opposing side, he might well end up with a nasty beating from enemy onlookers).[82]

Since knocking an opponent into the canal resulted in just as much of a victory as simply drawing blood (Saint Disdier in fact called it a "double victory"), fighters also aimed at forcing their rivals off the narrow surface of the bridge. Should punches alone not suffice, they might resort to pushing, tripping, or even dragging one another by their long hair. Such tactics were generally frowned upon by spectators, however, who considered them "more like wrestling than boxing." They could in any case turn out to be counterproductive, for while pushing his opponent a fighter was more than likely to be grabbed himself, with the result that both duelists could tumble into the water together. In that event, it was customary that the two swim back to their own sides and, dripping wet, return to the *arengo* to begin the fight again.[83]

Although enthusiastic young men were both the initiators and the most aggressive participants in most *battagliole*, the true art of the *pugni*, most observers agreed, was best understood by more mature men. Acquiring the skills needed for the *arengo* and the building of a factional reputation took time, and the most respected duelists tended to be older artisans, perhaps twenty-five to thirty years of age.[84] Young men, with the eyes of all the city upon them, tended to behave rather wildly in the *arengo*, to the extent that some, enraged or perhaps disappointed, even ended up attacking the audience itself. Sometimes older duelists would refuse to fight against such aggressive youths, who were moreover not often permitted to serve as *capi* or *padrini* because they were considered too *bizzarri et ostinati* in their conduct.[85] Mature fighters not only knew better how to limit and direct their aggressions into the fighting itself, they were also more skilled at aiming and landing their punches appropriately. The proficiency of such older masters as Manone ("Big Hands") of San Nicolò and Capo Michiele of the Arsenal greatly pleased the audience and went a long way to making an art out of the *pugni*: "both [were] over forty years of age, having been in their youth ferocious rivals: in the first *cimento* their punches were of equal force and passion, and being mature men, [the blows] fell heavily upon their faces, causing the highest admiration from the public."[86]

An intense and long-standing personal rivalry like that of Manone and Capo Michiele could intensify the kind of widespread interest that matches between factional champions usually aroused. Just the rumor that two such antagonists would be returning to the bridge again to continue their rivalry was enough to bring enthusiasts of the *pugni* flocking to the site—even on a workday and with none of the preliminary skirmishes or display that usually helped stimulate factional passions.[87] Clearly, much of the attraction of such matches lay in the hope that the skills of two experienced antagonists could only be enhanced by their mutual dislike. At least there can be little question that the protagonists themselves knew how to keep the level of popular curiosity and excitement high. Challenges were noisily exchanged in public places—at inns, the fish markets, or even on the Grand Canal—and were often accompanied by theatrical insults, slaps, or curses.[88] At the bridge itself, these antagonists worked to wring as much drama as they could from their confrontation, dressing for the occasion in their own distinctive fighting outfits and sometimes bringing their own personal *padrini* in tow.[89]

What sort of aesthetic or professional standards did followers of the *pugni* expect these skillful and experienced performers to maintain? Audi-

ences appear to have been especially pleased by protagonists who were tough
enough to stand their ground as they gave and took blows to the face
unflinchingly: strong on their feet, and striking out cleanly without too
much dancing or fencing around (*troppo gioco nella scherma*).[90] Defensive
skills, while admired, were less important than demonstrable courage; grap-
pling and wrestling were condemned less as unfair fighting than as a
coward's way of avoiding his rival's punches; when duelists refused to dis-
engage, it was termed "more a contest of force than fists." Passion and
ferocity were the natural attributes of a fighter, but a good duelist would
not allow himself to be turned into a beast. Grabbing an opponent by the
hair and yanking him around, kicking him in the genitals, or—worst of
all—kicking or punching him when he was down were "unfair acts, highly
censurable wrongs and injustices not [to be] permitted at the bridge"—a
sign of the bizarre excesses of youth rather than the practiced conduct of
a mature fighter.[91] Knowing that such conduct could not only prove personally dangerous but might also provoke onlookers to violence, experienced duelists controlled their fighting, giving one another the kind of
solid blows that both exciting combat and factional honor required. If
occasionally, as the Chronicler of the *pugni* suspected, some carried their
sense of showmanship to the logical conclusion of agreeing beforehand
to pull their punches a bit, it was only with the end of assuring a better (if
less bruising) spectacle, one in which duelists might delight onlookers by
exchanging a rain of apparently punishing blows, while "their faces
remained as uninjured as if they were [each] a quintain."[92]

Once the last round of a *mostra* had been fought, the two duelists
signaled the end of their combat by exchanging an embrace and a "frater-
nal kiss"—gestures that many made at the beginning of a match as well. It
was the duty of the *padrini* to see that this ritual sign of peace was given,
and indeed they themselves often kissed as part of the ceremonies surrounding the beginning of the afternoon's series of *mostre*. These initial and final
kisses drew a kind of liminal boundary around the violence of the *cimento*.
The kiss that introduced combat served to indicate that both duelists
welcomed the fight, but also that previous grudges and rancors should
not be allowed to intrude into the *cimento* itself, to the extent that they
caused the participants to behave like beasts. The closing kiss sealed the
violence that had passed, so that the duelists could leave behind the injuries they had given and received at the *arengo* without turning them into
a later vendetta.[93] It was indeed a continuing source of amazement to
foreign observers—in an honor-conscious age where a physical blow in
any situation was deemed so insulting as to naturally demand a response
that was usually escalating and often fatal—that "so much anger and considerable injury could so quickly and in an instant convert itself into a kiss
so affectionate."[94] Yet Venetian enthusiasts of the *pugni*, while no less sensitive than others to the demands of honor, prided themselves that in this
peculiarly Venetian ritual the knowledge of how to bury the animosities

aroused by one-on-one combat was as important as skillfulness in throwing a straight punch.[95]

Despite all their accompanying display and ferocity, *mostre* thus turn out to have been fairly benign affairs—clearly involving nothing like the lengthy and merciless poundings that would later be so characteristic of British prizefighting.[96] Indeed, in Venice many *cimenti* were over almost before they had begun, on the occasions when one fighter tumbled his adversary off the bridge into the water at the first charge or managed to draw blood with an early punch. Since each duelist's *padrino* was watching his rival closely for bleeding and was ready at the slightest signs of red to claim a victory, fights could be quickly halted, sometimes even when both participants were still eager to continue.[97] Perhaps the difference between the British and Venetian forms of boxing lay partly in the economics of the ring: Venetians did not battle for a purse, but instead in a quest for honor. Unless personal animosities kept them fighting, participants had little reason to keep on attacking each other once the appearance of blood had signaled a victor; certainly, there was no cash prize waiting for the man who could beat his opponent senseless.[98] Economic incentives were weak because men came forward to the *arengo* as much as representatives of their faction or neighborhood as on their own behalf. Even the principal fighters, who might have received contributions, if not indeed regular salaries, from wealthy patrons of the *pugni*, never really detached themselves from their community ties to become either independent professionals or the creatures of patrician enthusiasts: the pull of faction was simply too strong.[99]

Furthermore, for Venetians—as indeed for people all over the Mediterranean basin—the other side of honor could only be shame. Duelists seem to have been drawn to the *arengo* less with the wish to destroy their opponents than to humiliate them, for as long as his rival ended up mortified a fighter could still claim his full measure of public recognition.[100] Shame effectively inflicted not only brought honor, however: it was also tremendously funny. Spectators and factional supporters came to the *battagliole* as much to be amused as to witness violent combat, and to this end the Venetian canal bridge was admirably suited. Narrow and slippery, bridges made precarious platforms for staging anything like a serious boxing match, and a slip, shove, or tumble into the water below made for both a resounding splash and a fighter's ultimate pratfall, a shaming that could be seen and enjoyed by thousands of jeering, whistling, and shouting spectators of both factions.[101]

When the *mostre* of the afternoon were concluded, the number of bouts won by each faction's duelists was tallied up: whichever side had won more could then claim an overall victory. In this way, the *mostre* served to further not only personal but also factional honor.[102] The disagreements, rancors, and rivalries that in the normal course of life inevitably boiled up between individual Venetian artisans, living packed so close together in their overcrowded city, could all find a focus and resolution in bridge duels involving a minimum of personal risk while promising a maximum of public exposure. At the same time, all members of the Castellani and Nicolotti could share in the glory (or shame) of the outcome even if they had never actually fought that day, and it was rare that even the losing side could not go home in the evening with the memory of at least one or two satisfying victories to assuage factional pride.[103]

The Battle for the Bridge

Yet even if the *mostre* were an effective means for workers to win honor and settle their grudges, such duels were not in themselves enough for most Venetians. In part, it may have simply been impossible to satisfy the needs of all those present with one-on-one duels: even if a hundred *mostre* were staged (and this was a rare occasion indeed), many hundreds more aspiring fighters would have been left out—and few at the bridges appear to have been the sort of men who were willing to enjoy secondhand pleasures and honors. Moreover, many devotees of the *pugni* plainly thought that the one-on-one duel was but a poor second best to what they thought to be their real business at the bridges: waging all-out factional war. "We have come here for the *frotta* and not to stage *mostre*," *padrini* and factional supporters would repeatedly complain, when annoying and adverse circumstances—the weakness of one of the sides, the presence of the *sbirri* of the Ten, or a simple shortage of time—had apparently conspired to deprive them of "the war they so greedily desired."[104] Most likely, the majority of fighters and spectators wanted both *mostre* and *frotte* together, each staged at moments that seemed appropriate and neither to the complete exclusion of the other. These two forms of the *battagliole* in fact turn out to have been closely connected in the minds of Venetians: really no more than two facets of the same factional warfare to which so many devoted their lives.

Since *mostre* were generally put on with "both armies facing each other and in close vicinity, [and] desirous of starting the *frotta* and of coming to blows," it did not take much to disrupt the fragile truce between the factions that made the boxing matches possible. The slightest evidence of misconduct in the *arengo*—a duelist who punched a rival who was down, for example—was often enough to trigger a massive attack by both sides.[105] The most frequent initiators of this sort of spontaneous *frotta* were in fact the *padrini* themselves. Although it seems to have been generally understood that the *padrini*, in their role of referees, saw themselves under no obligation to be unbiased or even especially fair—many brazenly lied in an effort to secure a victory—certain excesses in their behavior could easily provoke their followers into beginning the *frotta*. In seeking to gain time for their own man to rest, many *padrini* would harass the opposing duelist by insisting that he was bloodied. Such a resort to "bickering rather than just reasons and valid judgements" would frequently set the two (or four) *padrini* to quarreling among themselves, and when (as almost inevitably happened) one *padrino* ended up so annoyed that he punched another, all pretense at factional truce generally vanished in an instant.[106]

As a result, it was a rare occasion when both factions actually managed to stage all the *mostre* upon which they had agreed at the beginning. If ten bouts had been planned, it was quite likely that only five or six would be held before someone lost control and threw an inappropriate punch, "and immediately a most impassioned and furious *frotta* [would be] set off." Sometimes the two sides could not even manage to get through the first *mostra* before they would both charge the *piazza di mezo* "to devour each other like rabid lions and tigers."[107] This result rarely disappointed either fighters or audience, and onlookers in particular were often so eager to see a *frotta* that they might actively attempt to disrupt the truce of the *mostra*. If the *padrini* and duelists failed to oblige them by misbehaving, spectators might sometimes go so far as to recruit a volunteer, who would enter the *arengo* under the guise of offering himself in *mostra* and then would take a punch at the opposing *padrino*.[108]

The *frotte* that followed could last anywhere from twenty minutes to two or three hours—until either one side had given up or it became too dark to continue. During this time the apparent control of the bridge might change hands a dozen times or more. Unlike the *mostre*, which was dominated by the figures of the *padrino* and the champion fighter, the real contestants in the *frotte* were the *capi* and their fighting squads, or *compagnie*. *Capi* were especially necessary for lining up the squads of fifty or more into tight formation that would come at the bridge from the *fondamente* on its right, left, and—if there was one—center (the *fille di destra*, *di zanco*, and *di mezo*). The intention was to continuously recharge the *piazza di mezo* with a steady flow of new fighters who could replace those who were being knocked off into the water or otherwise eliminated; as gaps developed in the mob on the bridge, these squads would be thrown into the battle, and their places back on the *fondamenta* would be taken by reserve units stationed behind them (Figure 2.6).[109]

The *padrini*, by contrast, usually quickly made for the sidelines once the *frotte* broke out, to safe positions from which they could serve as the generals of the battles, offering overall coordination of the movements of their followers. They were the ones who decided when, or if, new squads should be called for, or whether an attack should focus primarily on the right or left flank.[110] Those who were clever in the "military arts" might also use the stratagem of keeping still other squads in hiding in a nearby warehouse until the proper moment: closely watching the enemy at the center of the bridge for signs of fatigue, they could then hope to win by sending fresh troops in a surprise shock assault against opposing companies that were already exhausted by long fighting.[111]

A certain amount of skillful leadership was thus important in managing the *frotta*. At the same time, however, the massed combat had its own sort of inexorable logic, against which even the most skilled *padrino* could

Figure 2.6 *Capi* directed their squads onto the bridge from either side; broadside
woodcut with verses, signed "Andrea Piazza, Eques," undated. (Museo Correr,
Archivio Fotografico, M. 37128)

hardly expect to make much impact. The constant pressure of the squads
streaming onto the bridge from either side tended to jam the entire span
with fighters—with perhaps as many as four or five hundred men on the
relatively small Ponte dei Pugni at San Barnabà—and the force of those
pressing from behind packed them together so tightly that usually it was
impossible even to take a swing (*vibrar un pugno*) at an enemy. Those on
the bridge were quickly clogged into a dense throng known as the *groppo*,
one of the central features of most *frotte*: for perhaps ten or fifteen minutes hundreds of men would be stuck together, pushing, shoving, or
butting with their heads, rather in the manner of a modern rugby scrum
(Figure 2.7).[112] The *groppo* was never stable for long, however. In their
enthusiasm, those behind would often leap on top of their trapped companions in an attempt to get at opponents on the other side. The result
was that the gridlocked "mountain of flesh" (*montagna di carne*) would
finally resolve itself in a sudden—and generally disastrous—collapse (*scioglimento*), as fifty, a hundred, or even two hundred or more men all fell in a
punching, kicking, biting knot into the canal below.[113]

Figure 2.7 The *groppo* was an immense shoving match from both sides of the bridge. (Museo Correr, Archivio Fotografico, *varie* 20164)

The dissolving of a *groppo* with its sudden shift in the battle's dynamics was an ideal time for leaders to send in fresh troops, the more so since many of the opposition's best fighters might well be out of action—floundering about in the water, or *trapassati* and cut off from combat on the far side of the bridge.[114] Should there not be enough men around to do the job, the *padrini* and *capi* might well lead the attack themselves, and they could be joined by some of the more excited *gente dei ferrarioli*, who would strip down to their silk *braghese* and wade into the battle. This was often the vital moment of the *frotta*, for even if occupying the bridge did not automatically mean a victory (a counterattack was always possible), it certainly carried a considerable psychological advantage. It was generally held that a bridge was easier to defend than to attack, especially if the occupiers had time enough to mass a substantial garrison. At moments like this, faced with a heavily defended bridge, many *padrini* would indeed decide to give up and cede the victory to their opponents. Yet their yielding was not always enough to end the battle, since often there were a few stubborn squads whose *capi* would refuse to quit, even after having been tumbled head-over-heels off the bridge and reduced to a confused and jumbled *montagna di carne* at the foot of the bridge.[115] Even the sounding of the Ave Maria, signaling the coming of night, did not always bring an end to the fighting, for although in the darkness no one could be sure at whom he was punching, nevertheless certain diehards might try to prolong the combat, bringing torches, lighted brands (*canne accese*), and candles out onto nearby balconies or onto the bridge itself, in the hope of producing a final *groppo* and a new chance at victory. Only when one faction finally had no more squads left and no more *capi* in a condition to lead them against a bridge occupied by their well-organized foe could the battle be said to be definitely over.[116]

The *frotte* thus turn out to have been much less restrained than the *mostre*, with little consensual opposition to participants giving free reign to their aggressions and to generally behaving like beasts.[117] The Chronicler sometimes seems to express a certain grudging admiration for "this Venetian *popolo*, that at the bridges behaved as though completely devoid of any reason or thought except to triumph, the one over the other." In the course of the melee men were punched and butted in the face until their teeth flew out; some had their ears chewed off, while an unlucky few had their testicles squeezed or bitten so hard that they fainted on the spot (Figure 2.8). Those who were caught in the violence of the *groppo* were not necessarily any safer once it dissolved: simply falling into the water during the frigid fall weather of the *battagliole* season was in itself risky, such that many were later incapacitated "more from the rigors of the cold than from the hot passion of the battle." Furthermore, the fighting often continued in the canal below, with those unlucky enough to have gone over first quite likely to be pushed head downward into the thick mud by those who followed. If the tide were high, they might drown; if it were low, they

Figure 2.8 *Frotta* on the Ponte di San Barnabà. (Museo Correr, Archivio Fotografico, *varie* 3419)

risked broken bones from those tumbling down on their heads.[118] Yet dangerous though it may have been to fall into the water, it was no safer to remain on the bridge itself, for the sudden shifting of bodies all along the *piazze* and the continuous pressure of those pushing from either end meant that many would fall and end up trampled and seriously injured.[119]

For artisans whose work required that they be physically fit, the risks of participating in the *battagliole* were as much economic as physical, for in their slow convalescence following an encounter, many of the seriously injured certainly lost days or even weeks of income before they could return to work. Worse than losing employment because of injury, of course, was the very real possibility of losing one's life. Almost every year a few unfortunates were killed, usually either from drowning or from being trampled under the feet of panicky onlookers. Occasionally real tragedies would take place, as in 1611, when a panic seized both fighters and audience, and in the ensuing stampede no fewer than twenty-six victims ended up trampled or suffocated in the mud of the Rio dei Carmini.[120] After even a minor battle the city appears to have been filled with the convalescing injured, who "for a long time were spitting blood [and] languishing from punches or falls." When walking about the city after an encounter, one could see on every hand the high cost that the cult of the *pugni* exacted on its followers, in

> the misfortunes and accidents so terribly damaging, not only to the people themselves but also often to the point of the total destruction of their own families: those most involved [in the *battagliole*] carrying on their faces practically from one year to the next the memories and unhappy marks: the scratches, sprains, teeth knocked out, dislocated jaws, gouged eyes, and finally, smashed ribs and crippled legs, to the point that many, in a few months' time, left this life.[121]

The Lords of the Bridges

The very real dangers of the *frotte* make its persistent popularity among both participants and spectators all the more intriguing—an opinion we can share with contemporary observers of the event, who were aware of the paradox that otherwise sober-minded Venetian artisans should continue to risk both their lives and their livelihoods seemingly just to amuse themselves. For all his enthusiasm for the event, even the Chronicler of the *pugni* sometimes had to admit that the bridges of the city "were like monkshood, that for a simple touch will contaminate and poison all who ever approaches them." That peaceable workers could so easily surrender themselves to such violence seemed to provide indications of deeper social problems: of a society where citizens "always lived unaccustomed to calmness [and were] easily reinfected with faction;" and where the natural hierarchies were so weakened that "when it comes to battling at the bridge, the Venetian people are so infuriated and enraged that they do not value their own

lives a penny—knowing neither reason nor respect, nor the required reverence for who commands them, they run as if blind to ruin and destruction,
heedless even of their own lives." When given the opportunity and excuse of
the *battagliole*, in short, Venetian workers appeared prone to go somewhat
berserk: driven insane by the excitement of the crowd, factional passions, the
quest for glory, and liberal doses of wine.[122]

Many contemporary observers of the *pugni*—even when they admired
the encounters—must have felt some of the unease that King Henry III
had expressed about the event: it was too much for a game and too little
for a real war. If participants were not fighting a true battle—with its
attendant hopes of conquest, spoils, and promotions in the field—how could
they sanely risk injuries or a squalid death in the mud or under the feet of
the crowd? Indeed, the assumption that such violent, popular entertainments represented a reckless waste of human life and resources persists:
in a modern-day sociology of sports that continues to treat such "folk"
sporting events as if they were manifestations of a social pathology that is
rooted in the somehow irregular character, family, or social backgrounds
of the participants.[123]

The weakness of these sociopathic interpretations of violent popular
sport lies in an initial assumption that there were no rewards sufficiently
strong to induce any but those who were basically irrational to run the
risks such activities presented. In fact, the *battagliole* did reward its devotees extremely well, although not always in the prosaic or quantifiable form
of cash and prizes. Instead, success at the bridges paid off in the coin of
status: those who excelled in fighting with their fists could expect to make
a name for themselves that would ensure them rank and respect among
the many enthusiasts of the *battagliole*. By the later seventeenth century,
men "who did well at the fights" (*che fan ben a' pugni*) could be said to
have inhabited a separate, sporting world, distinguished by its own complex system of hierarchies and values. It was an alternative universe that
flourished in parallel to the everyday artisans' world of work, family, and
neighborhood—complete and rewarding enough in its own way to induce
thousands of otherwise normal citizens to throw themselves into the mael-
strom of the bridges in quest of the honors to be won there.

Fighters ambitious to make their way in the world of the *pugni* sought
reputation not by specializing in the *frotte* or the *mostre* alone, but by
excelling alternatively in both—another indication that these apparently
distinct forms of combat were in fact closely linked. Young men, eager
"to succeed in their turn as a militia brave and courageous in the disciplines of war," tried first to establish a name for themselves in the open-
ended combat of the *frotte*. Here, as in the youthful *scorrerie*, there was
ample good reason to believe that individual skill or initiative might give
one a chance at gaining recognition—by leading an impromptu charge,
by repelling attacks, or even by knocking out an enemy *padrino* with a
lucky (and perhaps illicit) punch. Having won a name as a skilled brawler

in the *frotte*, a fighter could then present himself at the *arengo*, not as an anonymous novice who might find himself humiliated when more established champions rejected him as too inexperienced, but as an worthy participant in his own right. Reputation in the *mostre*, in turn, was apparently essential for a fighter who wished to establish himself as a *capo*, recruiting and training the squad of neighbors with whom he would gain further glory in the thick of the *frotte*.[124] Finally, the experienced and successful *capi* were the ones, as we have seen, who would in time be the most likely to win the right to call themselves *padrini*, the factionwide chiefs who provided leadership in both *frotte* and *mostre*: making the decisions that set the strategy during the melee, and having the final say in awarding victory and reputation to those ambitious young duelists who were coming up in their turn.[125]

To its successful devotees, the cult of the *pugni* gave a status that went well beyond anything that could have been won by simple physical superiority. Saint Disdier called the *padrini* "serieux et notables Bourgeois," and although, as will be seen, the actual work of these otherwise ordinary artisans would certainly have never justified placing them among the bourgeoisie, they did enjoy some of the respect and prerogatives normally accorded to those of the respectable middle class.[126] *Padrini* may have occasionally had to impose their commands with brute force, but most of them enjoyed sufficient status in their faction that they could expect to be obeyed: if a youthful hothead should object too loudly or violently, he risked a thrashing from his own teammates, or even perpetual banishment from the bridges.[127] The *padrini* of each faction, together with some of the leading *capi*, formed an elite group that the Chronicler sometimes referred to collectively as *caporioni principalissimi*. There were a dozen or so of these esteemed individuals at any one time, men who had both the honor and the responsibility of meeting with their equals from the other side to arrange the details for future *battagliole*; the lunches where they met in some neutral territory such as the Rialto could well be convivial, but they progressed with much the same formal care as encounters between the ambassadors of two warring powers.[128]

The *padrini* were also especially honored to represent and speak on behalf of the factions to those Venetian aristocrats who followed the *battagliole*. Theirs was a working relationship: many patricians were virtually besotted with the excitement of the *pugni*, and realized that to get close to the action of the bridges they would have to cultivate the *padrini* of their faction. As a result, *padrini* were frequent guests at noble palaces, and sometimes at their tables, meeting for strategy sessions and serving as the conduit for the disbursement of money for the factions. A few of these men managed to rise to a still higher sort of renown, where for a time they might enjoy the overall command of their entire factional army, with the title *commandante generale*. Perhaps the rank and fame of these workers was somewhat informal and transitory (the position seems to have generally been only for a single battle), but for the time of their glory those

few fortunate workers could expect to be lionized by nobles and commoners alike as they went about the city, basking in a reputation that in a certain sense even transcended factionalism itself.[129]

Although these *padrini commandanti* or *commandanti generale* enjoyed
the honor of leading their factions into battle, they do not appear to have
occupied the highest ranges of the hierarchy of the *pugni*. Holding a status
even above these factional potentates was a handful of aged veterans, men
who were clearly too old for combat but who were known to the Chronicler as "the revered old ones of the factions" (*i vecchi venerandi delle
fattioni*). These heroes of past battles may have had their fighting years
behind them, but they nevertheless remained active as the governors and
(one might say) the high priests of the cult of the *pugni*. They had won
the respect they enjoyed both through skill and sheer survival: "[E]steemed
for their honorable state of rank and authority, but above all for their
memorable valor and example in the battles of their times . . . the old *Capi
di Guerra* were revered, bowed to, and feared by everyone, including those
of the opposing faction." Appropriately, in a society that traditionally respected its elders, the *vecchi* were honored with the titles of *stimatissimo*
or *reverendissimo*; they passed their days in factional banquets and planning sessions, or as the guests at the palaces of noble *parteggiani* of the
pugni. Yet their rank was by no means an empty or idle title, for these
septuagenarians could still wield considerable influence over their factions,
a status incarnated in the hortatory address that one of them would customarily give to his assembled troops before a major battle. During the
actual fighting these *vecchi* would usually leave the battleground and retire
to a sort of general headquarters a few hundred meters from the bridge.
There they would continue their efforts on behalf of their faction: planning and conferring with their side's *padrini*, sending out spies, and receiving ambassadorial visits from the opposing faction. When necessary, they
were available to give their faction's *padrini* and *capi* pithy advice based
on the experiences "they had acquired in similar cases during battles in olden
days." Old though they may have been, however, these *vecchi* were far from
feeble, and when the occasion seemed to require it they were more than
ready to reprimand an obstreperous young warrior with a sharp punch in
the mouth.[130]

Significantly, the reputation these *vecchi delle fattioni* had won at the
bridges also guaranteed them respect and position in everyday social life.
At least some of these patriarchs of the *pugni* exercised a leadership role in
their own parishes; taking a place among other respected old men of the
community, with whom they shared the honorific title of *bara*, or "elder."
Little enough is known about this informal side of community governance
in Venice, but it would seem that the *bare* in many parishes, either on their
own or in consultation with the state's neighborhood representative (the
capo di contrada), would busy themselves in settling and defusing local
disputes before they could attract the attentions of higher magistrates. This
role of community sage and peacemaker was particularly appropriate for

the *vecchi delle fattioni*, for having themselves won great reputation in the *pugni*, they would have well understood how to deal with the questions of honor that were forever flaring up in their communities. As virtual village elders, respected by all sides, these *vecchi* could be essential in assuaging the aggrieved feelings of offended champions and brokering an honorable peace between rivals who otherwise might have turned their disputes into a widening circle of vendetta.[131]

Offering the possibility of both the immediate glories of combat and the lifelong honors of a role within its elaborate leadership hierarchy, the ludic world of the *pugni* must have seemed highly attractive to many ordinary Venetian men, the more so for the lack of any comparable status to be won in the usual everyday world of work and neighborhood. By the mid-1600s most sectors of the Venetian economy were mired in decline, and the average worker's hopes of finding fortune or reputation through the successful pursuit of his craft had for the most part vanished with the prosperous years of the previous century. In an earlier era, even those artisans whose trades gave them few serious hopes of amassing significant wealth would—like most craftsmen throughout early modern Europe—have at least enjoyed some compensating honors coming to them through their corporate lives from their confraternities or the processions, offices, or rituals that enlivened their guilds. In seventeenth-century Venice, however, with underemployment a fact of life, workers increasingly had to make their way through poorly paid service jobs and in manual labor, activities that granted them little in the way of prestige, corporate sodality, or even a subsistence wage.[132]

Certain worker contingents at the bridges, it is true, were drawn from highly organized and self-conscious corporate groups, in particular, the fishermen of San Nicolò, the shipbuilders of the Arsenal, and the mirror makers of San Canciano parish. Yet the great majority of those attracted to the *pugni* followed very different trades, often of the sort typically associated with weak or nonexistent corporate ties. Many of the best fighters came from among Venice's laborers: the longshoremen (*bastasi*), porters (*facchini*), and commercial boatmen (*burchielli* or *piateri*) who had the brawn to do well at the bridges but who were also forbidden by the state from forming their own guilds.[133] A great number of less robust workers, belonging to guilds requiring little skill and confering small status, also proved quite willing to abandon their meager professions for days or even weeks to pursue the honors of the *pugni*. The bridges were crowded with cobblers, tinkers, biscuit bakers, and barbers; fruit, chicken, and lasagna sellers; cattle slaughterers, grain sifters, and wine carriers; tailors, weavers, and window makers; feather hawkers, rag dealers, cesspool cleaners, and lottery ticket agents—along with a host of other humble occupations. If the state had allocated corporate status to many of their trades, it was more with the aim to keep these service workers fragmented, more readily taxed, and held accountable for military service. In the customary sense of the word, they were "guildsmen" in name only, possessing no craft traditions, political powers, or economic influence; for many of them, their guild membership was barely more than a convenient fiction to cover their various activities as specialized beggars, in a society where servility had largely replaced industry or trade as the focus of human activities.[134]

Servants were also often to be found at the *battagliole*: hardly surprising in an era when even minor nobles maintained small armies of retainers for status reasons. The presence of the elite's private gondoliers—burly men who provided all-purpose muscle for their masters, much as coachmen did elsewhere—was apparently so marked at the bridges that Saint Disdier mistakenly concluded that they were the ones "who had the reputations as the best fist fighters." There was, clearly, a much wider range of working poor involved at the bridges, but the Chronicler of the *pugni* did record a number of fighters and even a few *padrini* who worked as *servitori* or *gondolieri*. The place of servants in the *battagliole* was clearly more complex than that of other workers, for many fought at the bridges with the awareness that their master was watching from a nearby balcony and perhaps wagering on their success. The drive to excel before the eyes of one's *paron* must have been strong, and indeed sometimes whole contingents of servants—perhaps belonging to a single master—would battle against other groups of domestics, carrying on what may have amounted to surrogate wars between the elites themselves.[135] At the same time, however, servants could be shrewd enough to see in the *pugni* a means of staking out a certain amount of personal independence relative to their master: Saint Disdier observed that many Venetian gondoliers would only enter into service if their contracts allowed them time off on Sunday afternoons to go to the bridges to make a name for themselves.[136]

Other devotees of the *pugni* were to be found still further down the social scale. The names of not a few fighters and *capi* turn up in the police records as violent men who were just as likely to be arrested for theft as for attacking or brawling with their neighbors. Some pugilists were no doubt poor enough to be driven to stealing, and certainly many had quick enough tempers that they would often find themselves in fights that had little to do with factionalism or the bridges. Perhaps because they were skilled at thrashing others, some of these toughs who had no other trade could evidently hope to attach themselves to the retinue of an obliging noble, in the capacity of professional thug (*bravo*) or even assassin. Tonin, a *caporione* from San Luca parish in the 1630s, was an inhabitant of this rather shadowy world. Speaking of him in the context of the *battagliole*, the Chronicler hailed Tonin as a *soldato famoso*, "one of the strongest and most glorious of warriors." Yet from the testimonies of his various victims there emerges the picture of another Tonin, one who seemingly acquired the skills that served him so well at the *pugni* through his life as local bully and sometimes killer-for-hire: "an assassin who only gets his bread by breaking the law and [who] lives by arms (although for appearances he keeps a tailor's shop), gathering about him at his expense a large gang of miscreants [*malviventi*] with whom he has assaulted and killed many."137

This role of the *pugni* in granting status to the lowly was most marked among those who rose to the position of *padrini*. Skill in combat and leadership could raise even the humblest workers to a stature where they might mingle with Venice's elites and even receive an occasional summons to come to the door (although not into the actual chamber) of the Council of Ten, when the state needed their help in arranging a battle for distinguished visitors. Thanks to the *pugni*, Venetian artisans of otherwise quite modest status were given heady opportunities of commanding troops, conducting diplomacy, and plotting battle strategy: among the ranks of the *padrini* were found a boatman, a picture-frame maker, a stonecutter, and any number of other low-prestige trades. One of these was a certain Giacomo, praised by the Chronicler as "one of the most famous and esteemed *padrini* of his faction. . . . the *capiorione principalissimo* of the Nicolotti." After Giacomo had the misfortune to be trampled to death in the midst of a *battagliola*, he was awarded one of the highest honors to which any Venetian might have aspired: a grand funeral cortege with more than a thousand mourners, each bearing a lighted candle in solemn procession, the sort of public recognition that would more typically have been bestowed on persons of noble birth or high office. Yet outside the cult of the *pugni* Giacomo would surely have been considered a nobody, for he was identified by profession as a mere *zavatin,* a used-shoe vendor.138

The *pugni* thus turn out to have been largely, if not primarily, the cult of Venice's socially disenfranchised. For these many humble and sometimes not very savory individuals, dedication to the bridges opened an alternative world of honor and respect. It could indeed be argued that the mounting enthusiasm for faction and the *battagliole* over the course of the sixteenth and seventeenth centuries had much to do with the increasing presence of this underclass on the Venetian urban scene.139 Like many cities of the early modern era, Venice was a magnet for impoverished immigrants, whose steady flood into the city could have only worsened the prospects for resident workers. Beyond providing them with a minimal amount of charitable sustenance, accompanied by the careful surveillance of a ferociously efficient police force, the Venetian state appears to have done little to socially accommodate its floating mass of working poor. State honors and recognition were reserved for the city's elite craftsmen—furriers, goldsmiths, silk merchants, printers, glass blowers, and their like—who enjoyed the right to march with fellow guildsmen in ducal processions or to display wares on sumptuous barges during state holidays. Consigned as they were to the audience as passive spectators on such occasions, it is small wonder that the city's marginal workers sought reputation elsewhere: in festive occasions of their own devising and especially in the *pugni*, Venice's ultimate popular forum for the creation and allocation of honor.140

In exploring the element of risk in another violent ritual, Clifford Geertz adapted Jeremy Bentham's term "deep play" to describe those social activities so risky and so consuming of human resources that the likely dangers of pursuing them would appear to have far outweighed any possible rewards or satisfactions. Yet although its apparent wastefulness might induce more utilitarian souls to condemn it, playing deeply—as Geertz went on to observe—could also serve a vital role in the vision a society produces of itself, by creating an ephemeral arena where deeper cultural agendas may be brought to the surface, contested, and resolved.[141] Venetian workers of the more humble sort, who enjoyed no particular place or status in their city's own self-vision, proceeded to construct such an arena on their own, creating the cult of the *pugni* and the violent play of the *battagliole*. Here they found their key to an alternative world from that of their meager daily allotment of work and subservience, a world in which an individual worker could embrace values and standards that might redefine him in terms of both personal accomplishment and factional honor.

That their play should be based on a considerable degree of risk apparently went without saying for these artisans. Any contest from which participants might expect to walk away unscathed was seen as essentially trivial, neither bringing true honor nor having the psychological force to provide their alternative world with importance. For this reason, workers in the *frotte* were permitted or even expected to engage in, a kind of beastly behavior that would have been considered dishonorable in one-on-one duels: thereby they both created the danger and exposed themselves to it. As a result, their Chronicler could safely and repeatedly assert that the *pugni* were "no mere amusement or an action of little importance": by risking themselves, Venetian workers made their conduct at the bridges matter, such that their ordinary identities in a world of closely prescribed conduct and class relationships emerged redefined from the contests.[142] At the same time, danger also gave meaning to reputation and hierarchy at the bridges, for honor was tempered and given weight by the real risks involved in winning it: the roles of *capo*, *padrino*, or *vecchio venerando* would never be taken for mere carnevalesque masques that might be assumed in fun and then lightly discarded.[143]

At the same time, there was little sense in playing deeply for those who did not do so publicly. Venetian artisans well understood that reputation was a middling thing when won by a private individual trapped in his own submerged world of the crowded urban landscape. If a contest of the *pugni* were to carry meaning, it would have to unfold not just before the eyes of companions and workmates (that would describe any ordinary street or workplace brawl), but also on Venice's most public stage: on the fighting bridge where contenders for reputation were necessarily exposed to the city's applause and jeers. The actions of spectators along the *fondamente* and up on balconies and rooftops make it clear that these onlookers knew that in their way they were as much participants in the *battagliole* as were the fighters down on the bridge. This active interplay between fighters and audience turned what might have otherwise seemed simply a violent circus or sporting event into a kind of dialogue, an exchange between the city's socially marginal and their surrounding world of neighbors, fellow workers, patricians, and curious foreigners.

To be sure, such a dialogue was never firmly defined, any more than was the fight itself. But if the details and structure of this public exchange between fighters and public can only be traced in rough outline, at least it is possible to discover what was being discussed. With their shouts, whistles, and applause, audience members sought to influence the workings of the contest developing before them, themselves guided by their own shared (though hardly universal) sense of what was appropriate to honor, custom, and good play. Onlookers' calls and jeers might encourage a reticent fighter to come forward and present himself in the *mostra*; they could be equally decisive in determining who would be awarded the victory, should a duel's outcome appear unclear. Likewise, vocal public support could be an important factor in a faction's decision to press for a *frotta* in the place of individual matches: it could also be crucial in giving the squads the determination to fight their way to victory.

Most important, however, was the audience's ability to establish by its presence the factional context in which the *battagliole* would be decided. The support or derision of onlookers enlarged the failures and triumphs of ordinary artisans to heroic proportions, further deepening their play by magnifying not only its physical dangers but the social risks as well: the prize of public honor to be sought and the shame of open humiliation to be avoided. On the other side of the dialogue, fighters laid a claim—through their performance and the abuse they suffered—to the honor that only this public could grant them. It was this need for reciprocity that kept the *pugni* out of doors, in the public eye, as a contingent of Nicolotti fighters once made quite clear, in walking away from a "private" *battagliola* that a noble fan had set up for them on a wooden bridge in his palace courtyard:

> To battle in this way in private renders neither glory nor reputation. The purpose of our combat and contests is not to kill each other or tear each other apart, but only, in the presence of the city, to win and to take possession of the bridge, with competition and with the usual audacity. If you were now to open the gates of this palace, in a moment [the courtyard] would be filled with two thousand people, who are those that are outside, waiting to see and to know the outcome of our brawls, *mostre*, and duels. Truly, private encounters such as this do not have the public applause desired by the Castellani and the Nicolotti.[144]

Ultimately, however, Venetian artisans played deeply and violently to find out who they were: to see how they might respond in a liberating scenario of disorder as unlike as imaginable to normal life in their regulated, watchful state—bound by caste, driven with servility, and fenced by the encroaching lagoon. Out on the public bridge, whether alone in a *mostra* or in the thick of a *frotta*, fighters and *caporioni* alike were released: free to attack, to flee, to remain steadfast, or to jump in the water, they were thrown in an instant through the range of feelings from rage to terror, from pity to revenge. To be able to claim a place in the world of the *pugni* was to reside beyond the limiting horizons of baroque Venice, where all these various and no longer useful facets of human character could be put back into their place. After the battle, these workers might be seen hobbling about the city, temporarily unfit to make a living but at least able to point to the scars on their bodies as indicators of just how well they had met the challenge of combat:

> Both sides would not so easily forget this war on the next occasion, because of the exterior signs which they bore: the scratches, bites, ruptures, missing teeth, swollen eyes, medications, and bruises that they wore on [their] faces as trophies, with [broken] arms at the neck for some days, as testimony to their obstinate pretensions . . . [as] Venetian plebes, indomitable in their competitions as warriors on the bridges.[145]

3

The Spoils of War

E per una corona di carton
Spegazzada da quattro coloretti
Sustentar cose che fà maledetti
I più boni impastai da st' afflition.

And for a cardboard crown
Daubed with a few middling colors,
Even the best people will ruin themselves
When they are caught up in this obsession.[1]

Throughout the early modern era the *pugni* captivated Venice. During the fall months of the *battagliole* season fascination for the event penetrated every corner of daily life, as people of all classes talked and indeed thought of little else for weeks at a time. It was a perpetual dialogue, mixing memories of previous encounters with expectations for future battles: in which the virtues of various *capi* and *padrini* were the subjects of wagers and fierce debates and where the chances of the champions who would meet in the next grudge match were discussed down to the finest detail. Apprentices avoided their work to argue about fighting styles and techniques, while their masters—those hundreds of fishermen, shipbuilders, porters, cobblers and butchers who would crowd the bridges on Sundays and holidays—argued and traded insults with one another when they met by chance in taverns and *campi* after work. These were no idle debates: when Venetians met and disagreed about the *pugni*, they could move quickly from words to blows to bloodshed, for these workers always had the knives, boathooks, cleavers, axes, and hammers of their trades close at hand. In the season of the *battagliole* these same passions were just as likely to seize the more cultivated members of society. Nobles politicking at the *broglio* and merchants doing business at the Mercerie or Rialto were no more restrained than ordinary working men in backing up their opinions with fists, daggers, or even pikes. Children, too, in back alleys all over the city, apparently liked nothing better than brawling over their favorite champions; and fishwives, like Anzola Nicolotta and Betta of Burano, were always more than ready "to come to words and then to deeds" in the name of the factions of their birth and of the champions who won them honor at the bridges. Foreign visitors might well find that the *pugni* provided them with their introduction to Venice even before they caught sight of the city itself. Those who came by barge along the Brenta Canal could find themselves addressed—as they prepared to disembark at Fusina for the gondola trip across the lagoon—by partisan placards, virtual billboards for the factions, showing one side symbolically held in chains and beaten by their captors, accompanied by a doggerel exhortation such as:

> Strangers, stay your feet:
> Those bound up here are those that build the fleet,
> Who though they resisted bowing to the Nicolotti,
> To this fate they've fallen, along with Zuecca and Gnesotti;
> When you return home again,
> To everyone there make it plain:
> That the Castellani, for all their pains,
> Are slaves of the Nicolotti and stay in chains![2]

Yet if these passions were aggressive, contentious, and frequently violent, they were also intensively festive. Venetian men and women of all classes delighted in gathering both to witness and to participate in the encounters: just coming together as Castellani and Nicolotti in their two enormous factional armies was a kind of celebration, a proud assertion of the city's popular spirit. Should one's faction, parish, or even favorite champion happen to come away victorious, it was cause for an almost limitless joy, to be broadcast about the city as loudly and as aggressively as possible. Officially (and then only after the largest encounters), the state allowed winners three evenings to celebrate their victory; in practice, many more nights were sometimes hardly enough for all the parishes, squads, and individuals who had triumphed in the *battagliola* to express their jubilation sufficiently. On the frequent occasions when battles ended inconclusively, the frustration on both sides was so great that a good deal of the city's normal work seemed to come to a halt in anticipation of another weekend meeting and another chance for the Castellani and the Nicolotti to duel each other again.

The Honor of Working Men

That the *battagliole* could arouse such passions and such fascination provided the proof, according to the Chronicler of the *pugni*, that these encounters were "important and not trivial affairs." Indeed, the stakes were high at the bridges: for many artisans and laborers of the city, men for whom honors were otherwise rare, the *mostre* and the *frotte* may well have offered their best, if not their only arena for winning and asserting public status. It was delightful to fight—everyone seemed to like beating on someone from across the canal; yet for most of the amateur warriors, thrashing an enemy in battle was secondary to winning honor and public recognition. Castellani and Nicolotti did not so much hate each other as love their own honor and wish to promote it at the expense of their opponents': "[T]he aim of our contests" as the Nicolotti once remarked, "is not to kill or tear each other apart but to win . . . glory and reputation in the presence of the city." It was a passion for winning that could drive fighters on both sides quite literally fighting mad when in the thick of a battle:

> In these matches, when it comes to a question of reputation, glory, and honor, the combatant is not a man but a Mars: it matters little or nothing if he has his face broken or scarred by fists, for it is enough for him just to please his faction and popular opinion and to hear the shouting of "Viva! Viva!"[3]

Such single-minded pursuit of status and reputation by ordinary workers is striking in an absolutist age, where the assertion and display of honor was typically the preserve of social elites. Nobles, bureaucrats, and guild officers held the monopoly on public honor in the early modern era: rights to precedence by virtue of their birth or of the Prince's special recognition of their services.[4] In baroque Venice this privileged group was embodied in law: they were the hereditary aristocrats and citizens (*cittadini*) of the city. As the Republic's *persone honorate*, they virtually defined the concept of honor itself. Thanks to a birthright nurtured by the practices of generations, these men and women incarnated and set the standards for honorable and proper conduct. Theirs was an elite's claim to public esteem, a sense of innate superiority deriving from lineage and an habitual closeness to the centers of state power. Even the meanest and least significant of their number (and there were many) was well aware of the deference owed them by commoners and the rights that were their due: the titles, special forms of address, political privileges, and even styles of clothing that were reserved for them alone.[5]

Accustomed to see honor and its associated privileges as a monopoly of their class, the Venetian elite would certainly have agreed with the jurist Cesare Beccaria when he asserted that working men did not interest themselves too much in affairs of honor, since "among common people . . . reputation is of less importance than it is to those of a higher rank." Artisans were generally considered too unsophisticated and too *villi* to feel any need for personal status or to crave precedence over their fellows. The expectation was that they would find enough honor in their work, and even there not so much as individuals but as members of a guild, exercising through their corporate solidarity and craft standards "the honest practice of work and . . . honest social, legal, and human behavior."[6] Yet Venetian workers certainly did pursue public honor, both for themselves as individuals and for the factional groups to which they belonged. Moreover, they claimed a right to recognition and a special social status in a context of their own devising: on top of a fighting bridge, in jousts and melees not all that different from those once favored by the medieval nobility for much the same purpose.

This use of the bridge *arengo* as the principal generator of worker honor may actually have occurred fairly late in the history of the *battagliole*. In sixteenth-century contests, when the fighting was still carried on with shields and sharpened sticks, participants appear to have been more intent on expressing and giving vent to their anger and aggression than on exploiting the matches as occasions for winning honor and public status. If this was so (and the evidence is quite sketchy), the cause may have been the style of battle itself: in these stick fights, where the danger of injury, mutilation, or death was quite real, even the most aggressive men would seem to have had to work themselves up to an extremely belligerent state before they were willing to attack. To overcome their natural wariness about rushing in to confront one another with fairly lethal weapons, stick fighters who met in the one-on-one *mostre* would attempt to provoke each other to anger by calling out a litany of insults and abuse that may have been partly ritualized formulas and partly spontaneous displays. Caravia, in describing the *battagliola* at the Servi in 1521, provides several examples of these aggressive exchanges, such as the one between Giagia of the Castellani and Tota for the Gnatti (that is, Nicolotti):

> Here on the Bridge of the Brothers of the Servi,
> The first to jump up were Tota and Giagia,
> Men, one could say, with nerves of steel.
> Giagia, the Gnatto, to provoke his rival,
> Said to him, "You're leaping around like the deer,
> What's with you, is your stomach feeling queer?"
> Tota, who had more heart than a dragon spitting,
> Called back, "Lick my ass while I'm shitting."
> Responded the Nicolotto, "I'll lick your rear
> With a six-foot pole, two-penny rascal of a pitch-eater."
> Giagia replied, "Keep on prattling and you'll get beaten
> Or maybe a black eye, no-account crab catcher."
> "Come on up here, wretch," said Tota,
> "And we'll have a little fighting, just us two."
> Giagia answered, "Let's go! I'm all ready,
> What are we waiting for? That some one plays us a tune?"[7]

Caravia's mock epic suggests that in these early *battagliole* as much time was spent in such taunting and insulting exchanges as in the actual fighting, while the duelists worked themselves up to the appropriate level of rage that would then discharge itself in rapid (and often fairly bloody) flurry of sticks. The abandoning of *canne* for *pugni* around 1590 made the *arengo* at the same time both a safer place and a more appropriate arena for the winning of honor. The custom of hurling insults continued, of course, but more in the form of heckling between gangs of factional partisans rather than purposeful provocations between duelists about to fight. The Chronicler of the *pugni* repeatedly noted how rival squads—especially of youths— would seek to incite each other in the early stages of the *battagliole*: calling out that their opponents were "gobblers of cabbage and beans" (*lovi da verze e da fasioli*—and therefore full of gas?) or by making the rude, sexual gesture of thrusting out their fists with the thumb between the first two fingers in the faces of their rivals (*facendo la figa negli occhi*).[8] These preliminary displays largely designed to inflate the level of rage and aggression among nervous fighters who might otherwise have feared to risk themselves. By the later seventeenth century, however, such ritual taunting was no longer practiced between those about to engage in a one-on-one boxing match. By then, experienced duelists, generally secure in their skills and their knowledge of the *pugni*, were presenting themselves not (in theory) out of anger or revenge, but to win glory and fame ("Oh, how much power," as the Chronicler once exclaimed, "has the [desire for] reputation!"). At such times there must have seemed little point in ridiculing one another beforehand with work-related jibes or sexually explicit threats: the promise of the honors of the *pugni* was in itself enough to induce both opponents to fight at their best.[9]

By the time of the Chronicler the cult of the *pugni* had made the significant step of separating anger and honor at the bridges, establishing the *arengo* more as a place for winning public praise and recognition than for venting anger and aggression. Champion fighters came to be referred to simply as *li honorati* (the honored ones), an indication that in this alternative world prowess alone could win a man the sorts of prerogatives and precedence that in the larger society would be restricted to patrician elites. When going about the city—particularly during the *battagliole* season, when factional passions ran high—they could expect the same show of respect that would be accorded to any passing Senator or Procurator; before a great battle, their public speeches might well attract greater popular interest than state proclamations.[10]

In the world of the *pugni*, a champion's assertions of honor may have been ultimately based on physical force, but, as in the parallel realm of the patrician elite, his claims to precedence also rested to a large extent on knowing how to act appropriately for one of his stature.[11] Above all, a fighter had to be willing to stand up for his faction with bravery and determination: in common parlance, he had to show himself as *generoso* and *risoluto*, for, as the Chronicler once noted, "The fighter who does not love encounters does not love honor, for those who do not defend the name [of their faction] clearly offend it." A *generoso* give freely of himself at the bridges, and only those who willingly did so would in consequence be counted among the *stimati*; those who could expect to claim the public's esteem. Thus, on the occasion of the visit of the cardinal de Lion, the Castellani were eager "to make themselves known as *generosi*," seeking to *pugnare da generoso*, to produce a "match [that would be] brave and worthy of universal praise and acclamation."[12]

Yet there was more to the notion of *generoso* than a simple willingness to do battle: courage without prudence or wisdom, after all, amounted to little more than the rashness that characterized reckless youths. The range of behavior at the bridges that was appropriate for warriors of honor was mapped out by a host of related terms: thus, the *generosi di guerre* were well trained (*allestiti*), to the point that they could indeed be called *aggueriti* (inured to war, or to suffering). Disciplined, they were also stubborn (*sodi*), willing to stand their ground even when seriously outnumbered. Perhaps most important, they also possessed *spiriti sensitivi*, that is, they were alert to the demands and the prerequisites of the honor they had won.[13] By extension, *generoso* could also mean quite literally "generous" in the more conventional sense, the *capi* of fighting squads were particulary known for their openhandedness in equipping and rewarding their men. For such leaders, liberality was in itself a means of claiming honor. The older noncombatant leaders, the *vecchi venerandi* (or *vecchioni*, the "great elders"), likewise merited the deference and respect of their factions, for the years they had generously given to the cult of the *pugni*, setting honorable precedents by "their memorable valor and example in the battles of their times."[14]

There was in all of this, a sense that *soldati generosi et honorati* were selfless and perhaps even somewhat ingenuous in their commitment to behavior appropriate to the *pugni*: "*sì generosi, liberi, sinceri* [so generous, open-hearted, and sincere] that they were without the slightest deceit."[15] Such champions would thus temper their natural bravery and eagerness to scrap with a sense of fairness and openness on the battlefield. In doing so they were giving public expression to those values of "fair play" that many scholars have assumed originated among eighteenth-century English sporting crowds but which clearly were already followed in Venice by the mid-1600s. Such "fair play" was vital in setting the ludic boundaries of the *pugni*, establishing a context of honorable behavior in which men might engage in the essentially dishonorable act of pummeling each other with their fists.

The responsibility for defining the *arengo* as a fighting zone where blows could be exchanged honorably fell primarily to the *padrini* on each side. Invariably drawn from among the champions on each side, these were the men who busied themselves "before the fight . . . [by] partitioning the *piazza* honorably and equally . . . [by] monitoring the location, setting the time, and adjusting the [fighters'] stance." The ultimate "fount of honor," however—in the world of the *pugni* as in society at large—was public opinion: the crowd at the bridges that through its applause, whistling, or waving of handkerchiefs finally determined whether duelists (or indeed the *padrini* themselves) had behaved correctly and honorably or had violated the communal sense of appropriate comportment by indulging in improper blows, arrogant conduct, or cowardly responses.[16]

Personifying the values of faction, fair play, and the warrior, the *honorati* provided a focus for the cult of the *pugni*, the celebration of which, by the later seventeenth century, was very much given over to recognizing these men as the worthies who had won their faction honor through leadership or triumph in battle. Each side had its champions around whom factional loyalties and partisanship tended to coalesce; usually these individuals served—sometimes for decades—as their faction's *padrini*—but even ordinary fighters who had participated in especially evocative duels and challenges could enjoy a fleeting renown. It is hardly remarkable that in a society so hierarchical and status-conscious as that of Venice, each side tended to create and turn to living heroes—rather than symbols, totems, or evocative images—in seeking a focus for its sense of factional identity and honor. Much as the doge and the Senate personified and represented the Republic to the external world, so these fighting champions served to incarnate the Nicolotti and Castellani spirit to their own partisans.

The best of these champions could attain the status of cult figures within their factions, with their faces depicted in paintings, cartoons, and effigies all over the city, and their names memorialized in poems or on placards (*cartelli*) pasted up on walls all around the factional boundaries. The Nicolotti champions, as well as most of the faction's leaders and best fighters, tended to come from the parish of San Nicolò, the fishing community that gave the side its name. Champions and cult figures among the Castellani had a more varied origin: many of them, like the famed Piero Moro, oarmaker from Santa Ternità parish, worked at the Arsenal, but others of lasting renown came from Sant' Agnese, the Giudecca, or from as far away as Burano.

Those who were most successful, or who perhaps appeared to best capture in their persons and actions the essence of their factions, could expect to find themselves lionized, in the manner of Tomè Panchia, the Nicolotti *capo principalissimo* from the late 1660s into the 1680s. A tobacconist and one of three brothers who all won esteem at the bridges as *capi* and *padrini*, Tomè would seem to have personified the best of the Nicolotti spirit.[17] He was apparently blunt, clear-thinking, and impassioned, yet also courteous and eloquent enough to enjoy the personal confidence of both the elders of San Nicolò and the Castellano patriarch of Venice. Stalwart in his duties as *padrino* to the point that he would willingly stand up to the principal Castellani duelists when he thought they had acted "against the proprieties of the *mostra*," he was also sufficiently brave in battle to lead many of the attacks himself.[18] Tomè Panchia was "revered and bowed to by all the Nicolotti militia," and partisans honored his leadership by celebrating his name wildly each time he led his faction to victory. A one-page broadside poem that circulated after the *battagliola* of 20 August 1679 gave him special recognition, quoting him and praising his leadership; a 1667 oil painting of another *frotta* carries a dedication to Panchia and his rival Toni the Baker and appears to have singled out the two, locked in combat in the midst of the anonymous mob (Figures 3.1 and 3.2).[19]

His face, or at least rough approximations of it, must have been familiar all over the city, for both Nicolotti and Castellani artists featured him prominently in the placards they produced and displayed for their victory celebrations. If such artworks were not especially sophisticated, they would

APLAVSO ALLA VITORIA CONSEGVIA el dì 20. AGOSTO 1679. DAI VALOROSI NICOLOTTI
Sul Ponte de San Bernabà.

1
GHe ne haueuimo vinti de ſto Meſe,
Voi dir d'Agoſto del ſerantanioue
Tempo, che per far veder bele impreſe
El Nicolotro, e'l Caſtelan ſe muoue
Quando, che ogn'vn le file à pur deſteſe
Per moſtrar del valor degne le proue
Stè à ſentir, che mi ſenza tante faue
Ve conterò el ſuceſſo in puoche otaue.

2
Comparſi al ponte i Nicoloti aſperti
Coragioſi al ſo poſto, e nò pì auanti
Seguri de portar Vittoria, e certi
Sempre co ſto penſier braui, e coſtanti
Intanto i Caſtellani i ſo concerti
Machinaua ; no sò, ſi for ſi i pianti
I preuedeua, ò pur ſi con inganno
Al ſolito ì tramaſſe el noſtro danno.

3
Dopò gran pezzo i xè cōparſi al Ponte,
Tartaro, e Ceghignola gran Paregni:
Mà ſe vedeua, che n'haueua fronte
De cimentarſe à ſi ſcabroſi ſegni :
Doppo d'auer tegnù le file ſconte
I à voleſto tentar i ſo deſegni:
Mà tanto pian, che no i zonzeua mai
Giuſto come alla Forca và i picai.

4
Si haueſſi viſto, come che i vegniua
A paſſo, a paſſo co ſà le Lumaghe,
Credemelo, che mai no i la compiua
Ogniun diſeua: Via fenila ſeggaie:
Cuſſì da cordo tutti al Ponte arriua;
Diſeua i Nicolotti: Gheſtu? ſtaghe:
Ga voleſto per dir là à vna parola,
Per tirarli là sù la Ceghignola .

5
Homeni da Caſtello ci ̀ n'hò à viſto
A vegnir sù co tanta bella Schiera
Da Muran, da Buran; mi ſon vn triſto,
Si no i paſſaua più de dieſe Miera
Zente, che podea certo far acquiſto
D'vna Citae, no che d'vna tal guerra
Oltre tanti Gneſotti, è Zuechini,
Che giera pien per tutto quei confini.

6
Subito che Tomè Panchia, è Birola
A vegnir i Caſtellani à vegnir ſuſo,
In tun iſtante ſenza dir parola,
Preſto i ſà deſpogià conforme l'vſo:
Cuſſì pian pian xe vegnù sù la ſola
De i Caſtellani, rouerſando il Muſo:
Se ſaluda i Paregni, no volen?
Panchia ghe diſe: olà ? che pretenden?

7
Tartaro parla : Nù volemo prima
Trè Moſtre, e pò tacar drento la frotta:
Tomè no ghè da rechie, perche ſtima
Daqualche ingano qualche bela botta:
Al fin lù ghe reſponde coſta rima:
Tiolè vna moſtra, è pò demo la rotta:
In tanto i Caſtellani à minchionando
Sù la Piazza del Ponte và vanzando.

8
Reſta da cordo. Via (diſe i Paregni)
Chi xè quei, che ſta moſtra gà da far?
Tartaro, è Ceghignola da i ſo ſegni
Se caua, e ſi ſcomenza zoſo à dar,
Panchia, è Birola, che xè homeni degni
Quando i vede la Frotta à ſcomenzar
Cō do pugni, e vna ſpenta i ga dà drento
Chei ghe nà trato in aqua cinquecento.

9
O che bel veder giuſto à mezo el ponte
Vn groppo, che mai più ſà viſto vn tal
In acqua ghe ne giera vn certo Monte
La più parte de quei dall'Arſenal
In tanto i Nicolotti col ſo fronte
Sa cazzà auanti, con coragio tal,
Che in tun momento ſenza remiſſion
I li hà butai de poſta zò in Caſſon.

10
El primo Pugno, che Tomè gà dao
Altri che Ceghignola no l'hà buo ;
In le coſte de poſta el gà tirao :
Da che ſaor, che l ſà lo cognoſſuo:
Cuſſì da ſto gran Pugno malmenao
In acqua zo del Ponte lè vegnuo
El gà ben dà la Caſſa, e in veritae
Si del corpo nol và, certo el ſà aſſae.

11
Vien quà Tomè ; dou'eſtu vita mia?
Fat'in quà, che te vogio dar vn baſo:
Sia tanto quella mare benedia,
Che rà fatto, che ſiela in tel Bombaſo:
Lodo in Eterno la to Gagiardia:
El to Brauo valor nò, che no taſo:
I to pugni ſà gnochi ſbreghi, e tagi
Pugni no i xè ; biſogna dirli magi .

12
Nò v'auè contentà vegnir vù tutti
In tanta quantitae con ſi gran fola
Vardè ſi ſè più della Volpe aſtutti,
Che hauè fatto vegnir fina i Pignola
Si ben, ch'i à poria via roſſi i Perfuetti
E che i ga ſtruca ſuora la Meola
Baſta mi sò, che i à bù certi Pignoi
Che fin, chel ſiò ghe dura i ſarà ſoi.

13
In tanto i Caſtellani à ſeguitao
Co ſforzi tali no ve poſſo dir:
Certo, e teguro , che i ſà decipao
Pur per veder ſul Ponte de ſortir:
Trè ore imagineue i ſa peſtao
Co mille forme i volea pur riuſcir
Dai tira para la ghè andà rouerſa
In Concluſion la Guerra xe ſta perſa.

14
Al fin i Caſtellani tutti quanti,
A dito andè, che venza ve la demo:
A baſarli ghe nè andà ſuſo tanti
Digando: nu per vù boni no ſemo:
Adeſo sì, che ve ſtimemo Atlanti ;
Per vn pezzo co vù no contendemo:
Haue venzo vna guerra, che mai più
Vogia ne vien ſul Ponte d'andar sù.

15
Cuſì co ſta Vitoria, è vegnù via
I Nicolotti pieni d'Allegrezza ?
Imagineue quella zente ardia
Si'l ſo cuor gera tutto contentezza ;
La zente Caſtellana ſbigoria
Dalla vergogna pieni de triſtezza
Andaua maledindo la ſo forte
I parea giuſto tante Gate morte .

16
Viua donca voi dir viua in Eterno
L'inuincibil valor dei Nicolotti ,
Canterò le ſo Glorie in Sempiterno
Me ſenta pur Zuechini, e anca i Gneſoti
E sì quei da Caſtello auerà à ſcherno
Le mie parole, e quei che ſupia i goti ,
Che i ſupia pur , che ghe dirò debo to
Che i ne vegna à ſupiar in tel Verao .

17
Al fin ve parlo ſchietto vegnì pur
Quanti , che ſè , che zà vù ſe Paroni
Greghi, Pignola, Armeni, ſe reduſi
Suodè pur le Feluche dei Schiaoni
Da Lio dalle Vignole ſe condut
Zente, e tutti i Chiozotti dai Meloni
Sì i fuſſe centomille , e nù duſento
No ſchiueremo mai de darue drento .

18
Feniſſo la Canzon, ſon ſtufo morto
Più matteria me vien, più che mi parlo
Da mì no ſtè à ſperar niſun conforto
L'honor à de chi lè ; biſogna darlo,
Mi vedo aſſie de vù col naſo ſtorto
Si l'auè, à voſtro dano, andè à drezzar lo
Va via la Muſa, e mi no gò pù vena
Buto via el Caramal, ſbrego la Pena .

IN VENETIA, CON LICENZA DEI SVPERIORI.   IL FINE.

Figure 3.2 Oil on canvas commemorating a *battagliola* at San Barnabà, with the inscription: "On the day of 22 October 1667. Commanders (*padregni*) Tome Panchia and Toni Forner dalla Carità." (Museo Correr, Archivio Fotografico, 21271)

have been clear and to the point for anyone who happened to see them: the Nicolotti *cartelli* often depicted Panchia as outfitted for battle (*in arnese*), posing over the defeated foe in symbolic dominance and identified with the fortunes and aspirations of his side. Although certainly revered by his partisans, Panchia's image was also used by Nicolotti artisans as part of their rude burlesques. Some supporters from San Giobbe parish, for example, once came up with a *cartello* that portrayed Panchia seated upon an inverted castle (thus, the defeated Castello) in which there was trapped a diminutive Castellano, who lamented:

> If Castello has its ass in the air
> We are to blame, for all our fear;
> But what I really cannot bear
> Is that Panchia has gone to crap up there.[20]

With his widespread reputation and public appeal, Tomè Panchia may have been somewhat exceptional—even a *padrino* of the Castellani, while exhorting his troops, once made the rather pathetic assertion that "in our Captain Toni the Baker we too have a Panchia truly strong and of great valor."[21] Nevertheless, the history of the *pugni* in the mid-seventeenth century could in large part be traced through reference to such factional heroes, whose images and words served as both symbols and rallying standards for their sides, and whom the Chronicler called "*i più nominati delle fattioni*": from Piero Moro, Sponzeretto, and Piero Arduin in the 1630s and 1640s, to Panchia, Mazzagatte, Bara Lucone, Paolino the Boatman, and Toni the Baker in the 1660s. In the satirical *cartelli* displayed at factional victory celebrations, they were depicted beating, teasing, or humiliating those of the other side: leading away chained prisoners or, like the chief Nicolotto duelist Mazzagatte, cracking a whip over a defeated opponent.[22] The public adulation of these champions was such that at times they achieved the status of popular cult figures, some even having their face and figure immortalized—not just in crude satirical sketches but occasionally in formal portraits in oils, posed in the warlike stances that had won them fame at the bridges (Figure 3.3). Such paintings, intended for public display about the city, made a champion's high stature clear to those in his faction; at the same time, as memorials created in a highly elite medium, they redounded to their subject's credit, enhancing still more to his already considerable reputation.

> [Paolino] the Boatman ... was in his day one of the most valorous and esteemed among the Castellano militia, especially among those of the Gnesotti and Zuecchini, and for his name and fame he was portrayed in a painting, in that posture and warlike stance with which he used to appear *in arnese* on the bridge, in the *mostre* and duels. Indeed, for its novelty it is quite often displayed in the Mercerie, on the occasions that [these streets] are adorned ... after the elections held for the Procurators or other observances.[23]

Figure 3.3 "Pugillatore," by Grevembroch, who added the comment: "One of the most valiant, who in past times distinguished himself in the matches of the favorites, was Bartolomeo Tartaro, once a boatman and then a guard at the prison; here we show his physique, as taken from the original portrait, so that posterity should not forget the look of such bold men, so vaunted within their families, almost as if they were great captains or heroes of battle." (Museo Correr, Archivio Fotografico, M. 24061)

It went almost without saying, however, that the more stature a champion achieved within his own faction, the more he would also find himself vilified by the opposing side. The honors of the *pugni* were appropriately generated by the conquest of a bridge or triumph in a duel. But they would certainly be enhanced if achieved at the expense of an enemy who was also shamed or embarrassed. Champion fighters represented the most accessible and indeed the most suitable figures for abusive treatment by the opposing faction, since they more than anyone else were understood to incarnate their side's honor, while providing the most well-known and generally recognizable targets. Seeking (successfully) to provoke their rivals, the Castellani once hung a *cartello* across Campo San Barnabà, showing smoke pouring from a victory crown, and Panchia, standing before the scene ready for battle but with his hands tied, exclaiming, "Oh, how my glory has gone up in smoke!" Another Castellani placard, hung in Campo San Gregorio, featured the Nicolotto champion Mazzagatte emerging soaking wet from the canal and begging to be spared a spanking from the caulking hammer of an Arsenal worker. The accompanying verse concluded:

> Alas! talk no more, responded Mazza Gatte, since
> My fanny's trembling from the hammer that he has;
> The glory shall be for the caulker;
> As for me, I'll be taking a bath like a fool![24]

A few decades earlier this symbolic mistreatment of opposition leaders had been much rougher, if less poetic, centering around the creation, abuse, and eventual destruction of their effigies. Although by 1667 it was considered "too vindictive" when Gnesotti youths hanged an effigy of Tomè Panchia in their *campo*, thirty years earlier the factional festivities of 1639 had included a whole range of such staged, symbolic acts, perhaps because the *battagliola* that year had ended inconclusively. With both sides claiming victory and local feelings running high, neighborhood groups seemed to be in competition to outdo both the opposing faction and each other in abusing enemy champions:

> Their continuous excitement could not be diverted . . . [and] not being able to give vent to their vengeful passions, they resolved that with hands and works they would at least satisfy themselves with the appearances; and thus the militia of Sant' Agnese hanged an effigy of Barbuzza in the middle of the bridge, and in the Campo of Santa Maria Formosa that of Vecchina of San Nicolò. At [San Piero de] Castello [an effigy of] Zanco Prizola was dragged behind the tail of a horse, to denigrate his dominance at the bridge, while at the Giudecca [an effigy of Piero] the Stonecutter was given the strappado, so that he would no longer go around making war. The Nicolotti, outraged by such affronts and derision, [responded] that evening when they were dancing the moresca, by burning over that same stage a statue full of firecrackers of Palao, [as] the one who had started the battle illicitly, adding below the saying, "THIS IS WHAT THE TEMERITY OF PALAO DESERVES."[25]

Such symbolic abuse of effigies stood in sharp contrast to the response of factional partisans when one of the Nicolotti or Castellani leaders actually died, whether in battle or by natural causes. On such occasions, factional urges to offend and disparage the opposition through symbolic humiliation of its chiefs were "converted into bowed heads and weeping to such an extent that one could not hear even one voice shouting out, as is customary in the battles."[26] Indeed, Caravia's dialect mock epic "La verra antiga dei Castellani, Canaruoli, e Gnatti" was as much a eulogy to the two slain *padrini* Giurco and Gnagni (whose names also appear in the original subtitle), as it was a poetic recounting of the bloody stick fight of 1521. Bawdy, dramatic, and clearly intended to be sung by ordinary citizens, the poem was written in 1550, a good thirty years after the actual battle; reprinted in 1587 and again in 1603, and extensively cited by the Chronicler of the *pugni* in 1670, it provides a good indication that factional champions like Giurco and Gnagni were still enjoying fame among their fellow Venetians a century and a half after their deaths.[27]

By the seventeenth century the funerals for fallen champions had became elaborate affairs. On such occasions both solidarity and piety were the theme, with partisans of both sides vying to show their respect, bereavement, and reverence: "[F]or such is the devotion of these people that when one of their leaders dies in battle . . . they reciprocally honor that corpse with a great many lights, and with humble prayers to God they consign him to the earth." After the Nicolotto *padrino* Giacomo the Furrier was stabbed to death during a factional argument, he was carried to his burial at his local church of San Giobbe at the head of "a procession of almost six hundred people, marching two by two with their devoted prayers"; for the funeral of Giacomo, a Nicolotto shoe dealer, more than a thousand turned out, including "three hundred from the Arsenal . . . each one with a lighted candle in his hand."[28]

A good deal of this pomp was no doubt designed primarily to assert the deceased's personal and factional stature. Yet these vast processions also effectively underscored a message of reconciliation: in death a champion transcended his role as a factional hero and instead could now serve as a shared icon to remind both the Castellani and Nicolotti that they were mutually Venetian citizens. In his deathbed exhortation to his fellow Castellani, Giurco, Caravia's fallen champion, ends "La verra antiga" on a very different note than the rude challenges which had begun the battle at the Servi:

> Do not be rashly saying that the Nicolotti
> Are more lazy or cowardly than you are,
> Since also among us there are some buffoons,
> And likewise not all of them are blockheads.
> None of us should vaunt himself more than the others:
> For in the end, are we all not patriots?
> All of us coined of the same flesh and bone,
> Grown up in these streets, these *campi* and parishes?
> Are we not all of one and the same nation:
> Sons of San Marco and his state?
> All that we have she has given to us:
> May God protect her and make her prosper!"[29]

If honor belonged to the victors in the *mostre*, those who were defeated were correspondingly shamed, often deeply, by their public failure. The Chronicler of the *pugni* repeatedly notes losing duelists (and factions) who left the bridge *molto mortificato*, with *poco honore*, and to the *discapito* (disadvantage) of their reputations.[30] Significantly, terms of humiliation and defeat occur even more frequently in the Chronicle than those concerned with the honors of victory: an indication of just how closely the quest for status at the bridges was conditioned and indeed controlled by an awareness of actual or potential shame. In the usage of the day, those who endured such public dishonor were less likely to be considered *vergognati*, with its overtones of sexual shame, than *mortificati*, which carried the connotations not only of being ashamed but also of having been physically (or, by extension, morally) wounded. Unlike the *generosi*—by nature energetic and vigorous—men who were *mortificati* could be reduced by this wounding to a virtual paralysis. This condition of not knowing how to respond to or cope with the burden of humiliating defeat was known as being *storno*, a kind of drunken confusion that was hardly surprising, considering the variety of conflicting emotions the breast of the vanquished. Not only was he "affronted, outraged, and injured," but at the same time he was also disappointed (*deluso*) from his failure, red-faced (*arrositto*), and filled with bitterness (*amarezza*) from the feeling of being ridiculed (*schernito*). When the defeated faction left the bridge, the men would go away "in a fever, grinding their teeth" but at the same time *muti e mortificati* (silent and ashamed) under the gaze of victors who were *allegri e trionfanti* (joyful and triumphant), highly pleased with these visible signs of impotence and frustration on the faces of their rivals.[31]

Certainly no one who lost at the *mostre* could expect to avoid embarrassment: spectators of the opposing faction were vocal and aggressive in their attempts to accentuate the loser's disgrace, since otherwise their side's victory would be incomplete, unsatisfactory.[32] The winning fighter himself would likewise spare no effort to exalt his triumph: "flaunting, flourishing, leaping, and dancing" on the slippery bridge surface, even when his defeated rival lay unconscious at his feet.[33] Many losers evidently found the mortification of their failure so "unbearable and insupportable" that they tried to cancel their shame by quickly seeking another duel for themselves, either with the fighter who had just bested them or with a new opponent. Some were indeed so unbalanced by their personal humiliation, that—even though bleeding and broken—they had to be physically prevented from trying to charge right back into the *arengo* for another chance, or sometimes from seeking to attack those that were mocking them among the enemy spectators. A few were even willing to accept the additional shame of loudly owning up to their initial defeat to the assembled spectators, in hopes of being permitted a second match.[34]

Yet significantly, fighters were humiliated at the bridges not so much because they had fought badly but simply because they had lost. Thus, a duelist who was bloodied by a chance blow to the nose or who unluckily slipped while fighting and fell into the water would feel shamed more or less to the same degree as one who gave up, fell down, and "begged in a great voice" for mercy, or who even fled the *arengo* altogether.[35] Surprisingly, although participants lamented their losses and gloated over their victories with equal intensity, a good deal of the outcome of any given contest was in fact ascribed to pure luck: at any time, it was held, the wheel of fortune (*ruota di Fortuna*) could turn against a faction or might always bring a recognized champion down.[36] That the sentiments of honor and shame could exert such powerful force under conditions of apparent chance is curious. Losers might attempt "to diminish their shame with excuses and lessen the pain with gestures, blaming their luck . . . [claiming that] the battle was prolonged beyond the proper time, and that if it had lasted as it was supposed to, they would have won," but such rationalizations were apparently of little help in shrugging off their loss or, by contrast, in denigrating the victory of their opponents.[37]

To some extent, fighters were humiliated by their defeats because they shared in a belief—which was certainly implicit throughout the Chronicle of the *pugni*—that even if *Fortuna* were blind, winners and (especially) losers deserved in some manner what they got. In practice this usually meant that hubris would get the better of arrogant champions, who, blinded by an inflated self-esteem, would eventually receive their comeuppance—the shame of which losers would feel even more sharply just because of their exaggerated feelings of self-esteem.[38]

In another way, however, the participants' sense of shame in the *pugni* appears so indiscriminate because a fighter could feel himself *mortificato* not only from an active failure—by putting on a poor show (*farla bruta*) during the duel—but also from the passive frustration of being denied the honors he so intensely desired. For most participants winning was the only thing, and in a context where everyone wished so passionately "to amass new glories and pile up laurels," blaming *malfortuna* was no satisfaction in the case of failure. It is true that an encounter could conclude in a draw, leaving neither party feeling especially dishonored; indeed, when highly sensitive champions were battling, their *padrini* sometimes arranged to declare a tie because they wanted to be sure that "neither the one nor the other should be degraded in merit or honor." Still, it was commonly held that if no one were greatly shamed in a drawn match, nor was anyone particularly honored, and for true champions a tie was no substitute for a clear-cut victory.[39]

Because they were in such high demand, the honors of the *pugni* were necessarily fleeting: in contrast to the public reputation of gentlemen, ensured by birth and the law and enduring for life, the status of these warrior aristocrats was always uncertain—sometimes brilliantly acquired but also just as easily lost. Only a few great leaders like Tomè Panchia or the *vecchioni* who were beyond the age of combat could expect to rest on their laurels, for there was always a host of ambitious youths eager to gain reputations of their own by bringing a champion down. Still-active fighters could never be sure that their hard-won reputations might not vanish in a single fight, like that of the hapless Nicolotti champion Barzaga, who was knocked down twice by his opponent, the Blacksmith, until finally:

> He fell down again, with scant reputation, and . . . left the *piazza* bent over, thinking more of the pain than of victory. And so his glory, which had flow-ered in him throughout the three years that he had come to the bridge, was lost with just three blows from the Blacksmith. . . . From which the fighter

can well learn that just a single felicitous success at war does not [thereby] make him fit for prizes and honors, any more than one flower makes the spring.[40]

Bedeviled by this insecure status, fighters were inevitably touchy about any imputation regarding the honor they believed they possessed. Few great gatherings at the bridges came off without someone feeling affronted with respect to his reputation, and in consequence usually eager for revenge. Perhaps for this as much as for any other reason, duelists had by the seventeenth century abandoned the custom of exchanging ritual insults before an encounter. Nevertheless, since the *battagliole* were perceived as fundamentally celebrations of and contests for honor and status, they continued to generate highly volatile situations, where honor would be offended and some form of vindication sought. In a very real sense, the pursuit of honor that was so central to the cult of the *pugni* could not be properly celebrated without giving rise to this resulting cycle of affront, revenge, gang warfare, and sometimes assassination.

Those *padrini* whose task it was to keep the *battagliole* from degenerating into simple brawls were well aware that the *pugni* had to take place under special conditions if the men of honor who competed were not to offend each other simply by the act of exchanging punches. To consecrate the *arengo* for the contest, they tried to make sure that the top *piazza* of the bridge was empty except for themselves and the two duelists, who were made to kiss symbolically before being carefully positioned in opposite corners.[41] Yet neither the *padrini* nor the various gentlemen enthusiasts who sought to keep the fighters under control could ever expect total success. There were always those who would try the patience of the *padrini*: members of the crowd who were constantly encroaching on the *arengo*, interfering with the match, or even taking a swing at the opposing champion. Significantly, such conduct was seen less as "against the rules" (literally, *fuori dell' ordine della Guerra*—there were, of course, very few such rules) than as "dishonest," "hardly honorable," or "worthy of blame."[42]

Since they were conceived of as violations more of honor than of abstract regulations, it is not surprising that such infractions were often taken as personal affronts by the individuals who were involved. The *padrini* in particular tended to treat their own reputations as tightly bound up with "fair play" during the matches and to see disobedience on the part of the fighters as a personal challenge to their honor. As a result, those onlookers and participants who rashly disrupted the *mostre* were less likely to find themselves ejected from the bridges (although this could happen) than to be suddenly challenged to an affair of honor by the *padrino* they had happened to insult.[43]

Onlookers seemed to have been most often tempted to intrude in the *arengo* when the *padrini* themselves were arguing, as if such noisy debates— or perhaps simply the delay—could drive already impatient spectators to lose control entirely. So it happened in 1668 when, as the *padrini* were contemptuously dismissing one another's claims about which fighter was bloodied, one Piero Garbuio ("Messy Pete") from Quintavalle abruptly stepped into the *arengo*, "put his hands on the chest of Valerio Facendina [in itself a highly insulting act], and pushed him in the water without any justification of Battle."[44] Such acts were of course much more sensitive if they directly involved the *padrini* in charge. Thus it happened with Nicolotto Radego, who refused to obey orders to keep off the bridge and instead took a swing at his *padrino*; with Zuane Testa, who upbraided the *padrino* Domenico Sottilo "in emotional and threatening words" for not refereeing properly; and with the duelists Chieppa and Verigola, who in their haste to rush into their match bowled over the hapless Castellani *padrino*.[45]

The immediate results of such blatant offenses was usually a spontaneous *frotta*, as both sides immediately charged the center of the bridge to avenge the wrong. It was generally held that a good, rousing brawl at this point might go a long way toward canceling out the factional dishonor occasioned by the original insulting infraction. The personal dishonor experienced by the offended *padrino* was not so easily assuaged, however.[46] Nor was it a simple matter to redress dishonor experienced on a variety of other occasions: when a champion was outraged at being denied the right to fight when he wished, when a duelist came out on the losing end of a decision by the *padrini* (his own as well as the opposition's), or when someone of honor felt he had received an unwarranted jostling from another fighter or even one of the spectators.[47] When men were highly sensitive about their reputations, words alone could cause offense just as easily as blows, and if the aggrieved parties were unable to find satisfaction immediately, they would leave the scene simmering with a sense of injustice.

> Then . . . Andrea Zaccher let it be known that he wished to mortify all the Nicolotti, no longer with fists and stones but with the blade of his machete, in particular [a Nicolotto called] the Genoese and those other Magoghe (as he put it), who at the bridge are only good at clowning around. These words were said so openly that they were overheard by Barbuzza, who as leader of all the Nicolotti turned to Zaccher with his hands on his hips, saying, "The Magoghe of San Nicolò are good enough to thrash you [Castellani] with fists and will also suffice to give all of you some good beatings and slashings, and I in particular will be their leader, and start with you." [Barbuzza then] drew his dagger . . . but being among a crowd of friends, they were separated, each of them departing saying, "We will discuss this later."[48]

On such occasions, "gnawing at himself" with frustration and his sense of public shame, the wronged fighter might set in motion a vendetta. Usually he proceeded by collecting around him *in setta* (that is, in a group, or sect) a number of supporters, men of status and honor themselves: if possible, sympathetic *padrini*, merchants, or even nobles.[49] Since a vendetta over honor wounded in the context of the *pugni* meant deciding to "avenge the affront with steel instead of with the fists," an offended champion and his men loaded themselves down with pikes, knives, and daggers of every description, although rarely with firearms, the carrying of which was strictly forbidden.[50]

Thus equipped and sometimes followed by a gang of eager youths whose work aprons were loaded with stones and iron balls, the offended champion went out into the streets: ostentatiously and belligerently parading about the city, brandishing his drawn weapons, vocally demanding satisfaction, sending out spies to discover his rival's movements, and—if he were especially serious—even taking his gang into the heart of the opposing faction's territory to seek out his enemy at home.[51] These open demonstrations of outrage would, of course, in short order provoke a reciprocal display from the offending party, who—both for his own safety and for personal honor—would soon begin collecting his own followers and likewise going about *in setta*. When the two antagonists were champions of the first order, their dispute could quickly turn into something of a cause célèbre that might capture the interest of the entire city.[52]

These highly visible, irate heroes of the *pugni* parading about the city very much resemble (and no doubt modeled themselves on) the more fractious nobles of the era, who were also accustomed to going about armed, with a retinue of *bravi* and servants, when looking for trouble or revenge (thus giving rise to the expression *caminar armati*). With both rivals so heavily armed—and not unwilling to plot out ambushes, if these promised success—such affairs had the potential to become quite bloody, and sometimes they were. When the large followings of the Castellani *padrino* Arpa and the Nicolotto baker Simonetto blundered across each other one Friday afternoon in 1632, in the Campo dei Carmini,

> These being men who were exceptionally skilled and who knew how to fight with knives, . . . with everyone wanting to defend their companions from insults, they started up a fierce battle that lasted until nearly the Ave Maria, with so much disturbance that people were throwing chairs and stools down from the balconies to break it up . . . but in fact every one of them ended up wounded, either more or less, [many] from stones and iron balls: indeed, [one of them] died the next day.[53]

Despite their vocal ferocity and display of weaponry, these worker vendettas were not always bloody. Although they could climax in an ambush or a fatal brawl, such disputes over offended honor might also go no further than the first stages of declaiming and posturing in the streets. Certainly, men were not always implacable about seeking to butcher one another in such affairs, in which case their friends and supporters could be more than willing to prevent a genuine confrontation: it was not unknown that the agents that each antagonist sent to spy out the movements of the other would on their own decide to bring back false information to keep the two opposing gangs from ever actually meeting.[54] The offended party was in any case often quite content to accept an apology rather than go through with his threats, the more so because of the legal risks both antagonists ran: the Council of Ten had quite stringent laws against anyone, noble or commoner, who made a showy pretense of going about *armato in setta*. If both adversaries showed openness to such a solution, entire squads of go-betweens—nobles, merchants, or other partisans of status (also worried that such violence might provoke the Ten into banning the *battagliole* entirely)—would soon be shuttling between them trying to work out an agreement.[55] In the best of cases they managed to work out a convenient fiction, "an honorable and arranged settlement," whereby the offender could apologize without losing too much honor himself. Such was the solution found for the dispute of honor that arose in 1668, after the Nicolotto Tomè Panchia had (so it was claimed) exceeded his authority as *padrino* by striking a Castellano champion during the duel:

> To avoid an armed brawl between these two *capi*, some gentlemen friends managed, with great skill and after many discussions and consultations, to effect an adjustment, which followed in this manner: that Panchia would say that, in the passion of the duel, he was aware of throwing a punch, but he did not know whom he had hit, whether Jani or Mazzagatte [the two duelists], but whichever it had been, he had not with hostility intended to affront either the one or the other. So a peace was made between them at the Convent of San Salvador, and everyone had lunch together at the house of Verigola Nicolotto, the paper dealer in Rialto.[56]

Behind these levels of posturing and bluffing that could verge on the burlesque, such confrontations between champions had a more serious purpose. In issuing their challenges and parading about the streets *in setta*, these men of sensitive honor were attempting to bring their disagreement out into the open as a means of maneuvering their claims for redress before public opinion: the traditional tribunal for deciding questions of reputation. In this way, wronged fighters sought to demonstrate the validity of their assertions of offended honor through the level of public support they could claim. A champion of high status with a worthy cause could expect to enlist the backing of gentlemen and *padrini*, who would both march with him and put pressure on his rival. Someone on less secure ground or of lesser reputation (and thus with less honor to defend) would have correspondingly less public support, and could end up like the unfortunate Castellano Passerin, "who, not having a great following, did not come out in public [*alle piazze*] but remained in hiding; [and] in the end was therefore forced to make peace."[57]

This public forum of the *pugni*—significantly guided by the *padrini*, *vecchioni*, gentlemen partisans, and other factional leaders, but also shaped by the less distinct *vox populi* of all those who went to the bridges—could prove quite effective in establishing which sorts of affronts were truly insults to honor and which were mere *pretentioni*. At the same time, this tribunal also sometimes managed to impose an equitable (and bloodless) settlement in such disputes. Public opinion could also help in confirming how the affairs of honor themselves ought to be pursued. It eventually came to be held that vindicating affronts was a personal matter, to be settled by the insulted individual, not by his friends, squad mates, or parish allies acting on his behalf (though close relations could be another matter). Thus, "the fighter [who] has not been offended in his own person, in his honor or his reputation, by common opinion never exposes himself to matches or personal duels against someone who has not affronted him." Likewise, only those who had been witnesses to the original provocation, it was thought, had the right or duty to march with the aggrieved champion.[58] It also was widely held by those who followed the *pugni* that *padrini* who were attacked while serving honorably as referees were generally in the right, just as those who failed to carry out their duties correctly were in the wrong and would get little popular support if someone should strike them in retaliation.[59]

Perhaps most important, by the mid-seventeenth century common public opinion began to hold that the disputes over honor that arose at the bridges were better resolved by dueling with fists rather than with steel; or as the Chronicler put it, "that when the pretenses of honor had their origins in the War, it made sense that they also be terminated with the War." Men who had offended one another during one *mostra* took to challenging each other to reestablish their honor by having another boxing match later, "in the presence of all the people of both factions," instead of pursuing a vendetta leading to a street brawl. Those with a sense of the dramatic (and perhaps a literary friend as well) might also seek to plead their case still more elegantly and openly, by posting a written challenge to meet and duel at the bridge, using a large *cartello*, which they pasted up or stuck on a lance point at the factional boundaries for all to see.[60]

Either way, these challenges represented a step that was highly satisfactory to the partisans of the *pugni*, who were always especially pleased to witness a match involving long-standing personal animosities. More importantly, the *pugni* would in time develop into a venue for resolving many of the various plebeian disputes over honor in the city, whether or not they had been originally generated at the bridges. This ability to become the general staging ground for settling questions of popular honor helps to explain why *battagliole* became steadily more frequent over the course of the seventeenth century, as duels were arranged in ever-expanding cycles between new or long-term rivals. Champions defeated one Sunday would, if they were physically able, quickly begin making plans to regain their lost honor by setting up a rematch the following weekend (or sometimes on a workday, if the humiliation of defeat were too strong to bear for an entire week).[61] At the same time, dozens of *disfide*, or challenges, stimulated not only by affronted honor at the bridges but also by the disagreements and confrontations that were touched off daily throughout the city, would also be arranged for the next Sunday's *battagliola*. So popular would the *pugni* become as the public forum for settling such questions that by the mid-seventeenth century it was not unusual for fifty or even a hundred *mostre* to be staged on a single Sunday afternoon, all dedicated to the public expression of the honor of working men.[62]

Naming and Belonging

The honors and reputation to be won at the *pugni*—those signs of a *vero guerriero*—were at their heart highly masculine: for Venetians, the war of the fists, like all warfare, was quintessentially the business of men. In consequence, to celebrate the *pugni* was to celebrate being male, to assert not only the strength, endurance, and aggression that were proper to men but also to proclaim how this maleness differed from the female and the childish. When local fighters, ready to do battle, marched two by two on their way to the fighting bridge, they declared their masculinity to the city at large, through their discipline, dress, and warlike chanting. Their processions would bring women and children flocking to nearby doors and balconies to salute them, cheer them on, perhaps to follow in their train— and ultimately to bear witness to this collective assertion of male distinctiveness.[63]

But what did being male mean to these warriors of the *battagliole*, who came to the bridges so highly conscious of their virility? Beyond the Chronicle of the *pugni* itself and its specific context of factional aggression, there is little enough available on early-modern working-class attitudes toward such questions of gender: this was not the sort of topic that captured the interests of seventeenth-century writers. But the culture of assertive masculinity was not unique to early modern Venice. Such demonstrative maleness is indeed one of the unifying and distinguishing features of what modern ethnographers consider the Mediterranean cultural basin. This great expanse of common human geography, stretching from Spain to the Levant and embracing the societies of southern France, the Balkans, the Maghreb, and Turkey, cuts across the religions, languages, and customs of many people, yet is still linked by ancient, shared cultural norms. Given the persistence of such deep cultural structures, it is not unreasonable to anticipate that behind the practices of male self-glorification associated with the *pugni* there can be found at least some of the same value systems that ethnographers have also identified in modern societies in such places as Greece, Albania, and southern Spain.

Customs of accentuated masculinity, whether they flourish in present-day Mediterranean village society or among seventeenth-century Venetian workers, are generally considered to be an expression of the vivid consciousness with which gender bipolarity is (and was) experienced in daily life. This sharp awareness of the sexes and their different roles and places in turn imposes itself on the urban landscape itself, effectively dividing social space into male and female realms. In early modern Venice—as is generally still true in many towns and villages around the present-day Mediterranean—male space was public space: men were dominant (and much more visible) in the streets, taverns, and *campi* of the city. Moreover, the

Chronicle of the *pugni* underscores how in Venice this sense of a masculine preserve was especially strong at the neighborhood bridges—the scene
of so much arguing, playing, and drinking by journeymen, *bravi*, and other
idle males. The household was correspondingly female territory, an enduring element of Mediterranean gender polarity that extends back to classical Greece. No doubt the Venetian worker considering himself the
paterfamilias and head of his house—much like his counterpart in many
modern villages. Nevertheless, he tended to leave the running of his household and the raising of his children almost entirely to his wife, female relatives, and the network of neighborhood women.[64] In charge of this inte-
rior realm, women of all ranks (though especially noblewomen) tended to
spend more of their time indoors, secluded from public view, except when
business took them out to the shop and marketplace or religious obligations called them to church.[65]

This gender division of social realms was both a reflection of and a
structural reinforcement for the high degree of social consciousness regarding the differing standards and prerogatives of the sexes. It also tended to
create special problems for young males, problems characteristic of many
modern Mediterranean societies. At a certain stage of their lives maturing
boys must make the difficult transition between these two social regions:
the protected female space of the family house, where they are born and
spend their first years in the company of women and girls; and the more
open and competitive male space of the streets, *piazze*, and bars where,
with little assistance from adults, they must eventually find their place among
men. The traditions of sexual segregation pose less daunting challenges
for girls, who not only expect no such major shift of social spheres but
who also benefit from adult female role models to provide guidance for
this, the major passage of their lives, that of marriage and leaving their
girlhood home to move to their husband's house.[66] Given that seventeenth-
century Venetians were at least as sensitive about the gender imperatives
of their living space as are most modern Mediterranean villagers, we can
safely assume that young men of the 1600s experienced such difficulties
of transition—in effect, one of the dominant problems associated with
coming of age in this cultural world.[67] For many Venetian youths the trials
of passage may well have been easier than they are today. In the past, after
all, the elaborate, formalized traditions of apprenticeship helped to guide
the transition to adulthood. At least for those youths whose fathers had
enrolled them in the more respectable Venetian guilds, some of the personal difficulties associated with this passage from the private household
to the public *campo* and workplace were institutionalized and therefore
deflected by the process of gaining a mastership and thus winning formal
observance of their adulthood. Other young men would have won a similar recognition when they managed to marry and set up a household for
themselves.[68]

Yet for thousands of young Venetian working youths, earning public
recognition of their transition to adult male status would have been far

more burdensome. Those young men who worked as day laborers, street vendors, porters, or any of scores of other low skilled trades labored in occupations that neither recognized any sort of masters (since they were indeed usually not even organized into guilds), nor provided enough income to establish an independent family. For youths from such backgrounds—increasingly common in the economically declining Venice of the 1600s—success at the bridges offered not only an attractive alternative to their ordinary working lives but also a highly visible, public means of claiming a place within the society of men.[69]

The *pugni* thus provided both an arena for Venetian workers to establish honor and reputation and the means by which youths of the city could hope to win a place in the world of men. It was a process that began quite early in life. Small boys, making their first sorties out of the female-dominated household, began their masculine re-orientation through joining local youth gangs and personally identifying with a favorite champion fighter of their faction or community, eagerly getting into brawls with neighboring boys to defend the name of their hero. Some evidently became so captivated by their chosen *capo* or *padrino* that they passed their time following him around the city as he went about on factional business.[70] Slightly older youths, not yet mature enough to fight at the bridges but familiar enough with the customs of the *pugni* to be known as *giovenotti di prima experienza*, would form factional gangs, whose incipient masculinity seems to have found its best espression in mounting those noisy group raids, or *scorrerie*, that took them—shouting and taunting—into the territories of their faction's enemies. In the process they demonstrated that they could violate the space (and thus the honor) of their rivals with impunity. From here it was but a small step for youths to attach themselves to feuding champions, marching about the city *in setta*, with their pockets, work aprons, or even sacks loaded up with stones and iron balls in anticipation of joining in a factional brawl.[71]

In some ways, these Venetian gangs were not so different from youth groups throughout premodern Europe, as well as in modern Mediterranean countries: naturally contentious and disruptive, these young Venetians would also continually push one another into ever more provocative acts—including stone throwing, gang wars, racing about with flaming brands, and singing rude songs about their neighbors—as each boy sought through exorbitantly aggressive behavior to magnify the distance between himself and the feminine household he was leaving behind.[72] Such has long been the privilege of youth groups everywhere, as boys took (and still take) advantage of the temporary marginality imposed on them by this transitional phase between the household and the streets to flout social rules and lay claim to whatever masculine honor they could find.[73] Yet in baroque Venice, where the entertainments of agonistic sport were not restricted by custom just to youths but were instead the traditional activity—if not the special prerogative—of the collective body of working men generally, these gangs had a relevance that went beyond simple street solidarity and carnivalesque amusement.[74] Such working-class youth groups in early modern Venice should also be considered as the training schools of the *pugni*: the boys who belonged to them were actively defining themselves with respect not only to the feminine household they were leaving behind but also to the particularly masculine world of the bridges that they hoped eventually to enter. Some adult partisans of the *pugni* sufficiently appreciated the role of such adolescent gangs as the testing grounds of maturing boys that these men would make it a point to observe their youthful duels and skirmishes— even if they were "of little importance"—and to encourage the most pugnacious of them "to show that they were youths of spirit, [who] . . . when their day came . . . would make a militia just as fierce and courageous in the disciplines of war."[75]

   The end of his adolescent training period came when a youth reached sufficient size and maturity that he managed to convince his neighborhood *caporione* to enroll him in the fighting squad of local men. He was evidently not fully part of the world of the *pugni*, however, until he had presented himself in the *mostre*. Such was their eagerness to complete this working-class rite of passage that many youths would eagerly try to shoulder their way into the *arengo* even when they were still too green and inexperienced, only to be humiliated and contemptuously dismissed by their *padrino*, "for impeding the *mostre* of the stronger and better known." Yet they were more than willing to risk the embarrassment of being chased off the bridge in the hope of winning a chance to pit themselves against a recognized champion, for anyone who defeated such a veteran could immediately gain the reputation of a *vero guerriero*. So eager were these novices for a chance to prove themselves that they would sometimes mob a famed duelist who offered himself at the *mostre*, winding up fighting bitterly among themselves over who would get the chance to meet such a champion in single combat.[76]

   This impatient urge to parlay success at the bridges into reputation and acceptance in the world of adult men is understandable, considering how few similarly overt and clear-cut proofs of their maturity were available to lower-class youths. It was an uncertain status, to be sure, like all the honors of the *pugni*, to be brilliantly won but just as easily lost in a single, humiliating defeat. Perhaps the very precariousness of the manhood to be won at the bridges explains why such young men flocked to the bridges with an almost desperate contentiousness, driven by the awareness that defeat would bring them not only shame but also a kind of emasculation before the eyes of the city. Youths who failed to win at the bridges lost any claims they might have had for membership in the masculine, public world of the *pugni*; worse yet, they could find on returning home that they were no longer welcomed in the feminine world of the household either:

> The losers . . . are so humiliated that there are those who do not even dare to
> return to their houses, because their womenfolk will sometimes close their

doors to them and drive them away, reproaching them for their cowardice with abusive terms [such as]: "Away from here, dishonorable, ignominious pig!"[77]

While they were struggling to conquer a place for themselves among the mature fighters, young contenders also tried to craft a persona that would go along with their new status at the bridges. For many, adopting a nickname or nom de guerre to flaunt while going into battle was a significant element of this new factional identity. Not that nicknaming was a practice limited to the bridges, for in these years before surnames became universal among ordinary Venetians it was quite common for workers to sport some sort of sobriquet in addition to their customary patronymic. Certainly, parallels to this frequent usage of nicknames (including family nicknames, handed down through generations) can be found in the present-day Mediterranean cultural basin, where such names have traditionally served as mnemonic aids, helped to enforce social norms, and censured misconduct in these close neighborhood worlds.[78] In premodern Venice the practice also no doubt flourished in good part through necessity, in a city that was so crowded and where the choice of given names was by custom so restricted that quite often no other means would have existed to identify individuals: sometimes both census takers and the police had to resort to entering nicknames in their records, presumably for the sake of clarity.[79] Yet whatever their social function, nicknames in Venice—as indeed in all societies—fell into certain patterns, depending on their inspiration. Some were evidently derived from objects or instruments associated with work—a fisherman of San Nicolò might well be named after a fish, (which he had once caught—or perhaps resembled); an artisan might be called after one of his tools. Other times men and women found themselves branded by terms recalling a physical defect or a behavioral quirk. A few unfortunates were marked by enigmatic, sometimes scatological expressions that most likely invoked a now-obscure play on words or an otherwise long-forgotten childhood misdeed.[80]

Nicknames, aptly coined and imaginatively manipulated, contributed to the festive and somewhat surreal air surrounding the *pugni*: many champions seemed to have special selves, larger-than-life, often grotesque identities when they strutted into the *arengo*. Openly and publicly used, such nicknames would seem to have had a broader social role in the Venetian world of the bridges than they have now, centuries later. In present-day Mediterranean village culture nicknames, though widely used, tend to be applied rather circumspectly, and never to their owner's face. When used in the *pugni*, by contrast, nicknames were not only known to everyone but they also evidently served as a form of personal advertisement: more nearly noms de guerre than private nicknames, they could well have been the signal that one had completed the transition from ordinary society to the alternative brotherhood of the *pugni*.[81] Some of these nicknames, it is true, simply referred to their owners' profession: with the better-known *padrini*, it would seem to have been enough for the Chronicler to refer to "*the* Doughnut-Seller" (Il Zavatin), "*the* Window-Maker" (Il Fenester), or "*the* Furrier" (Il Varoter) for contemporaries to have understood whom he was speaking about.[82] But a great many fighters sported sobriquets that were clearly tailor-made for the bridges, nicknames whose pugnacious or gruesome associations would have been especially evocative of the warrior image appropriate to the *pugni*. Some of these epithets may have been simply fortuitous (or formative) childhood nicknames that made particularly good noms de guerre: physical descriptions such as Manone ("Big Hand"), Grinta ("Grimace"), Garrofalo ("Fist"), or Denton ("Big Tooth"); or behavioral characterizations, calling to mind the kind of ferocity, agility, or general nastiness that seemed appropriate for the bridges: Tienduro ("Hold Tough"), Saltafosse ("Ditch Jumper"), Gaiardo ("Stalwart"), or Beverin ("Poison"). Moreover, some of the most renowned fighters at the *mostre*—where bluffing and intimidation were especially important—sported noms de guerre that seem especially designed to impress and, if possible, dismay opponents: thus, Azzalà ("Made of Steel"), Bota ("Blow"), Mangiamundi ("World Eater"), Magnamorti ("Eats the Dead"), Mazza Homeni ("Man Killer"), Mazza Bravure ("Destroyer of Boldness"), Morte ("Death"), and Omocidio ("Murder").[83]

These nicknames of the *pugni* were highly public, the common property of everyone who frequented the bridges. Fighters were refered to by their noms de guerre not only by those who came to watch the encounters but also on the placards and banners produced for victory celebrations. Poets who wrote of the *battagliole* seemed to delight in filling their texts with long lists of such fighters' names, perhaps to amuse and astonish their readers with the bizarre inventiveness of Venetian workers.[84] Such baroque and extravagant noms de guerre were in a sense carnival masks, probably striking most contemporaries as they do modern readers—as exaggerated burlesques. Yet nicknames were not simple caprice. Unquestionably they would also have served to heighten the dramatic sense of the moment: much more would appear to have been at stake in a duel between Teramoto ("Earthquake") and Zuzzateste ("Sucker of Heads") or between Miseria ("Misery") and Drago ("Dragon") than in a straightforward fight between Zorzi and Zuan, the Venetian equivalents of George and John.[85] That these were somehow more than ordinary men further reinforced the connotations of ludic space at the bridge: that special context that allowed opponents to beat at each other without insult to honor or the need of seeking later revenge. At the same time, a champion with a nickname was still close to his roots among the working people: his nickname signified that he remained in a familiar relationship with his supporters, much as do modern-day matadors with their circle of bull-ring aficionados.[86]

This interplay between champions and their public by means of such noms de guerre was in effect a two-way process. Fighters attempted to impress each other and the crowd with the ferocity of their nicknames while spectators in their turn would seize upon these same names as a means of mocking and commenting on the participants themselves. The Chronicler of the *pugni* was certainly only reflecting popular custom when he exploited the humorous possibilities that such nicknames presented by punning upon them in the context of the narrative moment: thus,

Zurli ["Flyweight"] lifted Grinta ["Grimace"] with a great grimace indeed.

Tieneduro ["Hold Tough"] was not in fact able to hold in all that tough.

Risi ["Laughs"] did not laugh at all but gave up the fight.

Folla l'uva ["Crushes the Grape"] fell down practically crushed.

Ballon ["Balloon"] departed inflated with ambition and glory.[87]

Playing around with their champions' nicknames allowed spectators to keep on terms of easy familiarity with their heroes; at the same time, by abusing fighters through their nicknames, onlookers could maintain a sense of participation in the battles and even of control over their outcome. Spectators might amuse themselves as they did when the Castellano Marco the Carpenter proved unexpectedly resistant to the repeated punches of the Nicolotto champion, Ceccho Panchietta: it was no surprise, they called out, since carpenters always had their faces covered with walnut planks. When the duelists Mastelletto and Tuttotattare came to a clinch, one grabbing his enemy by the hair, the other by the neck, and with their heads tilted back gave each other repeated punches to the face, it was said that "they seemed like the two Moors that strike the hours at [the clocktower of] San Marco."[88] The sharper wits on the rooftops and quays were constantly calling out puns involving the nicknames of the fighters before them, to the great amusement of the crowd. No one could resist jesting with the apparently fortuitous match between Naso ("Nose") and the bizarrely named Tre Riose de Cul ("Three Asshole Roses," that is, "Three Farts"):

[I]n the end, receiving as many blows in the face as in the sides, Naso did not find the smell too good from Tre Riose . . . and left bleeding and quite humiliated; it was a match truly much applauded by the people, as much for the meeting of names as for the *mostra*, since the nose has the property of smelling, and the roses [that] of odor.[89]

This running commentary by the crowd went beyond just making puns, however, for during the *battagliole* the crowd could also exercise its right to give new names to participants, nicknames that were truly a product of the bridges. Once, after the young Castellano duelist Sille had been badly knocked about by his long-standing rival Mazzagatte, he could do no more than hunker low on his hams in the *arengo*. He looks "like a chicken scratching," one Nicolotto wag called out, and so, the Chronicler concluded, "Sille acquired the name 'Cuffete' [Little Pecker], for he cleaned up the *piazza* just like the hens."[90]

The most common targets of such play with names were, not surprisingly, either those whose nicknames especially invited mockery or those who were themselves known as especially touchy, arrogant, and demonstrative while in the *arengo*. One young Castellano champion who seems to have combined all these qualities was nicknamed Frate ("the Friar"), the special hero of the Giudecca squads. Possibly because of his occupation (he was a servant) or perhaps because, although still young, he was extremely proud, (having already made a name for himself in the rough-and-tumble *frotte*, and expecting his place among the top duelists of the *mostre*), Frate found himself the repeated target of Nicolotti partisans, who relentlessly sought to give him his comeuppance.[91] He was the first of the duelists to present himself at the grand encounter at San Barnabà on 23 October 1667, but:

> Before coming to the clinch, he was annoyed by his shoes, which he threw off the bridge into the water; [then] he met his Nicolotto adversary with ferocity, but in the first round he was knocked by the force of the blows into the water. This first match was a prodigious woe to the Castellani, who got still more disheartened when the Nicolotti laughed, shouted, and called out that this Friar was not of an order that went barefoot [*scalzo*], which was why it was a good thing that he had gone to fetch his shoes.

When Frate presented himself against Mazzagatte a year later, before the Princess Colonna on 15 September 1668, things went no better for him; although he initially landed a few punches to his rival's face, in the second round he was tumbled off the bridge again. This time, however,

> [t]here were voices going around that it was a Nicolotto [onlooker] who had pushed him in the water, with the result that Frate, completely soaked, was unable to bear such insult and injury to his self-esteem, and wet as he was, he returned to the bridge and by biting his finger, he threatened Peo of San Gregorio, the one who was supposed to have pushed him in. But the Nicolotti onlookers leaped up with rather abusive and offensive words, laughing at him that he should change his name, and not call himself Frate any longer, but Frà Aquario ["Brother Aquarius"], since . . . he was always falling in the water.

The Nicolotti crowd continued to play with this theme, for when, at an encounter several weeks later, Frate was challenged and did not step forward immediately, the wits in the audience

> [m]ortified the Castellani with jeers and whistling, calling out that Frà Acquario had gone to confession but had become lost; that anyone who found him should lead him to the vestry; that there he would be able to find [more] courteous treatment, and other similar insults and humiliations.[92]

Nicknames and noms de guerre thus turn out to have been distinctly two-edged in the context of the bridges. A young contender who presented himself at the *arengo* with a fighting name that he had won or had given himself could more effectively assert his claim for a place among adult males. If he succeeded in his battles and continued to comport himself in ways appropriate to a champion, his nom de guerre could be immortalized by poets and spectators alike. If, however, he let his arrogance run away with itself and ended up (justly) thrashed, the crowd was more than ready to pounce on his nickname as an easy target for cutting him down to size. Nicknames, like all the honors of the *pugni*, were ultimately subject to the tribunal of public opinion, and while partisans clearly enjoyed having factional heroes and champions who sported suitably ferocious names, their mockery of pretense and misconduct makes it evident that they also wished to make sure that their local hero—lionized at home and patronized by elites—did not start to see himself as "above the usages of the bridges".[93] It was not a kind of mockery designed to crush, but was more "deflatory" than "egalitarian," as John Davis has called such teasing in modern Andalucia: "For it pricks the pretentious and takes them down a peg or two—it does not assert the equality of all men's honour: it asserts that some men are not so much more honorable than the rest as they claim to be."[94]

The Pride of the Neighborhood

If the cult of the *pugni* rewarded the individual fighter, granting citywide prestige to the mature champion as well as public recognition of his manly status to a young contender, its honors were also intensely important to Venetians collectively. Men, women, and children of all classes closely followed the aspirations and successes of their local *capi*, neighborhood fighting squads, and entire faction in what might be considered widening circles of group identification with the *pugni*. Their role was not simply that of passive spectators, for communities in the city also assertively celebrated the triumphs of their favorites as an expression of their own local honor, each neighborhood competing with and seeking to outdo all the others through a variety of celebrations and festivities. Partly planned and partly spontaneous, such group displays were the product of worker creativity and elite wealth, providing glittering examples of tenacious popular culture in a city otherwise long since dominated by patrician tastes in processions and ceremonials.

These collective festivities had varying orientations, depending on whether they were held before or after an encounter. The hours just before the battle actually began—usually between two and three o'clock in the afternoon—was typically given over to celebrations of a factionwide nature, as part of the general gathering of each force. Large-scale *guerre ordinate*, usually prearranged days ahead of time, were sure to draw fighters and their followers from all over the city, its lagoon, and up the Brenta Canal to beyond Padua. The coming together of two such great factional hosts— each side numbering up to ten or fifteen thousand participants and spectators combined—was in itself a distinctly festive event: as both factions steadily grew in size with the arrival of new squads, companions normally living far apart would recognize one another, shouting out the hopes for the eventual victory that ran high on both sides.

Filled with the wine generously supplied by their supporters, the men of the factions made much of their gathering and arrival at the battle site, waving banners, singing, and playing musical instruments to mark their passage. Of the two sides, the Castellani were able to make the more extravagant show of their passage, since they tended to come to the chosen bridge by water. With the Venetians' ingrained sense of how the adroit use of boats could enhance any processional occasion, the Castellani would gather in a staging area beforehand (usually at the quays near the Arsenal) and, bringing together a great array of barks, longboats, gondolas, and sailboats of every sort, would sail and row in a majestic, if rather raucous, flotilla to the chosen bridge:

> At the first warning [of the Nicolotti arrival] the [Castellani] supporters hurriedly jumped into a great number of boats and launches, filling them with horns, drums, and castanets, making a very great racket, shouting "Viva! Viva! Castello!" . . . [I]n coming up the Grand Canal, they also picked up a great many sailors of the fleet and a squad of two hundred Dalmatians, whom they towed along behind in dinghies. . . . At the same time, there emerged from the canals of Santa Giustina and San Lorenzo an infinity of other boats and skiffs of the Buranesi, the Muranesi, from the Lido and other neighboring islands; and these uniting themselves with the Castellani boats made a grand armada, and running along with exceptional noise and shouting, they passed before Piazza San Marco, flags flying, ever shouting "Viva! Viva Castellani!"[95]

The highpoint of these preliminary festivities of joining together was often a rousing address by the leader of each faction—known as the *caporione principalissimo* (or sometimes the *commandante generale*)—to his assembled troops.[96] Adhering to the traditional forms of prebattle orations everywhere and speaking in the idiosyncratic jargons of their particular district—the Nicolotti chiefs in the patois of the fishermen and the leaders from the shipbuilders in their own *linguaggio arsenalesco*—these commanders worked with the themes that were most likely to stimulate their men to do their best in the *battagliola* to come. After thanking his troops for the honor of his election as chief, each might invoke the icons and historic protectors of his faction: the Castellani, their ties to the Arsenal and the Lion of San Marco; the Nicolotti, their own traditional leader (known as the "Doge of the Nicolotti") and their historic association with San Nicolò. Factional traditions were further strengthened by calling to mind great victories of the past, especially if they involved the humiliation or even the death of the enemy: the Nicolotto leader Zamaria Pitteri recalled with real relish that the battle of 1606 had ended in the deaths of no fewer than fifty Castellani; the Arsenal chief Piero Moro evoked the memories of Castellani *scorrerie* in 1628 that had so frightened the Nicolotti of San

Baseio that "just at our appearance they locked their doors and their balconies, and did not know in what hole to hide themselves."[97] Beside elabo-
rating on the theme of his faction's claims to honor—through its size,
ferocity, and ability to intimidate the enemy—the commanding general
might also pause in his exhortations and proceed to business that was at
the same time practical and ritually important: presenting the overall combat leaders and each of the *capi* to the troops, giving tactical advice to the
capi themselves, and encouraging the younger fighters. He then concluded
by predicting a victory that would be all the sweeter for the simultaneous
humiliation of the opposition, and then led his men in a final cheer, as
did Tomè Panchia in 1667:

> On, on, dear sons! On brave Nicolotti youth: heart, soul, and courage! To
> the *frotte*, to the struggles at the bridge, to the vendetta, to the slaughter,
> everyone follow me! Everybody get with your squads and *capi*, run to glory
> and the laurels of victory. Viva Nicolotti! Viva! Viva![98]

In contrast to the great mass celebrations that preceded the *battagliole*, the
victory festivities staged after an encounter tended to be much more
fragmented, largely the inspiration of local residents in their own parish
or neighborhood *campo*. Parish fetes were a long-standing tradition in
Venice: open-air community parties featuring drinking, dancing, bull-
baitings, and fireworks that were generally paid for by local notables interested in publicly honoring a neighborhood or family occasion. Though
they involved many of the same elements, festivities for the *battagliole* were
at the same time fundamentally different than such casual celebrations.
Ordinary parish fetes were understood to be put on at the sufferance of
the state; the patricians and merchants who staged them were required to
go beforehand to the Council of Ten and (after paying the appropriate
fees and, very likely, a few bribes as well) receive state permission in the
form of an official *licenza*.[99] Festivals that followed the *battagliole*, in contrast, had something about them of a customary popular right and called
for no such need to secure a license. Tradition held that after important
bridge battles the parishes of the winning faction could hold celebrations
for the three succeeding evenings, rather in the manner (or perhaps as a
parody) of ceremonial triumphs customarily awarded to victorious naval
commanders and condottieri.[100] Perhaps originally offered as the state's
reward to its workers, for going to the time and expense of mounting a
large-scale *guerra ordinata* for the amusement of visiting dignitaries, by
the mid-seventeenth century the Chronicler of the *pugni* could single these
celebrations out as one of the distinctive features of the *battagliole*:

> [The *pugni*] are distinguished by [their receiving] the concession of the Prince,
> which permits the victorious side in the war to hold festivals for three con-
> tinuous evenings, and at least sometimes for entire weeks . . . all of which is
> conceded because You, Oh sons of Warriors, are faithful children of San
> Marco.[101]

Well aware that in their case the celebrations of the *pugni* were to be seen more as right of victory rather than as a favor to be purchased, and often sure that powerful *prottetori auttorevoli* from their local elites would protect them, Venetian commoners were far from shy about claiming the honors and pleasures they assumed that winning had guaranteed them. After smaller encounters, when the state might be less willing to grant the customary three evenings of carousing, local groups might well go ahead and hold their festivities without such permission. Usually (although not always) they would get away with such unlicensed celebrations. It was also not uncommon for revelers to extend the official three evenings of festivity to a week or more. As long as such merrymaking did not too blatantly attract the attentions of the Ten, it was possible that neighborhood groups could indeed get away with dedicating an entire month of Sundays and holidays to celebrating the victory of their faction.[102]

The victory celebrations of the winning faction usually began directly after the battle had finished: with the crowds of fighters and spectators streaming home singing, dancing, and stopping off at taverns on their way. Participants may have been far from home, but since neighbors tended to stick together in their local fighting squads throughout the *battagliola*, in a sense the community spirit of the winners' festivities was already established before the men and their supporters had returned to their parish *campo*.[103] The most immediate expression of their joy in coming home triumphant was often to light a bonfire in the middle of this open space: burning old boats, rushes, or scrap lumber made a natural focus for neighborhood crowds on cool fall evenings, and also served as an obvious beacon to broadcast the parish's jubilation to both allied communities and factional enemies.[104] In their enthusiasm, partisans might also break into the local campanile and start ringing the church bells or the tocsin, although this was strictly forbidden (and the parish priest might already have removed the clappers to forestall them).[105] There might also be some impromptu dancing and music making, as the newly returned victors would set to playing drums and flutes (along with whistles, fifes, and castanets if they were Castellani sailors). A stage might be hastily thrown together out of barrels and planks so that some one could "beat the *moresca*," the sword dance so popular with Venetians.[106]

Spontaneous, noisy, and evidently well attended, the victory festivities held immediately after a battle were nevertheless still fairly modest affairs compared to those that would be staged on succeeding days. The more elaborate, planned victory festivities which communities took for their allotted three evenings of celebration were occasions for local merchants and other notables to publicly demonstrate their support for the *pugni* and their parish pride at the same time.[107] As men already accustomed to financing both their neighborhood's fighting squads and its fetes, these local patrons were essential for bearing the expense for such necessities as food and drink, making sure that there was plenty to go around for the streams of local partisans and their guests, who crowded the outdoor tables "on one side eating lasagnas . . . on the other, eels in milk." These neighborhood elites were also no doubt the ones who bore the costs for the fireworks, the "rockets, firecrackers, and bombs" that were an important feature of any respectable festival. Great numbers would typically be shot off during these victory fetes, whether in continuous salvoes or in occasional mass displays of fifty or a hundred bombs (*mascoli*) all discharged together. Having shown enough public generosity to keep their plebeian neighbors out dancing till midnight or later, these promoters of the *pugni* and the parish would move their own celebrations indoors, "into [their] many private houses, with the banquets [for] friends and relatives, dancing and feasting until broad daylight."[108]

These local celebrations of the *pugni* were a time for the renewal of community bonds, both through the pleasures of eating, drinking, and dancing together and through the mingling of the neighborhood's disparate social classes, united in this moment of victory. The Chronicler observed with apparent approval that these were occasions when elites were accustomed to parade the streets in public, and noblewomen and girls— as a rule seldom seen out of doors—would show themselves at their palace windows, richly dressed and saluting those below. Neighbors of all classes also united in their desires to use the festivities of the *pugni* as a chance to impress outsiders with their community and its spirit: it was noted with considerable pride when a parish managed to attract "the first lords (*cavallieri*) and gentlewomen of the city" to its revelries. To make sure that there was more than just free food and drink to lure them, local craftsmen would hastily turn the ordinary streets and structures of the neighborhood into "regal pavilions" that would be a worthy backdrop for the victory celebration. The courtyards and *campi* where the dancing, bull-baiting, and feasting were to be held were set off with great temporary doorways (*portoni*), outlined with torches, and filled with tents and shows. The palaces overlooking the festivities (for some nobles maintained houses even in these peripheral parishes) were lavishly adorned as well, with colorful carpeting and textiles "of the most varied and finest sort" hung from the windows.[109] Appropriately enough for a festival celebrating the *battagliole sui ponti*, special attention was given to the bridges of the neighborhood: their steps were covered with tapestries, while vases filled with flowers and oranges were erected on each of their corners, together with towering pyramids, wrapped all over with damask, colored paper, and flying banners. If local wealth and craftsmanship permitted, the whole bridge might be turned into a festive structure not much less extravagant that those put up for the great state processions: thus, in 1667 the Nicolotti made the Ponte dei Arzere into "the form of a triumphal rotunda held up by eight figures and [covered] above with colored fabrics of the greatest extravagance," while the Ponte di San Nicolò

> had no reason at all to feel jealous of that of the Arzere, for it was decked out with six spires interwoven with quite gracious colors; and the parapets of wooden planks, wrapped in rich cloths seemed to make a garden, with all the

vases of flowers and oranges, and with so many banners scintillating on every
side.[110]

The result was an open-air ballroom, delineated by decorative ephem-
era and brought to life by music, thanks to bands featuring various com-
binations of trumpets, fifes, drums, and flutes (with castanets and bagpipes
sometimes included as well).[111] The music played at these occasions served
not only to amuse the merrymakers but also to focus the more formal
activities that were the highlight of such celebrations. Bull- and bear-baitings
as well as the occasional burning of a enemy *capo* in effigy would be staged
against a musical background of "trumpets and drums made almost hoarse
by [trying to play over all] the shouting and calling." Music was also the
organizing force behind the mass processions in which these parish festivities often culminated. Typical in this respect were the Cannareggiotti,
who celebrated the Nicolotti victory of 1667 by sending out a squad of
drummers to trace out their neighborhood boundaries, marching up one
fondamenta and down the other of the Cannareggio Canal, playing all the
while and drawing after them crowds of children and forests of flags and
standards.[112]

The purpose of such processions was usually the opportunity they
afforded for the exhibition and display of the community's victory crown,
or *corona*. As the Chronicler of the *pugni* observed, "[B]ecause in triumph
a crown signifies the victory obtained, so also these squads [*militie*] had a
crown hung up . . . to announce themselves as victors to the world." Evidently only brought out to celebrate a triumph at the bridges, these crowns
helped further to distinguish these festivities of the *pugni* from ordinary
local fetes. They were prominently shown off, suspended high in the air
by cables or on a long pole over the parish *campo*, an adjoining canal, or
a major bridge. They were evidently fairly large—probably between two
and four feet in diameter—and were composed of silver and gold paper,
perhaps of the same robust sort that the fighters used to fashion their breastplates for the *frotte*.[113] Within the limits of available wealth and craftsmanship, a parish's crown would be decorated with the greatest opulence and
brilliance possible. Its surfaces might be covered with small mirrors, ham-
mered tin, or gold leaf, interwoven with strips of tinsel (*oro cantarino*) to
increase their glitter. Some were also adorned with a cloud of festoons,
wreaths, banners, or other baroque flourishes such as colored arches sporting grotesque masks. One, possessed by the Cannareggiotti, was pierced
in the middle by "a gigantic sword, silvered to its golden scabbard and
tinted red with blood"; another, "blazing like the sun with mirrors and
tinsel," was held by a winged Mercury.[114]

Victory crowns were made to look "of the richest and highest value,"
and they were indeed precious: less for the materials they contained than
for the workmanship that went into them and for their ability to focus
local pride and identity. Larger communities, like that of the Cannareggiotti,

might own several, perhaps constructed and saved up over the years; some were apparently privately owned, while others seem to have belonged to the neighborhood.[115] Brought out and placed on public display for the three days after a victory, they were a kind of secular relic: it was not unknown for partisans to compose poems and madrigals in their honor. At the climax of each evening's festivities the crowns would be placed on a litter surrounded by torches or by bundles of tall, costly candles and paraded about the parish or neighborhood, in a procession that drew together the community behind an accompanying entourage of trumpeters and drummers.[116] Afterward, very much in the manner of religious relics, the parish crown or crowns would be stored in safety—"replaced in the most appropriate and honorable place, prepared as a memorial of the [community's] triumph," in anticipation of being brought out again for some future victory.[117]

Their ability to focus community identity gave victory crowns a special significance for Venetians, who already possessed a strong sense of local consciousness. Crowns in fact seem to have served something of a double function in the victory processions in which they were displayed, for not only were they shown off to the city to broadcast a neighborhood's part in winning the recent *battagliola* but they also served as a means for the community to assert its own identity by ritually and publically delineating its boundaries (*confini della contrada*). The residents of San Nicolò thus traced out their neighborhood territories by carrying their crown on a litter from its original place of display in the Court of the Two Wells out to the far end of their parish, at Santa Marta, "and then came [back] by way of the Arzere, a very long and extensive road, to the continuous accompaniment of trumpets and drums." The Cannareggiotti used the occasion both to proclaim their own geographic identity and to underscore an alliance with their neighbors at San Giobbe: carrying their crown the length of their community territory, from the Ponte delle Guglie up to the Ponte di San Giobbe, they then united it with the crown of the Giobbini and then carried the two together in a grand procession up and down the Canal of the Cannareggio. A similar and even more elaborate observance was carried out by the partisans of San Girolamo:

> Then, at eight in the evening, [with] two hundred flaming torches, they swarmed over the *fondamenta*, after which they took up the crown hanging at San Girolamo, with sixteen bundles of sixteen-*lire* candles, and carried it with just respect to the sound of trumpets and drums, with many standards and waving flags up to the [bridge of] the Servi, where they picked up the other crown, with another sixteen bundles [of candles], to the accompaniment of the detonation of fifty bombs in the *campo*. Showing off their triumph up to the Misericordia, they then returned back to San Girolamo, [where] they renewed with another fifty [bomb] blasts their happiness and festivities, replacing said crowns in a place [that was] prepared, appropriate, and praise-worthy, in memory of the victory consigned [to them].[118]

Crowns also stimulated a sense of unity within a community by projecting its sense of honor and accomplishment to the city at large. After a victory parishioners might decide to load their crown into a wide workboat (*peota*) and row up and down the Grand Canal, showing off this pride of their neighborhood to the assertive sounds of chanting, cheering, and the blowing of horns. Crowns might also be ceremonially presented—or at least loaned—by one community to another. Usually one of the principal fighting parishes would make such a ceremonial visit, perhaps wishing to honor an ally for its special contributions in winning the day, or perhaps to underscore the bonds that held the whole faction together. Thus, the Gnesotti once took one of their crowns to Murano, "to recognize the glory of the Muranesi, who after many years' [absence] had come with many people to wage this war"; similarly, the men of Cannareggio, "dressed in Persian costumes," carried a crown over to Mestre, on the mainland, "to honor those [of Mestre] and Marghera, who had come to fight the war."[119]

Crowns had a more aggressive side as well, however. Their display, as part of a community's ritual claim to the honors of victory, was also intended to humiliate and provoke the enemy. Crowns were paraded and displayed in part to shame the losers, a taunting that for the victors represented one of the most desirable honors of the *pugni*. Winners drove the point home by hanging their victory crowns together with placards that heaped mockery and insults on the fighters and the *capi* of the opposing side. When partisans like the Gnesotti and Cannareggiotti ostensibly held ceremonial excursions to carry a crown to their factional allies, they also had the not especially hidden aim of enraging their recently defeated opponents as much as possible. Whenever the enemy was spied en route, the rowers would eagerly set to waving their banners, blowing horns, setting off rockets, and shouting abuse to attract the attention of their rivals. Indeed, the victors of a *battagliola* might well dispense with all pretext of displaying their crowns as an honor to themselves or their allies and seek instead to use them simply as provocations, hanging them at their parish boundaries and sometimes carrying them in noisy processions along factional dividing lines, in the hope that these symbols of victory would be seen and resented by their irascible opponents.[120] Crowns displayed in this manner, so obviously aggressive and provocative, often sparked off disputes and brawls, especially since there were many factional partisans eager to pass rapidly from argument to violence in their defense:

> In San Vio parish, while they were celebrating and hanging out a crown, there passed by chance at the Ponte di Ca' Foscari Gerolamo the Stonecutter, a Nicolotto leader of some importance . . . and while he was admiring the said crown, he was accosted by Moro Fante, a Castellano, who said to him, "Signor *Capo*, maybe you have come to enjoy our victory and witness your own humiliation?" Gerolamo hotly replied, "Victories are victories when they are won fairly and honorably," at which [the latter], without speaking, gave him a punch in the face, at the same time pulling out a dagger.[121]

The symbol of a community's honor claimed through victory, crowns were notably totemic objects for a popular cult that was otherwise grounded in the human dimension, whether in the individual hero or the fighting squad. Significantly, such totems, unlike human champions, needed to be protected from all forms of violation—whether from the simple insults of someone like Gerolamo the Stonecutter or the concerted efforts of enemy gangs that would seek to steal, vandalize, or destroy them—lest they thereby be turned into equally forceful symbols of a neighborhood's dishonor. It is not surprising, then, that when the Cannareggiotti made their ceremonial procession to Mestre, they took care to load their boats not only with the usual festive implements—trumpets, drums, banners, and costumes—but also with arms, rocks, and pikes "because they suspected that the Castellani would come and attack them in the swampy canals [leading to Mestre]." Likewise, after winning the *guerra ordinata* of 1637, the Nicolotti posted guards as a matter of routine, "always going armed about their borders at night, fearing that the Castellani would come and steal the crowns that they had hung in all the *campi* to celebrate a triumph that was taken badly, indeed hated by the Castellani people."[122]

Such fears were not without foundation, for gangs of youths were always disposed to launch raids on enemy territory, and crowns made good targets for their attacks. Sometimes the raiding parties might be caught in the act: a Nicolotti squad from Santi Apostoli once came upon a gang of *arsenalotti* intent on trying to cut down the local crown with long poles tipped with hooks; more numerous and better armed, the Nicolotti had the pleasure of routing their enemies and forcing most of them to drop their poles and flee by jumping into the Grand Canal.[123] Yet with so many crowns displayed about the city, inevitably some of these raiders succeeded: finding a poorly defended crown, they might pull it down and "trampling on it with their feet, break it into a thousand pieces." Still more satisfying for those who could get away with it was to kidnap a rival community's crown, as the Castellani managed to do in 1639:

> [A]t night they stole one crown from the Ponte del Noal [in Santa Fosca parish] and another at San Polo, and by day they carried these on poles as triumphs all over Castello, even cruising on the Canal of the Giudecca with a *peota* and an armed sloop, to the sound of fifes and castanets, shouting loudly "Viva, Viva Castellani!," [all of] which provoked a great disturbance among those of San Nicolò.[124]

Like the crowns that were their central symbol, community victory celebrations turn out to have expressed both local pride and a purposeful provocation. In the context of the *pugni*, neighborhood fete and public aggression went very much together: no parish would have thought to celebrate and congratulate itself publicly through such festivals and merrymaking without also seeking to humiliate (or at least tease) a rival neighborhood. Yet so attractive were these parish parties to the city at large that antagonizing one's enemies was never too difficult: sullen visitors from the other side were often on hand, having come by to watch (and sometimes participate in) the feasting, dancing, and bullbaiting. Superficially innocent entertainment, in the context of the *pugni* all these local celebrations could become insulting and provocative when pursued brazenly and aggressively, "in the face" (*in faccia loro*) of those from the other side.[125] Lest the implications be lost on the spectators, there were always plenty of local youths who were quick to make the point, badgering enemy visitors to make them admit their own faction's inferiority, in a kind of ritual of public mockery known as *cercando la manza*. If their teasing failed to cause a reaction, local partisans were always more than willing to try to incite a disturbance for the evening's finale by moving in a drunken mob to the (recently reaffirmed) borders of their neighborhood to test their opponents by continuously shouting "Viva Nicolotti!" or "Viva Castellani!" across the canal.[126]

Such aggressive impulses, so central to these community celebrations, were very often successul in provoking just the sort of retaliation that was evidently sought: besides stealing or smashing the local crown, vengeful gangs from the opposing faction might also respond by brawling during the festivities themselves or even making off with the bull in the middle of a baiting.[127] As a result, the Chiefs of the Council of Ten often ended up sending out the Captains and their *sbirri* to suppress these local fetes all over the city: confiscating the various crowns, banners and standards, putting out the bonfires, and breaking up any wooden bleachers or stages they happened to find.[128]

Yet to focus too intently (as the Ten evidently did) on the factional provocations and retaliations that these victory festivals generated can obscure the fact that community celebrations of the *pugni* were as much about local pride as they were about factional antagonisms. Victory at the bridges provided the occasion for every neighborhood on the winning side to promote its own *bella reputatione*. While, with their crowns, bands, and banners, they proclaimed their loyalty as Castellani or Nicolotti, parishioners were at the same time expressing their satisfaction in belonging to a particular enclave in the city. Such pride, like all matters of honor in baroque Venice, was asserted forcefully, turning community fetes and dances into competitive events (what the Chronicler called *feste a gara*)—as much between parishes of the same faction as with those of the other side. The entire business of hanging out crowns, constructing decorations, and arranging music was carried out with a keen awareness that allies, even more than opponents, would be coming by to observe the results and had to be impressed by local efforts. One neighborhood's successes stimulated a rival to try still harder, to outdo all others in decorating its bridges and *campo* or in giving away ever more ornate crowns to friendly parishes. Indeed, the long succession of Nicolotti celebrations in 1667 came about largely because supposedly allied communities were in such competition with one another that each determined that "those [festivals] of the past would not be able to measure up with their own, if they were put face to face."[129]

Local communities in baroque Venice thus could be said to have sought their own honor from the cult of the *pugni*, pursuing status and rank among all the other neighborhoods of the city much in the same way that individual fighters did: through display, largesse, and aggressive self-assertion against all rivals—including their supposed allies.[130] That sometimes entire neighborhoods tried to promote themselves and establish *reputatione* through their festivals of the *pugni* is hardly to be wondered at, for these were mostly communities that, much like the fighters themselves, were peripheral to the city's more official and respectable world, the patrician social center around San Marco and the Rialto. Indeed, few places in Venice were (and are) more removed from the general flow of life than such parishes as San Nicolò, San Piero di Castello, or San Giobbe in Cannareggio: where little of Venice's grander life of encounters, processions, masques, and commerce ever intruded, and where the desire to stage festivities that would attract "the first lords and ladies of the city" must have been correspondingly all the more acute.

Peripheral communities and marginal men: both were striving for identity within the city at large. To do so, these outsiders turned to their self-fashioned world of the *pugni*, a force for socialization that in the end gave form to the whole course of their otherwise unremarkable lives. Men were indeed "born to the bridges," for whole lineages of fighters would establish themselves in the legends of the factions. As youths, though they passed with their age group through the stages of childish gangs and immature brawlers, the process of coming of age in the *pugni* was ultimately one that stressed and rewarded the individual as he received his nom de guerre, presented himself in the *mostre*, and eventually joined the company of those men *ghe monta sul ponte*. When fighters came to select their partners in marriage and coparenting, they were, by contrast, establishing, celebrating, and extending their family ties within the restricted local community: it was a time of demarcation and exclusion for which the *pugni* provided a perfect reinforcement for the endogamic imperatives of Venetian parish life. Finally, in death, the follower of the *pugni* moved to the largest possible stage, that of all of Venice, where he was reconciled and reunited in recognition of common values that were underscored at the end of his life.

Venetians of the center—patricians, gentlewomen, merchants, professionals, clergy, and the better guildsmen—relied on the great institutions of early modern life to guide them through this process of socialization. For these men and women at the core of Venetian society, the rites of birth, coming of age, marriage, and death were the responsibilities and proprietory activities of their guilds, confraternities, or parish churches; the making of connections and setting of limits that distinguished such key transitional moments of their lives were in consequence legitimized by recognized ritual and sacred protection.[131] For those Venetian laborers, street vendors, servants, and thugs who passed their lives largely outside the embrace of such institutions, the *pugni* provided a process of socialization that appears every bit as encompassing and a good deal more exciting than the rituals of priests and confrères. It was the genius of this alternative world, cobbled together by workers out of the discarded remnants of the authoritarian culture in which they lived, that it could be made to subsume moments of personal transition that were as vital for the self-definition of these marginal citizens as they were for the elites of the city. The *pugni* showered many Venetian workers with honor and reputation, but perhaps the true spoils of the War of the Fists was this sense of place and social identity with which it rewarded its followers.

The View from the Balcony

Su per balconi, fondamente, altane,
Se se rideva no ve digo gnente
A veder ghe xe sempre certe lane,
Nobili e altri che sta a dar la mente.

Up on the balconies, sunroofs, and quays
One would always see certain swells:
Nobles and others free with their opinions;
To say you would laugh, doesn't begin to tell it.[1]

Hugely popular and openly staged throughout the early modern era, the *battagliole* were nevertheless in theory completely illegal and only to be put on with the special permission of the state. The Venetian government had taken this stance at least as early as 1505, when the Council of Ten issued a *proclama* threatening anyone "who dared to gather or make war at the bridges" with three hoists on the strappado and—at the Ten's discretion—a possible whipping as well. To make sure its intentions about illicit *battagliole* were perfectly clear, the Ten posted this and later edicts against such gatherings not only at Piazza San Marco and the Rialto—the usual places for displaying proclamations—but also in those outlying neighborhoods where Castellani and Nicolotti partisans customarily gathered.[2] Before long, however, it became clear to the Ten that enthusiasts of the *pugni* would "continue to carry on the *battagliole* . . . because of the light penalties [involved]," so the punishments for those who sought to amuse themselves at the bridges without permission were steadily increased. The state's escalating battle against the *pugni* culminated with the edict of 29 November 1644, which proclaimed:

> That no one should dare make this said war under the irremissible penalty of assuredly being condemned to serve as a shackled oarsman in a prison galley for five years, or . . . being unfit for such service, to be confined in one of the . . . Ten's prisons barred to the light for a space of seven years. Should he flee [arrest], let him be banished from this City of Venice and its territories for fifteen years.

Determined to show Venetian workers that it took these illicit *battagliole* seriously, the Ten essentially turned any sort of unlicensed participation in the *guerre di pugni* into a serious felony, imposing the same sort of punishments that were usually handed out to smugglers, thieves, and even murderers. Provisions were also made to send regular police patrols to "the usual places" where factional enthusiasts gathered, to make sure that anyone who dared to *montar sui ponti* would be quickly arrested, or at least reported to the Ten. Following its customary practice, the Ten also tried to encourage private citizens to become informers, offering as much as three hundred *lire di piccioli* to those who would denounce or help police hunt down those neighbors who persisted in flaunting these edicts.[3]

Despite all their apparent ferocity, these attempts by the state to suppress the *pugni* as a popular, spontaneous entertainment hardly enjoyed an unqualified success. There is, if anything, every indication that in the two centuries following the ban of 1505 bridge encounters grew steadily larger and occurred more frequently, as the maturing and eventual decadence of the Venetian economy and social geography made involvement in the *pugni* increasingly more attractive to the city's workers. Whereas in the sixteenth century important *battagliole* were apparently mounted only two or three times a decade, by the 1660s and 1670s bridge wars involving over a thousand fighters had become virtual monthly events during the fall battle season. Despite the continuing efforts of the Ten to subject the *pugni* to some sort of state control, the popular cult became persistently more localist and plebeian, drawing ever more inspiration from that energetic corner of worker culture that survived outside the government's manipulative reach.[4]

In large part, these efforts by the Venetian state to regulate the *battagliole* failed to have much effect because the workers of the city proved largely oblivious to even the most draconian threats. When the battle season was at its height, and the Nicolotti and Castellani "armies" seethed with the passion to contest a fighting bridge, "it was impossible to hold back a Venetian populace so crazy and so resolved in [having its] wars, that . . . In the manner of a dog let loose from the chain that runs to attack the bear or the bull, so too [the people] run to the brawls, duels, and *frotte*, without any regard for the laws or prohibitions."[5]

Nevertheless, more than just blind determination on the part of local workers was frustrating the Ten in its attempts to tame Venetian factionalism and turn the *battagliole* into something more like the other stage-managed festivities that were celebrated in the city.[6] In the centuries when the *battagliole* flourished, no level of Venetian society was altogether immune from the attractions of faction and bridge battles: nobles, gentlewomen, rich merchants and priests all followed the *pugni*, often as passionately as any longshoreman or fisherman. Such elites were not shy about using whatever power, wealth, and influence they possessed to promote their own faction and the *pugni* in general. When their pursuit of the pleasures of the *battagliole* brought them into conflict with the Ten and its mission to promote public order, more often than not these patricians simply tried to get around the law. After all, the running of the state was in their hands, and even if the judicial code was ultimately designed to ensure their own continued existence as islands of privilege in a working-class sea, many Venetian elites were quite willing to subvert both the Ten and the police on whose efficiency the legal system ultimately depended if in doing so the next *battagliola* might take place without interference.

Certainly, the persistent survival of the *pugni* owed a good deal to this subversion of public authority by the very elites entrusted to protect it. Yet the endurance of illegal and violent *battagliole* can also be traced elsewhere, to weaknesses contradictions intrinsic to Venice's approach to law enforcement, and indeed to the nature of Venetian law itself. The system's traditionalist norms, based on a thousand-year-old society of orders, often turned out to be unresponsive or even completely unworkable when confronted with an aroused public, intent on structuring and realizing its own pleasures. When approached in terms of Venice's wider social context, the plebeian pleasures of the *battagliole* take on a new relevance, not only as a reminder of the widespread and lasting appeal of popular culture but also as a demonstration of just how complicated and indeed tentative government unity and control could be in one of early modern Europe's most authoritarian and tightly regulated states.

The Pastime of Aristocrats

In his late seventeenth-century guidebook to Venice, Alexandre Saint Disdier observed that, while factionalism and the *battagliole* were universal passions in the city, the motives that might drive a man to the bridges varied depending on his class. "As for the nobility," he noted, "there is a delight [in seeing] these fights and battles, while for the common people it is an affair of reputation and of importance." It was a social division that reflected itself in the spacial arrangement of the battle site: artisans fought and risked themselves on the bridge and its approaches, while elites watched and responded with shouts of amusement and encouragement from rented balconies or from their own moored boats. Yet at the same time, these patricians were not simply passive onlookers at the *battagliole*, for they took their pleasures as seriously as their honor: even in their apparently auxiliary role as supporters and fans (*parteggiani e fauttori*) of the event, Venetian gentlemen played an essential part in the promotion and success of the *pugni*.[7]

At one time, the aristocrats of Venice had been more personally involved in the *battagliole*. "In these old-style wars [of the 1580s]," the Chronicler of the *pugni* observed, "the more fiery and pugnacious nobles were accustomed to go to the bridges . . . armed with light helmets, heavy gloves, and cutlasses, to serve [their faction] as *auttorevoli padrini*." By the mid-seventeenth century, however, patricians had largely given up such active leadership of the factions during actual combat. They never took part in the one-on-one duels of the *mostre*, and Saint Disdier appears to have been somewhat shocked to report that on occasion, "[o]ne can even see some nobles so zealous for the glory of their faction that . . . they descend to the bridge, put aside their clothes, and box [*ont fait les coups des poings*] at the head of the *frotta*." In Venice, as elsewhere, an ever more cultivated nobility was in the process of a "tilt toward civility," in which such raucous amusementss as coming to blows with common artisans were being abandoned for more genteel conduct. No gentleman could expect to gain the sort of honor that was won with the sword by fighting with his fists; probably the most he could hope for, according to Saint Disdier, "was at least to set an example that would make [workers] fight more honorably." By the 1660s patricians who still felt such a passion for the *pugni* that they were unable to stay out of these brawls began for appearances' sake to come to the bridges in disguise, to prevent disapproving friends from recognizing them. Afterward they sometimes had "to hide themselves in their houses to protect their reputations until with bandages and lotions they had healed their facial injuries . . . and lameness."[8]

Yet while many Venetian nobles by the late 1600s may have considered it somewhat declassé to involve themselves directly in physical combat at the bridges, their enthusiasm for the *pugni* does not appear to have lessened as a consequence. Rather, aristocrats found ways to express their partisan spirit that were more in keeping with fashionable ideas of conduct appropriate to the state of *nobiltà*. Among these was a connoisseurship for the *battagliole* as spectacle, an interest in fighting and battle strategies that was completely suitable for a class that was traditionally trained if not defined by the military arts. With their knowledgeable appreciation of the skills and tactics customary to warfare, gentlemen flocked to witness this mock combat of the "armies" of the Nicolotti and Castellani, clapping their hands with pleasure at the successes of their side and calling out "*O Gran Forza, Gran Valore!*" to encourage their factional favorites.[9]

Their enthusiasm for this particularly Venetian form of popular combat, combined with their sense of what was permissible or appropriate on the bridge, allowed some aristocrats to take an active role in the *battagliole*, though more as referees than as the active fighters their ancestors had been. Not infrequently, the only way an encounter could get started was if a few such gentlemen from both sides came onto the bridge, separated the shouting soldiers, and forced each faction to retreat to its proper position (*dovuti confini*). When daggers made their sudden appearance on the bridge (the sight of even one could cause hundreds to be drawn in an instant) or when rocks began to be thrown from surrounding rooftops, local nobles could also be effective at inducing the factions to quiet down: even when forced to hold their cloaks over their heads for protection, such men seem to have enjoyed more respect and commanded more authority than the *padrini* or indeed the police themselves.[10]

Those nobles who preferred the relative safety of their boats or balconies to the bridge itself still sought to keep the *battagliole* progressing in what they considered a proper manner. They yelled, cheered, and called out directions or support to the fighters. On occasion it was their shouted negotiations with those on the other side that established how many—if any—*mostre* would be staged. Perhaps aware that their voices would usually be lost in the roar of plebeian onlookers, however, nobles might also resort to a visual signal, by waving their white handkerchiefs or neckcloths (*stolle*). These especially apt symbols of gentility—whose customary display at the bridges may have originated when the French king Henry III waved his on behalf of the Nicolotti in 1574—would have been all the more effective against the dark backdrop of patrician *ferrarioli*. An attention-getting device, the unfurled white handkerchief was a quick way of establishing noble authority in a crowd of commoners; gentlemen waved theirs in unison at the bridges as a favorite means of communicating what they considered appropriate or wished to see done by those who were fighting (Figure 4.1).[11] In this sense, the display of the white cloths was intended "as a sign of peace" meant to persuade the two sides to settle down and stop their arguing or stone throwing so that the encounter could

Figure 4.1 Nobles waved their handkerchiefs as a comment on the action. (Museo Correr, Archivio Fotografico, not catalogued)

get under way. But brandishing handkerchiefs could invoke a host of other often rather subtle messages as well. They might, for example, be waved when their owners wanted to criticize or comment on the fighting: to show approval or enthusiasm for their champion's conduct in the *mostra*, to influence the decision of the *padrini*, to urge on the attack, or to show appreciation for the spectacular dissolution of a *groppo* of fighters. Moreover, when hundreds of gentlemen on one side waved their handkerchiefs in unison, they might well be signaling not to the fighters on the bridge but to the noble spectators of the opposition, to challenge them to select and send forth a duelist or perhaps to admit they had been defeated. Handkerchiefs shaken rapidly (*fazzoletti scrolati*), could also be a sign of contempt—a visual insult meant to signal enemy spectators that their fighters on the bridge were weak or lacking in bravery.[12]

Everywhere conscious of their public image, gentlemen spectators at the bridges found the *battagliole* a particularly suitable arena for the aristocratic art of self-display. Nobles fought tenaciously with commoners and often with each other for the right to occupy the windows and balconies closest to the bridge. Certainly they wanted the best possible view, but a prime location also ensured that those who occupied it were on prominent display directly above the battle site.[13] That they were willing to pay wildly profligate sums of forty or more ducats just to sit in such a spot could only redound to their public credit—embellishing their reputations for aristocratic largesse, even as with their ostentatious presence they granted further prestige to the plebeian contest that they had come to observe.[14]

Another form of display that was compatible with nobility was gambling, and gentlemen bet heavily and publicly at the *battagliole*—as indeed they did at most other occasions. At the bridges, however, gambling could be seen as particularly suitable for gentlemen, for it brought the aristocratic attributes of display and largesse together with connoisseurship, giving nobles who wagered the chance to demonstrate their own bravado while at the same time asserting their factional loyalties, showing support for a favored champion, and revealing their own understanding of the arts of the *pugni*.[15] On the frequent occasions when their opinions or their wagers led to disagreements, gentlemen also carried out their arguments with a fine sense of show—loudly insulting one another and sometimes drawing their swords not only at the battle site itself but also afterwards, in such highly public and particularly aristocratic preserves as the *broglio* before the ducal palace (Figure 2.8, lower right, p. 77). What would have normally been unpardonable (or even illegal) conduct between noblemen was apparently accepted and understood in the special context of the *pugni*:

> It became ever more amazing to witness the racket and the uproar that was being made above in the windows [over the bridge] between some of the first citizens [*persone primarie*] of the city, abusing each other with mordacious words and sometimes with insults that would not have been bearable if not in such places, on occasions such as this.[16]

Eager to see their side win—especially if they had just bet heavily on the outcome—both Venetian and foreign nobles also considered it appropriate to encourage their faction with promises of gifts in the case of victory: dinners and prizes for the winning *capi* and *padrini* or costly ceremonial crowns that would be hung in the donor's local *campo*.[17] Moreover, gentlemen would also act as factional patrons by giving money and gifts to individual favorites or fighting squads. This might be simply a matter of making cash payments, but some nobles would go so far as to virtually turn their palaces over to their local fighting contingents, opening their doors and their kitchens to all the neighborhood youths and apprentices, who were in any case too excited by the coming battle to be able to work and earn their bread.[18] Aristocratic support of favorite champions often took the form of enlisting well-known fighters into service as gondoliers or house servants. Here there seemed to be something of a tradeoff: pugilists would agree to sport the livery of their noble patron in exchange for being given time off on battle days: it was an inconvenience that these aristocrats were evidently willing to accept, in anticipation of going about the city with a famous fighter or two accompanying them as their lackeys. The marquis of Fluentes, ambassador of Spain and an ardent Nicolotto, had two such champions as his gondoliers, one of them a very large and very powerful African servant known simply as "The Black Moor" (*il Moro Negro*). The Chronicler of the *pugni* did not seem to consider it odd that such an obvious outsider could gain honor and a certain fame by fighting and defeating Castellani challengers; he did, however, observe that the Moor was quite sensitive to the need of putting on a good exhibit for his master and, if necessary, would take on the servants of nobles who were rivals to the marquis, to allow these aristocrats to spar with each another at one remove.[19]

In such ways noble interests in the cult of the *pugni* coincided with the larger world of patron–client networks that defined the relationships between aristocrats and artisans in Venice. Yet the flow of power and obligation was not all one way where the bridges were concerned. Gentlemen who supported particular champions during the *battagliole* could easily find themselves drawn into the quarrels and vendettas that regularly broke out when their clients felt insulted or unfairly abused by rival fighters. Noble prestige and authority could be vital in calming down such antagonisms between individuals. When the dispute was between *capi principali* of the factions, gentlemen could end up acting as go-betweens, scurrying from one proud and outraged fighter to the other, in the hope of working out an acceptable peace.[20]

Aristocratic patrons of the *pugni* also used the status and authority of their class to further the complex maneuvers that were often necessary to make sure that large-scale, prearranged battles (those known as *guerre ordinate*) were actually staged. Since the plebeian leaders of the Castellani and Nicolotti firmly believed that any means of gaining a victory was per-

fectly legitimate, they also saw no reason not to try and gain as much preliminary advantage for their faction as possible. These *capi* and *padrini*
hoped above all to gain pre-emptory control of the battle site: at the very
least, leaders on each side sought to start the contest with an overwhelming
numerical edge, but they might well try other ploys, such as arranging for
their squads to arrive early, repeatedly switching bridges to confuse their
opponents, or even altering the bridge, *fondamente*, or surrounding buildings physically to gain the advantage.[21] Certainly, many nobles were perfectly willing to go along with such schemes, some of the more under-
handed of which were apparently dreamed up by patricians themselves. Yet
at least a certain number of the *pugni's* aristocratic followers also tried to
impose some minimal conditions of initial equality on the *battagliole*. Their
interest, although it may only have been to protect their own wagers, was
to ensure that however the battle ended, it would at least be with a clear-
cut result, such that "the resulting glory," as Saint Disdier put it, "would
reside entirely with the victorious party."[22]

Ideally, each side would be "at a number sufficient to resist the enemy,
from which should succeed a hard and contentious battle that would give
the greatest pleasure and satisfactions to their excellencies." To accomplish
this goal gentlemen were often quite busy behind the scenes, before the
actual battle. In their efforts to "goad the principal *capi* into making a
war that was equally matched and sincerely begun" they apparently spent
entire days trying to get the opposing *padrini* and *caporioni* to sit down
amicably together—sometimes at a local tavern, for a long and drunken
lunch; sometimes more formally, at a patrician *palazzo*—to work out an
agreement concerning the time and place of their eventual contest.[23] Such
seemingly simple details—the *battagliole* were almost inevitably staged at
midafternoon on a Sunday or holiday, and in any case only three or four
fighting bridges were under serious consideration—could easily become
insurmountable obstacles for contention when each faction's *padrini* were
trying to squeeze the maximum gain out of the choice. At these times,
when the fighters were themselves at such an impasse, the authority and
status of noble arbitrators could be important or even vital in assuring that
an encounter was ever held at all.

Their negotiations frequently followed curious and tortuous routes,
as some of Venice's principal citizens—often desperately eager to have the
battle come off—tried to coerce and cajole an agreement out of artisans
who could turn out to be as wary and hardheaded as they were humble
of origin. Sometimes the circumstances permitted direct action: on one
occasion, as noted earlier, a group of gentlemen chased down the Nicolotti
fishing fleet out at sea and was able to persuade the stubborn fishermen
to return and stage a battle by first cutting their nets and then promising
to make up for their losses with generous cash gifts. Other times, however, even nobles lacked the power to persuade the *padrini*, who, while
keeping up the appearance of studious—even slavish—respect for the blan-

dishments of their superiors, were also sufficiently aware of their factional responsibilities that they could not be budged.[24]

Such was the outcome of the near-heroic—and ultimately futile—efforts of the patriarch of Venice and his fellow members of the Dolfin family to arrange a *battagliola* for the visiting Cardinal Chigi. In the weeks before the cardinal's arrival, the Dolfin "gave all of themselves, exerting their maximum influence to work out the arrangements so these two armies would be ready to battle in the customary way," inviting the Nicolotti and Castellani *caporioni* to Ca' Dolfin for no fewer than four lengthy conferences.[25] Though repeatedly "reassured with reverent expressions by the *padrini* that they were ready to obey their every command," the patriarch and his relatives soon discovered that "in this business there were hidden many difficulties." Despite his most persuasive efforts—which included sending some of the *cavallieri Dolfini* to inspect potential bridge sites and even personally going out in disguise to track down and plead with a leading *padrino* in the man's tobacco shop—the patriarch was unable to bring the stubborn factional leaders to an agreement. Indeed, while apparently maintaining every outward sign of respect, the *caporioni* were in fact themselves busily trying to shift the responsibility for making difficult and unpopular decisions off on the patriarch.[26]

Also active as patrons and supporters of the *pugni* were the many members of the city's large merchant community: men who in the closely delineated hierarchy of Venetian society would have been considered commoners but some of whom were far wealthier than many local nobles. Certainly more respectable than even the top fighters of the factions but still far beneath the Republic's titled nobility in terms of social status, these merchants, shopkeepers of quality, professional men, and the like, were not quite of either class at the bridges.[27] Unlike titled gentlemen and aristocrats, some of these men continued to present themselves at the *mostre* well into the seventeenth century, searching to support their faction and to make a reputation boxing one-on-one against any worker who cared to defend himself. As a rule, they were even more enthusiastic about taking part in the *frotte*, and at crucial moments it was quite common for them to throw off their black *ferarrioli* and eagerly wade into the thick of the fight. When word flashed through their quarters around the Rialto and the Mercerie that, contrary to custom, a battle was about to be held on a workday, many of these otherwise sober citizens would become so excited by the prospect that they would barely take the time to close up their *botteghe*, but went racing off to San Barnabà or San Marziale, dressing themselves in their silver breastplates and fighting caps as they ran.[28]

Lacking the prestige and authority of aristocrats, middle-class devotees of the *pugni* did not presume to the leadership roles of patrons or arbitrators for the factions; in any case, many were too embroiled in the actual fighting to find the time. Perhaps in compensation, some of the wealthier tradesmen were correspondingly all the more eager to make a mark and to express their loyalties by supporting their faction financially. It appears that the expensive business of outfitting, feeding, and providing prizes for the squads fell less to the ostentatious Venetian nobility than to a few otherwise rather obscure merchants: men who faithfully gave away thousands of ducats every year, yet who were still businessmen enough to complain bitterly when a canceled battle caused their donated food and drink to spoil.[29] For prearranged battles, a half dozen or so of these supporters on each side would form themselves into an informal committee for the purpose of collecting a pool (*cumulo*) of funds. When the *battagliole* promised to be large, three hundred ducats or more might be gathered through the combined contributions of such men as Dr. Parenda, "bitter defender of the Nicolotti, also with his open purse"; Filippo Mangone, a cobbler and "famous Nicolotto, *con prodiga mano*"; and the Castellani merchants Bortolo Orsetti, "esteemed . . . for his important shops and full of money" and Alvise Armelini, "who squandered his gold on behalf of the Castellani." It was said that in his years as a factional supporter Armelini had "spent more than twelve thousand *scudi* [perhaps 25,000 ducats] to sustain the glory and the reputation of the Castellani militia."[30]

Yet, even while supporting the factions with their largesse, most merchants evidently continued to identify themselves more with the plebeian than with the aristocratic spirit of the *pugni*, as the inclination of some shopkeepers to seek personal reputation through active fighting would seem to indicate. Eager to put their own houses at the disposal of the factions, these middle-class enthusiasts were apparently on altogether more friendly and personal terms with their side's *capi* and *padrini* than were noble patrons. They often invited the *caporioni* by simply to make a social occasion, rather than just for negotiations over battle arrangements or truces.[31] Instead of seeing themselves as arbitrators, in the aristocratic manner, of the endless vendettas between principal *capi*, at least some of these businessmen chose to actively take sides, to the extent of even joining these feuding champions in their armed retinue, marching about the city with them as they sought their revenge.[32] It was a different matter, however, when factional brawls erupted in those parts of the city that these tradesmen particularly considered their own territory: in the Mercerie, the Rialto, or (on one occasion) in the Ghetto. At such times merchants took an active role in breaking up the brawl: not with aristocratic handkerchiefs or words of peace, but with long-handled pitchforks or boat hooks that they kept close at hand on the walls of their shops.[33]

Both by fighting with and paying for their factions, these merchants were essential to the continued vitality of the *pugni*. The most fanatical of them devoted their entire adult lives to the bridges, both supporting their particular side and championing the neighborhood boosterism that was so central to the world of the *battagliole*. Their enthusiasm for the local squad was such that some went so far as to personally incite their own apprentices and shop helpers to factional passions—even though they knew that as a result most of these youths would be worth almost nothing as workers for days before and after the battle.[34] In the process, they could heighten the self-identity and focus of their communities and provide a key link between the loyalties of the *pugni* and those of the neighborhood. The best of them were men like

> Signore Martin, mercer at the sign of the Unicorn, who was a dogged defender of the Nicolotti sect, supporting and protecting them with his purse, with advice in the time of the great battles, and—in his youth—with his own body, when it was necessary. Having reached the age of around seventy-five, he finished his life, and he left in his will that as a sign of affection there should be set aside every year fifteen donations of twenty ducats each to be given to the young girls of the parish of San Nicolò; that is, to the most needy, who would be chosen by lot and who should [then] be favored and enjoy for his charity and affection this particular legacy, so that they might pray to God for his soul.[35]

Such elite involvement in the *pugni* was not limited just to the restricted circle of the Venetian patriciate, for foreign nobles also busied themselves with both the city's factionalism and its champion fighters. Some of Venice's best pugilists turned up in the retinues of such resident foreigners as the ambassadors of Malta and of Spain; the latter employing two of the strongest Nicolotti fighters to row in his gondola. The Marquis Spada, a Roman aristocrat and Bolognese senator, took such interest in the affairs of the bridges that he donated four of his own soldiers to act as the personal bodyguard of one of the Nicolotti *padrini*. Quite possibly, the sporting enthusiasms of these dignitaries may have been a convenient mask for their larger interests and rivalries: diplomacy, as it were, carried on by other means. Apparently it was the Spanish ambassador's long-lasting support for the Nicolotti cause that moved French diplomats in the city to back the Castellani: as dignitaries of these two great powers ranged themselves to cheer on their factions from the opposite sides of the bridge, it might well seem that they had transferred the substance of their international rivalries to a small Venetian canal. Even foreigners who were not caught up in such intrigues often found themselves taking sides and getting involved in violent and highly partisan arguments over the merits of their chosen faction or favorite champion. Such visitors were evidently more likely than local elites or even Venetian workers to back up their arguments with weapons: they and were forever drawing their swords or brandishing pistols, and in consequence sometimes set off brawls that ended up with their getting attacked by townsmen of both factions.[36]

Visiting nobles who conceived a passion for the *pugni* were instrumental in spreading the fame of the *battagliole* to courts and cities all over Europe, to the extent that more than a few princes and delegates on state visits to Venice would—like Cardinal Chigi—particularly request that a demonstration of this uniquely Venetian entertainment be included in their official program.[37] During the period covered by the Chronicle of the *pugni*, such specially arranged, state-sponsored *battagliole* were regular events in Venice's ceremonial calendar: staged, for example, at the request of the French ambassador, Marshall Créqui, in 1636; for the Cardinal de Lion in 1637; and for Prince Giovanni Battista Borghese and his wife in 1669. Other battles were put on to entertain various diplomatic missions, including a combined delegation of Russian and Italian princes in 1668 and a Spanish envoy returning through Venice from Germany in 1670.[38]

Yet even when such visitors had heard of the *battagliole* beforehand, they were inevitably struck—according to the Chronicler—by the scale and ferocity of the real thing. The Cardinal de Lion, together with his entire entourage, expressed voluble admiration for the fighting squads that arrived "in such military order and so well regulated"; loudly applauded a *frotta* "that was much more memorable and incredible than what he had [previously] heard of or believed"; and finally went to meet the losers, to offer them his own postbattle analysis of the reasons for their defeat.[39] His first sight of a *groppo* of fighters so delighted the French marshall Créqui that he clapped his hands like a child, shouting encouragement to both sides at once; as the battle came to an end in the near-darkness, the marshal was said to have made the sign of the cross over the scene, "in amazement that the Venetian people could be so dogged, just to win the fleeting reward of two paces of earth and stone."[40]

Even if the *battagliole* were often brutal and always violent, they apparently appealed no less to female than to male visitors. Princesses and duchesses routinely accompanied their husbands to the bridges, and on occasion battles were staged specifically in their honor.[41] Although highborn ladies managed to restrain themselves from the kind of fractious displays put on by many visiting noblemen, nevertheless some of these women earned reputations as enthusiastic partisans of the *Pugni* (Figure 4.2). Writing of the *guerra ordinata* arranged for the Russian ambassador and his entourage of Italian nobles, the Chronicler observed that "these assaults and battles had been authorized to entice and gratify [all] the above-mentioned personages, but in particular for the benefit of the Princess Colonna, who enjoyed [them] above all." The princess in fact took so much pleasure in her first experience with the *pugni* that she positively coerced the *caporioni* of both factions to stage another encounter the following Sunday, just for her sake. Declaring her support for the Nicolotti, the princess set to waving her handkerchief on behalf of her faction *con molta allegria* from the moment the *frotta* began, "enjoying exceedingly the sight of a people so unrestrained and of encounters so warlike."[42]

The Pugni *Out of Control*

When so many glittering dignitaries were to be found in the audience, fighters of every rank, from raw youths to experienced *padrini*, prepared for and went to the encounter fairly intoxicated with the excitement of knowing that they would be competing on what had in effect become an

Figure 4.2 Noblewomen watched the encounters from balconies and windows draped with tapestries: *Guerra dei pugni* by Giacomo Franco, *Habiti d'huomeni et donne venetiane con la processione della serenissima signoria et altri particolari, cioeè triomfi, feste, ceremonie publiche della nobilissima città di Venetia* (Venice, 1602). (Museo Correr, Archivio Fotografico, M. 8035)

national stage. The hope of gaining some fleeting recognition or approval from the *personaggi* looking down at them—and, in the case of victory, possibly a cash prize as well—drove "even the least soldier to assert himself as if he were a *capo*, to show that he had no equal in his heart for daring and courage." Fighting before assembled notables in 1668, men would repeatedly plunge into the *mostre* and the *frotte*, "ambitious for the fame, desiring that their names should continue to be celebrated even in Asia, carried to the Muscovites by the [Russian] ambassador and to the Roman territories by the Prince and Princess Colonna."[43]

Battagliole on such a grand scale were not put on only for visiting notables, however. A good many patricians influential in government circles were also enthusiasts of the *pugni*, and they too would often arrange to include a bridge battle in the program of major state celebrations. Thus, amid all the *feste, giostre, e solennità*—the regattas, naval battles, processions, and public banquets—put on for the coronation of the Dogaresse Zilia Dandola in 1557 and Morosina Morosini in 1597, large-scale clashes were held between the factions every day for weeks.[44] Bridge battles might be ordered for civic commemorations, such as the series of encounters held in 1632 as part of the celebrations to mark the passing of the plague.[45] Since the encounters had so many martial overtones, the Venetian government seemingly liked to stage *battagliole* during the public *trionfi* that were held to celebrate military victories and diplomatic successes. The Chronicler of the *pugni* recorded two such occasions in connection with the beginning of the War of Candia:—for the fortuitous assassination of Sultan Ibrahim I and for the (temporary) recovery from the Turks of the islet of San Todaro in Crete.[46]

Such preplanned encounters, whether staged for visitors or for the republic's own ceremonial purposes, were usually of an altogether different order than the typical Sunday afternoon *frotte* between Castellani and Nicolotti squads. Possibly held outside the normal fall fighting season—and sometimes on a workday as well—state *battagliole* were highly popular with all classes of Venetians and brought out the factions and their supporters in greater than the usual numbers. The preparation for these battles could be prodigious, such that the *caporioni* once complained that having only three days warning was completely inadequate. When such a battle was scheduled for the popular fighting day of Santo Steffano (26 December)—as it was on the occasion of the downfall of Sultan Ibrahim—the solemnities of Christmas itself were effectively forgotten in the rush to make ready. Fighters eager to outfit themselves for the *frotte* hastily bought up all the available canvas and heavy pasteboard (*cartone*) locally available, keeping their neighborhood tailors working around the clock to sew the material into decorative chest coverings:

> They [the fighters] watched the shops of the tailors to make sure that without exception they kept at their cutting, working, and sewing of *cassi* and *busti* of double, padded canvas, and likewise of heavy cardboard: indeed, the shops of the paper sellers were entirely stripped of their cardboard, down to the very last sheet.[47]

Before such encounters, the Chronicler noted, "the city was upside-down with excitement . . . and in the shops neither apprentices nor journeymen were to be seen, for every one had given up [both] work and their own self-interests." Those of the Nicolotti fishing community virtually abandoned their regular work, "such that on the Friday and Saturday [beforehand] the fish markets of Rialto and San Marco were empty not only of fishermen but also of every sort of fish." Meanwhile, the Castellani, apparently under the impression that they had been charged with carrying out a state enterprise, would feel free to commandeer space in the government's own Arsenal to hold their preliminary strategy sessions.[48] Well aware that "those that are in the greater number for the most part end up lords of the *piazza di mezo* and all the bridge," both factions also busied themselves sending emissaries, fighting gear, and money to their allies on Venice's island and *terraferma* suburbs, while representative from these same outlying squads ceremoniously came to the city to inspect the battle site.[49]

Perennially concerned about public disorder, the Council of Ten was particularly nervous about allowing such a monstrous, brawling, and highly volatile popular event as the prearranged *battagliole* to disrupt the state's orderly ceremonial schedules. The Ten was indeed the magistracy that ultimately canceled the Dolfins' promised and much hoped-for battle for Cardinal Chigi, perhaps after remembering that more than a few earlier *guerre ordinate*, such as the one put on for Marshal Créqui, had rapidly disintegrated into a riot of stone throwing and knife fights. Nevertheless, the normally cautious Ten could also see the logic in permitting the city's *pugni* enthusiasts to organize such large-scale, festive battles. Even the hard-headed septuagenarians who generally ran this and other key magistracies of Venice appeared to have clung to the somewhat naive sentiment that the *battagliole* could effectively demonstrate the warlike character of the Republic both to her own citizens and to those visitors from the many larger states that increasingly loomed on all sides.[50] Perhaps more practically, it was also held that such battles were in some way recreational concessions by the state to its people, given in the hope that the latter would respond by wholeheartedly lending their support to the aristocratic regime—in particular, by paying their taxes more willingly.[51]

Attempting at the same time to keep such events under control the Ten also made a point of taking certain precautions in the days prior to the battle. The *caporioni* of both factions might be summoned to the steps of the Ducal Palace or to the door of the *Collegio* beforehand, for a lecture and a warning "that this [battle] should be carried out with the least scandal and uproar possible, [and] rather with the greatest effort and application, so that it should turn out to the satisfaction [of visitors and the state]."[52] Each of the *padrini* was warned that he would be held personally responsible if things got out of control and that there would be "thunderbolts of retribution" (*fulmini de' castighi*) should the encounter dissolve into a riot that would shame the Republic before its guests.[53]

Even though these leaders would thereupon leave the Ducal Palace making humble promises to control their men, their actual ability (not to mention their desire) to keep the event from running away with itself remains very much in question. Although certainly the most respected and usually among the strongest and most feared of the combatants, a half dozen or so *padrini* acting alone in the midst of a *battagliola* stood little

chance of restraining factional mobs of five hundred to a thousand fighters each. Perhaps a few were sufficiently intimidated by the Ten or motivated by their own notions of propriety to actually try to do so; usually
by shouting their commands above the roar of the crowd, or by attacking
those frenzied fighters who refused to obey and physically dragging them
off the bridge.[54] Nevertheless, it is doubtful that most factional leaders
were really all that committed to producing an orderly, choreographed
battagliola. Some recognized their own powerlessness in facing down "a
people so inflamed for war . . . that they do not know commands, admo-
nitions, advice, or threats," and wisely decided to slip away to positions of
relative safety, watching from a distance during the most chaotic part of
the combat. Others, caught up in their own factional loyalties and the desire
to keep up a good fighting reputation, were themselves swept away by the
passions of the moment and ended up more likely to foment than to bridle
the excitement of their followers.[55]

If the *padrini* did not or could not control their fighters, neither could
noble supporters ensure that the two opposing "armies" would not end
up as rampaging mobs.[56] From the moment they left their own neighborhoods, fighters were indeed working up their passions and aggressions for
the battle ahead. Charging to the chosen bridge in groups of fifty or more,
these marauding young men soon picked up dozens of other enthusiasts
along the way, together with a large and noisy following of women and
children. Sometimes racing full speed along the *fondamente* and sometimes
blocked by the mass of their own numbers in the narrow alleys, they kept
themselves animated and excited by shouting, singing, and banging on
doors and shutters until they could be heard all over the city. Any
obstruction in their path was likely to be shoved aside or simply demolished: doors, gates, even stone walls were torn down if they blocked the
mob's free passage to the bridge.[57] Noblemen who lived on the route to
the battle site had reason to fear that their palaces would provide a tempt-
ing shortcut to the bridge; though they might order their servants to bar
their doors to the crowds, few had enough retainers to keep their doors
from being kicked in should the passing troops decide to make the effort.[58]
Nor were fighters above some casual looting on their way to the battle
site, as unfortunate tradesmen could discover, when their shops offered a
shortcut to the bridge:

> Suddenly, all the main body [of fighters] took off and went to Baker's Alley
> [Calle del forner] in order to pass, as they usually do, through the [baker's]
> house to the Fondamenta. . . . The baker, having barred his door because he
> had just then taken the bread out of his oven, did not want to open up, fear-
> ing that the soldiers would eat it. Seeing this obstacle, [the fighters] sought
> to tear the door down; in the end it was opened—to the baker's great dam-
> age, however, because not having the time to hide it all in a secure place,
> that which he had feared happened: in passing, each soldier was able to carry
> off a loaf for himself.[59]

Such disorder was minor compared with the chaos that routinely occurred at the battle site itself, however. When fighters found themselves left by the flow of battle on the wrong side of the bridge, they would often try to avoid the roundabout trip back by land and instead charge directly across the canal, using the tightly packed boats and gondolas of the audience as stepping stones. Should dozens of men all get this idea at once—as often happened—the results could be catastrophic, as the narrow craft overturned everywhere, spilling not only the fighters but also the spectators, and sometimes trapping the more unfortunate under the water.[60] The collision of fighters and audience on land could be equally dangerous: those rushing to the bridge had no compunction about forcing their way through the crowd, trampling underfoot onlookers who were slow to make way or shoving those gathered along the *fondamente* into the canal until, when the battle was over, the waters would be littered with "lost hats and *ferarrioli* that floated in great abundance."[61]

Venetian bridge battles were particularly threatening to civic order and public safety because participants were so willing to intensify their violence. The mobs at the fighting bridge could escalate their encounter from "the punches and the *mostre* that should be done, as was determined and agreed," to knives and rocks with dazzling suddenness. Perhaps because they were strictly forbidden from carrying any sort of firearm, it was quite normal for Venetians of all classes to go about armed with a wide variety of knives and cutting weapons. Even fighters stripped down *in arnese* and ready for the *mostre* appear to have kept a dagger about them just in case; most participants indeed needed little provocation to draw their weapon, for a sudden thrust against an opponent or even against someone in the audience. Onlookers in their turn were always ready to charge onto the bridge, prompt to dispute an unpopular decision or act, "with knives and daggers in hand and mantles or cloaks wrapped about the arm." It was such crazed aggression by the Nicolotto Pasqualin Gritti and three companions armed "with great, naked knives" that caused the entire audience to panic at the Ponte dei Carmini in September 1611, with the result that twenty-six died, "drowned, trampled, and suffocated in the mud."[62]

But probably the most dangerous form of violence at the bridges was the rock-throwing duel: combat which by its very nature drew in both fighters and spectators and was as likely to claim bystanders as those directly involved. Stone-throwing battles were not generally initiated by those actually at the bridge but rather by members of the audience. It did not take much to induce the individuals or gangs seated on the surrounding rooftops to express their disapproval of the action below by tearing loose the roof tiles (*coppi*) that they were sitting on and hurling them down at the crowd: the Chronicler indeed suspected that sometimes they were sent up to the roofs by their factional leaders just for that purpose.[63] Those below responded by prying up the paving stones of the streets and quays with their knives, flinging them with deadly effect both at their tormentors overhead and their opponents across the canal.[64] On one occasion, at the Ponte di San Barnabà, partisans on the ground managed to dig up all the paving stones that covered the entire hundred meters of Fondamenta degli Alberti, while another time those up above "stripped the houses completely of all their tiles."[65] When these encounters got out of hand, they could turn into full-scale urban wars, as enraged gangs shouted, "Go on! Go on! Kill them! Kill them!" (*Dai Dai! Ammazza! Ammazza!*) and charged each other, throwing stones at a furious pace from both sides of the bridge. Once rocks began to be thrown there was little hope of ever re-establishing sufficient order to start the *battagliola* again, and indeed there was a saying that "rocks and roof tiles ruin the war" (*sassi e coppi fano vano la Guerra*):

> Then, by evil fortune, a rash Castellano threw two rocks that happened to land on the bridge. These had hardly fallen than immediately everyone fled, along the quays and out of their boats, people falling one on top of the other, because already—also from the Corte del Tagliapietra [Nicolotti headquarters]—the stones were beginning to fly through the air; and in that uproar the armies scattered, as one saw a hundred shields and a hundred daggers—on land as much as among the boats on the water—such that it seemed to be a different war, [one] of swords, knives, and daggers.[66]

This predilection of the *battagliole* for violence and riot, plus the often obvious inability of factional leaders to control their troops while at the bridges, inevitably made the *pugni* the particular target of the Council of Ten. While the Ten was obsessively concerned with all expressions of collective or public disorder, it was usually willing to leave the policing of most popular celebrations and neighborhood fetes to the local elites who put them on and to the parish *capi di contrada*.[67] Due to the size and sheer unpredictability of the *pugni*, however, no other magistracy in the city would have been able to wield the necessary authority for keeping order at the bridges.[68] The preservation of public order and the suppression of popular unrest were mandates that the Council of Ten had exercised since the early fourteenth century, when it was first set up to protect Venice's new nobility from attack or subversion. Closed to all but the inner circle of first-rank patrician families, the Ten was designed to address matters of state security unencumbered by the niceties of normal, legal procedure; allowing none of the "lively debate" that characterized other Venetian courts, its members conducted their hearings in strict secrecy, giving those who fell afoul of their justice neither benefit of counsel nor the possibility of appeal.[69] Thus, the Council operated with what were in effect permanent emergency powers and was a highly efficient, extralegal authority for purging the Republic of subversive and treasonous plots. From around the beginning of the sixteenth century the Ten began to turn these special powers to the problems posed by popular factionalism and the *pugni*.[70]

To ensure that its edicts and directives would be enforced, the Ten had its own police force: six (later eight) Captains, known as the *Capitani delle barche longhe,* each in charge of ten to fifteen police agents, or *sbirri,* all under the overall command of a *Capitanio Grande.*[71] Not of the nobility, the Captains were still evidently quite impressive figures, traveling about the city dressed in red and wrapped in the mantles of their office, at the head of their heavily armed squads; "each one with three or four pistols or blunderbusses hanging from their belt" (Figure 4.3). Highly visible, they were effective symbols of the Ten's power, patroling the canals of the city in the Council's special vessels, the so-called *barche longhe* that fairly bristled with pikes and muskets, prominently flying the red and gold banner of the Republic at their prow.[72]

When rumors began to reach them that the factions were preparing for battle (or when state authorities were arranging for a *guerra ordinata* that they hoped to keep within acceptable limits), it was customary that the Ten would order two or more of its Captains to proceed with their squads to the bridge in question, either to drive off or to restrain the gathering enthusiasts, as the situation required.[73] That this rather imposing task of crowd control should have fallen to police squads rather than to soldiers is only to be expected in a city that possessed neither a permanent military garrison nor a militia that could effectively do such a job.[74] Nevertheless, it is surprising that a few dozen police could have been expected to control thousands of fighters and factional partisans: those who ruled the city could only have assumed that Venetian commoners held their state in sufficient awe and esteem that they would automatically respect the commands of its agents. Such a vision of popular obedience and wise governance continued to hold sway with the Republic's admirers in later years. The nineteenth-century essayist Alessandro Zanotti dismissed the *battagliole* as "so much hubbub [that] stopped immediately, as if by a magic spell, at the appearance of a gondola of the Council of Ten, flying the banner of Saint Mark at the prow, [at which] everyone returned home or went elsewhere, amidst the cheers and the whistles."[75]

Certainly most ordinary Venetians had ample respect—if not outright fear—for the Captains, who were hardly the sort of benevolent guardians that Zanetti's passage would imply. As befit the enforcers of a secretive magistracy claiming almost limitless powers, the Captains enjoyed wide discretion in how they exercised their authority about the city, carrying out their policing duties all the more assiduously for knowing that the Ten guaranteed them a bounty for each of the arrests they made, a reward to be raised by selling the possessions of their prisoners.[76] Kept well informed about every activity in their districts by their personal networks of spies, the Captains were empowered to stop, search, and arrest anyone—worker, noble, or visitor—whom they considered suspicious; when pursuing fugitives they and their *sbirri* were free to break down the doors of private houses without warning or warrant and to chase their prey to the limits of (and sometimes beyond) the Republic's territories.[77]

Yet even with all their considerable authority, the Captains were not always able to deal effectively with the *battagliole*—certainly not with the

easy efficiency with which Zanotti and others have credited them. Their system of policing, with its concentrated, mobile, and heavily armed forces backed up by spy networks and a draconian judicial system, was effective enough at protecting the city's peace from brawlers, breaking up minor gatherings, and picking up those carrying concealed weapons. The *battagliole*, however, presented problems of law enforcement on an altogether different scale.

The first of the Captains' difficulties lay in negotiating the maze of canals and narrow alleys making up Venice's unique topography. When thousands of onlookers mobbed to a single bridge, the Ten's well-armed *barche longhe* lost their effective threat of bringing the force of the state directly to the scene of the disturbance, for the canal granting access to the battle site would be impenetrable, choked from one bank to the other by a wall of *gondole* and *peote* belonging to spectators. Should they try to clear themselves a path by forcing those responsible to move their boats out of the way, the Captains would quickly discover that "they were not able to discover even one owner of said vessels."[78]

As a result, the Captains generally would have had no option but to leave the relative security of their armed vessels and try to make their way to the bridge along the packed narrow streets, pushing through the crowds by brute force. But here they were often frustrated by the masses of onlookers and fighters, who, while feigning obedience to authority, still managed to find ways to keep the Captains and their *sbiraglia* from actually arriving at the bridge site. A mob of fans would pretend to be blocked

Figure 4.3 The *Capitanio Grande* and Captain of the
Council of Ten, "who have the duty to see that the city
is purged of wicked men . . . in order to keep the plebs
of the realm peaceful"; Grevembroch. (Museo Correr,
Archivio Fotografico, 24026 and 24031)

by others up ahead, obstructing the police's progress through the narrow
alleys, "such that rage and protests served them little."[79] Unable to see
past those in front of them, Captains were easily fooled by the calls of the
crowd into thinking that the factions had abandoned the contest or changed
their original bridge for another. Sometimes large groups of fighters spent
the afternoon charging from bridge to bridge, with the hope of leading
the Captains in a chase that would leave them too exhausted to break
up the battle when it actually occurred.[80]

Moreover, the Captains and their squads sometimes had other obligations, that could keep them from being on hand at all during a *battagliola*.
Occasionally the Ten would instruct them to patrol only certain bridges—
orders they scrupulously followed, even when the factions quickly caught
on and scheduled full-scale encounters at other sites.[81] In addition, the
Captains' duties at ceremonial events could keep them out of circulation
for a few days at the end of each month, when they were ordered to pre-
side at the ducal palace—probably for the monthly rotation of one of the
Ten's three executive Chiefs (*Capi*).[82] On certain holidays their presence

was also required at Piazza San Marco in order to control the crowds; such days were ideal occasions for those who wished to schedule a *battagliola*. On workdays the Captains were typically to be found patroling the Rialto and the city's main markets; usually during the week there was less risk of a battle breaking out, since fewer workers would be idling around the bridges. On occasion, however, encounters would be purposely scheduled during lunchtime or late in the afternoon on weekdays, in the knowledge that some workers would be available at these times but the Captains would not be so likely to show up.[83]

Even those Captains who did manage to reach the battle site could find themselves openly challenged. Their power at the bridges was conditional, based in part on their personal reputation and in part on circumstances—crowds seemed more willing to quiet down and break up on some popular religious holidays, for example, and less inclined to abandon their *pretentioni et sdegni* when large numbers of patrician enthusiasts were present to urge them on.[84] The state authority that he supposedly represented was not always enough to protect a Captain when he pushed his way to the center of a bridge and tried to drag combatants apart by sheer force. At the very least, he could expect to be derided and mocked by those who refused to render "the required obedience and respect," and who instead called out insults from the safety of the crowd. If he were not careful, fighters worked into a frenzy of factional excitement might well tear his cloak of office to pieces, punch him in the face, or trample him underfoot. It might be the fate of a less-experienced Captain—the *novello nella carica* who still imagined that his office gave him the right to arrogantly abuse disobedient combatants—to find himself bodily lifted up and thrown off the bridge into the canal below.[85]

Indeed, it may well have been primarily for self-defense that Captains came to the bridges so well armed: with swords, pistols, and a protective layer of *zacco*, or chain mail, under their tunics.[86] It was rare that they or their *sbirri* would aggressively attack—or even threaten—the crowd with their weapons; the wiser (or at least more cautious) Captains tried whenever possible to avoid descending to the level of those they were trying to control, lest they get drawn into a shoving or punching match with fighters who had become irrational with wine or factional excitement. Even the open display of their muskets and pistols—the very weapons that granted them unmistakable superiority over the public—was apparently to be avoided: brandishing a pistol or discharging it over the heads of the crowd might have had the satisfying effect of causing fighters and spectators to throw themselves to the ground or flee, but it could just as likely cause the disorder to spread and intensify, by provoking a *sassata* of paving stones or roof tiles to rain down on the bridge from all sides.[87]

Caught in the midst of a large and often hostile mob and recognizing the difficulty (and the personal danger) involved in attempting to subdue participants by direct force, Captains often tended to restrain the *battagliole* by means of threats and intimidation, attempting to impose their will on fighters in much the same way they did with suspects in the city at large. While it was difficult to arrest disorderly fighters in the thick of an excited crowd, the Captains could at least make a point of letting the particularly unruly or fractious know that they had been recognized. By loudly calling out their names or singling them out with obvious gestures—pointing at offenders, ostentatiously biting a finger in their direction, or taking down their names—Captains made it clear to the persistently disobedient that they were known, and "that they should desist with such presumptuousness or they would [be] . . . thrown in prison." Even though rowdy fighters might manage to leave the bridge untouched by the law, a few nights later they could well be rudely awakened at home, their doors smashed down in a midnight raid and they themselves arrested by the same *sbirri* they had so recently mocked.[88]

Such policing tactics were intended less to forcibly break up a *battagliola* than to coerce participants into desisting on their own, under the threat of a later, inevitable retribution. Certainly they had some success: the mere arrival of the Captains could have a direct and chilling effect on the popular ardor for the *pugni*, the more so when a few days later some of the more obviously unruly were suddenly arrested.[89] On the other hand, those who fell into the Captains' nets appear more often than not to have been only minor fighters: the sort of rank amateurs who were the most inclined to forget their self-control in the midst of the battle and commit such excessive and blatantly illegal acts as assaulting a Captain personally.[90] The leaders of the factions—the *padrini* and *caporioni*—were generally more circumspect in how they dealt with the officers of the Ten. When called upon by the Captains to help control their fighting squads, they would appear to cooperate, even if their efforts were often more feigned than real. On other occasions, such as when the Captains were particularly aggressive in attempting to stop the fighting, the *padrini* of both sides might keep on their dark cloaks and simply fade out of sight, blending in with the other *gente dei ferrarioli* in the audience.[91]

Even when *padrini* chose to disobey the Captains and continue to urge on their troops, it was not always so easy to capture them by means of the usual midnight raids. Enjoying close ties and held in high regard by their fellow workers, these leaders of the *pugni* tended to live surrounded by protective neighbors out in the poorer fringes of the city: in the fishing quarter of San Nicolò, in the *arsenalotti* district around San Pietro di Castello, or out in the working-class zones of Cannaregio or the Giudecca. Should the Captains and their *sbirri* try to capture fugitive *caporioni* by venturing at night out into districts that were, for the minions of law and order, essentially hostile territories, they risked stirring up a far stronger popular reaction than they could ever hope to contain:

> Truly the Captains employed every effort to imprison the *capi*, to the extent that they went with many armed men one night to the Giudecca to lay hands on some *capi*, whom by means of their spies they had located at a tavern. Such that, when Menego Cavallotto [a Castellani *capo*] came out, the *sbiraglia*

were immediately upon him, but being armed, he bravely defended himself. At [the sound of] such noise and uproar there came out others, armed with pikes, knives, and stones, chasing away the Captains . . . [and causing] the others to jump in the water or flee in their boats, unable to resist the furor of stones and the blow of arms, since everyone rushed out of their houses with the greatest racket, shouting, "Kill them! Kill them!" These officers were finally forced to shoot off two muskets (in the air, however) to intimidate such audacious and enraged people, [at which] everyone retreated, no longer either pursued or persecuted.[92]

Moreover, the factional *caporioni* were men who enjoyed aristocratic as well as popular protection. Even the highly secretive Ten was not altogether secure from leaks through the bureaucrats and nobles working at its fringes (and sometimes within its chambers), for many of these were staunch partisans of the *pugni*. As a result, it was a rare occasion when the names of disobedient *capi* and *padrini* denounced to the Ten by its Captains were not soon circulating beyond the Council's closed halls. When the Captains were subsequently sent out on their punitive raids, "to arrest the fomenters of so much tumult and disorder," they more often than not found that the houses of the *caporioni* were empty—as these leaders, with timely warning, had already hidden themselves, "some in the courts of the ambassadors, others in monasteries and the most secret houses, and this one or that one in the houses of the [noble] protectors of the factions."[93]

Venetian nobles were willing to go much further, however, to undermine the authority of the magistracy which, more than any other in Venice, seems to have existed particularly to guarantee their own primacy. Those *caporioni* unlucky enough to have fallen into the hands of the Captains could still usually hope to escape the usual torments of three hoists (*strappi*) on the strappado (that is, to be hoisted from behind by the wrists and released with a sudden jerk) or the lengthy prison terms that were the fate of lesser fighters and brawlers.[94] Rather than languish in the Ten's jails for years, factional leaders were generally freed within a short time, thanks to the personal intervention of aristocratic patrons. Those gentlemen who wished to intercede on behalf of their worker clients could find colleagues with the appropriate powers at the usual noble conclaves that came together under the arches of the ducal palace in the *broglio,* that long-recognized, informal forum for patrician caucusing and vote selling that would also appear to have encompassed such nonpolitical activities as these negotiations over the *battagliole.*[95]

To win their case, interested patricians were prepared to pay fines or bribes personally, although undoubtedly political favors were also exchanged to win the release of captive *padrini.* When they were successful, their clients might serve only a month or two of the seven years officially demanded by the Ten; indeed, some might go free within just a few days. Likewise, timely intervention could protect a well-connected *caporioni* from the strappado, even when the device had already been ostentatiously put on display for his punishment in Piazza San Marco.[96] If aristocratic partisans could not manage to get a prisoner let off completely, they could sometimes at least succeed in having the hoisting cord shortened, "such that he [would] not be lifted very far off of the ground."[97]

Besides this willingness to bend the Ten's justice for the benefit of their plebeian clients, some aristocratic enthusiasts of the *pugni* were also quite prepared to take on the Council's Captains personally, should these officials interfere too boldly in the progress of the fighting. Drawn from the popular classes, Captains would inevitably have had an uneasy relationship with their noble betters in the strictly hierarchical Republic. Although all citizens were in theory equally subject to their and the Ten's powers, younger noblemen tended to consider abusing and provoking these plebeian policemen as something between a prerogative and a sport.[98] They would join with the plebs at impeding the *shiraglia* from arriving at the battle site, feigning outrage that ordinary police would dare to push past and "annoy the nobility in the public streets." At the bridges, their sense of natural superiority sometimes induced gentlemen to assault the Captains outright, if they thought that they were about to be denied the pleasure of a battle. Once, in the middle of such an argument over whether the *battagliola* would be allowed to continue, one young blood boldly stepped up to the stubborn Captain and ripped the mustache right off his face.[99] Several times conniving (if less violent) nobles managed to lure an obstructive Captain away from the bridge with blandishments and promises, only to lock him up in a nearby storeroom (*magazino*) for the duration of the conflict.[100]

Assaulting such a high officer of the state would have been a serious crime if committed by workers, but when perpetrated by young nobles such an act took on a somewhat different cast. There is every indication that their aristocratic elders were often willing to wink at this sort of provocative behavior, dismissing it as youthful pranks, the more so when they were committed in the ludic atmosphere of the bridges. Thus, even after Giovanni Francesco Lippomano and Marcantonio Pisani had publicly sworn at the Captains for trying to stop a battle at the Ponte dei Pugni and then proceeded to attack one of them—"one punching him and the other pulling his beard and both together spitting on him . . . and finally carrying him off to a house where they locked him up so that he could not carry out his duties"—these two noble rogues were handed a punishment that could only be described as mild: they were banished to the garrison city of Palma to do a year's-paid military service.[101]

Caught as they were between enormous and often frenzied mobs of plebeian fighters and gangs of impudent and provocative young noblemen, it is no wonder that many Captains were reluctant to carry out their duties at the bridges.[102] Some were so unwilling to get involved in all the risks and difficulties presented by the *battagliole*—they were, after all, favorite targets for those throwing stones from the safety of the rooftops—that the Chiefs of the Ten had to threaten them with the loss of their position and

cloak of office to force them to go at all. Aware that failing to stop a battle
as ordered could well result in their own imprisonment or even the
strappado, Captains often responded to the commands of the Ten by pre-
varicating.[103] Those with an eye for their own safety might go into hiding
after failing to stop a *battagliola*; others tried to mislead their masters by
making false or incomplete reports, refusing to give the names of factional
leaders—perhaps to avoid being sent out on the dangerous mission of later
having to arrest them in a midnight raid—or sometimes even pretending
that no battle had ever taken place at all.[104]

Facing an implacable vengeance from the Ten if they failed in their
duties, yet perhaps equally convinced that actively trying to break up illicit
battagliole was ultimately futile as well as personally dangerous, the more
inventive Captains sought ways to frustrate the factions without actually
coming between them.[105] Among the most creative in both preventing
battles and in keeping himself well away from the thick of the fighting
was one Barbanegra, the *Capitanio grande* of the 1630s and 40s. Believ-
ing that "once the two factions were united at the bridge, there would be
no means of preventing a battle, not even with artillery," Barbanegra tried
to keep the two sides from ever meeting each other, by such schemes as
posting armed guards to block key bridges along the route the factional
armies had to follow to reach the battle site.[106] Another time he came up
with the novel idea of foiling an impending encounter by securing two
gondolas side by side under the bridge of San Marziale, with the result that
the boats

> stuck beyond the bridge with their *ferri* [the decorative but also sharp metal
> tips at either end], that is with the stern at one side and the prow at the other,
> threatening, with such a placement of steel, dangers to the lives of those
> who in the *frotte* are accustomed to fall in the water.

Barbanegra evidently assumed that no one aware of such a danger
underneath would risk brawling on the bridge, but his plan was ultimately
frustrated: fighters were too excited even to notice the risks they were
running, and in the end two (probably patrician) *maschere* disguised as
bishops rowed to where the gondolas were secured and—over the loud
protests of the police nearby—released and towed the boats away.[107]
Perhaps because they posed such difficulties (and possible embarrassments),
such imaginative solutions for controlling the *pugni* were not to the liking
of all the Captains; many were content to rely on methods that, in effect,
aimed more at simply obstructing the *battagliole* than stopping them altogether. Both the Captains and their masters at the Ten, for example, followed the practice of using spies and informers to expose those who were
making plans for an encounter. Moreover, when word began to spread that
a *battagliola* was imminent, the Captains could be sent with all their forces
to occupy the most likely fighting bridge, preventing the two factions from
making physical contact.[108] The Ten would in any case soon know when
an elaborate, large-scale battle was in the works, simply by the masses of

enthusiasts who for days beforehand would be vying to place their boats as close as possible to the designated bridge, and by the entrepreneurs who were filling all the adjoining quays with grandstands and benches for paying spectators. On such occasions, it was a simple matter for the Captains and their squads of *sbirri* to arrive at the battle site early on the assigned day and knock down the stands and tow away the boats moored nearby.[109] Such tactics no doubt annoyed partisans of the factions; they could do little to bring the *pugni* under real control, however, as long as other fighting bridges remained available for those thousands who wished to pass their Sunday afternoons at the *battagliole*.[110]

The Ambiguities of Absolutism

The Venetian state's often ineffectual response to the *battagliole* cannot be blamed wholly on the failure of the state police. Clearly the Ten, with its Captains, spies, and *sbirri*, had an impressive force at its disposal and generally knew how to use it: compared to the other European states of its day, Venice was an especially well controlled community, where little happened that was not soon known and dealt with by the authorities.[111] Contemporaries noted how strictly, not to say harshly, laws were enforced within the city, especially those concerned with sedition, riot, or public violence. Centuries of living in what was, in effect, a police state had taught ordinary Venetians a healthy respect for authority: indeed, most workers turn out to have been more than willing to abandon "their beloved pretensions to fight and brawl at the bridges" once they were faced with a truly concerted police crackdown. Often, after the Ten had ordered a sharp repressive response—with the usual armed patrols, arrests, jailings, and tortures—all trace of popular factional enthusiasms seemed to disappear virtually overnight, and "both the factions were terrified, no longer daring to go near the [fighting] bridge . . . [such that] for months not only did no one do battle, but they did not even talk about it."[112]

Why was the Ten, perennially hostile toward popular disruptions of all kinds, with a clear ability to make its authority felt, and well feared by the populace at large, unable to suppress the *pugni* once and for all? As has already been seen, the staged, mass violence of the *battagliole* continued for over two hundred years largely because of the particular interplay between fighters and their fans. When, under the risk of actual or imminent state repression, fighters started to show signs of losing their enthusiasm for the *pugni* and its honors, there were always plenty of "civilian" enthusiasts of the *battagliole* around who were eager to build up their courage again. Some of these *fattionari* and *fauttori* were neighbors or family members (including wives), who would mock the reluctant warriors for their cowardliness; perhaps more important were the noble and mercantile fans, who were not only prompt to foment their favorites' factional rivalries but at the same time promised them protection from the law. When their fear of the Captains once made the Nicolotti *padrini* reluctant to join in a battle, "[t]hey were reproved for their timidity by all the people and by the *protettori d'auttorità*, who expressly promised them that [if they fought] there would not be made any report in consequence, either by the Captain or by anybody else."[113]

This complicity between fighters and their supporters was abetted by the ways in which the state itself was pervaded by the *pugni*, however. Factionalism and factional passions, far from being just the concern of simple artisans and a few youthful nobles, also had a way of seducing those bureaucrats and patricians who staffed the city's government at all levels. It was a corruption of faction that became especially crucial when it affected the policing forces of the Ten, which at times it clearly did. Not only the *sbiraglie* but also the Captains themselves all belonged to one or the other faction, simply by virtue of having been born in either Castellani or Nicolotti territory. Many had close family ties to principal fighters as well. The Ten was certainly quite aware that its police had such loyalties, for it maintained a policy of assigning Captains and *sbirri* to oversee only their own respective factions—at one time they went so far as to choose as Captain for the Nicolotti a man who had actually been a renowned fighter for that side.[114] Probably the Ten had little choice in the matter: a Captain from the opposing faction would have provoked even more hostility than normal; at least if he were sent to police those of his own side he might hope to exercise some influence over the fighters:

> "The squads of San Nicolò . . . came to disembark on the canal behind the church [of San Marziale], with the greatest tumult and impetus, but Captain Tiraferro, who was at the bridge of Santa Fosca, came forward and obstructed the landing of the greater part, [by] soothing this indomitable and esteemed people with friendly words, since he too was a Nicolotto, promising them every favor at the [appropriate] time and place.[115]

Still, such policing tactics had risks of their own. The gangs of *sbirri*, probably never too well disciplined in any case, might well find themselves during the course of a *battagliola* in close contact with their own neighbors and friends among the fighters. When factional passion ran hot enough at the bridges, and these *sbirri* were swept away from the immediate control of their Captain, many of them could end up forgetting that they were agents of the state, and, tossing away their responsibilities along with their cloaks of office, they could wade into the battle as Castellani or Nicolotti, punching their enemies in the name of factional honor.[116] All police, whether Captains or *sbirri*, also had a tendency to take physical and verbal affronts personally, but the insult was all the stronger if it had come from someone of the opposing faction. The ordinary business of policing, especially the midnight raids for which the Captains of the Ten were so renowned, could under such circumstances turn into active vendettas, in which these police pushed the limits even of their own widely defined powers as they went after their prey with particular relish and ferocity.[117]

Such factional prejudices were not limited simply to the Captains and their *sbirri*, however. There are ample signs that some of the inner circle of nobility—those who customarily monopolized key positions of authority in the Collegio and the Senate, as well as in the Ten—also sometimes dabbled at being Castellani and Nicolotti. Not that these aged nobles ever got especially heated in their factional passions; the sharp words and occasional fights over faction that periodically disturbed the *broglio* were doubtless the responsibility of younger nobles. For the most part the more elderly aristocrats indulged their loyalties in the manner of the patriarch of Venice, artfully promoting their factional animosities and personal rivalries through a complex mixture of high diplomacy and local politics.[118]

Their outward factional loyalty may have seemed relatively mild, but it was still sufficiently strong to tempt some members of the elite away from their otherwise intense devotion for promoting and protecting a unified, hierarchical, and absolutist state. It may in fact have been precisely the ambivalence of such patricians about the *pugni* that left the Venetian government without any consistent policy on how to deal with the Castellani and Nicolotti, particularly when a majority of the Ten—and especially of its three Chiefs—passed by the luck of politics and the draw into the hands of oligarchs who enjoyed the battles. There is little question that the *caporioni* of the factions—well informed of affairs in government by their own patrician confidants—had a clear idea who these key individuals were and what sort of response could be expected should a battle be attempted. *Battagliole* were evidently planned around the knowledge of who might be in command of the Ten, either by waiting until a majority of sympathetic chiefs had taken control at the beginning of the month or by holding as many fights as possible before the end of the month, when less agreeable executives would be taking over.[119]

In the months when sympathizers of factionalism and the *pugni* predominated among the Ten or its Chiefs, the official policy of rigid restrictions against battles and factional brawling might relax considerably. Unless forced to do so in response to an especially disruptive battle, such patricians tended not to order their Captains to go to the bridges, either to impede or to break up encounters. In turn, the Captains would punctiliously stay away from potential battle sites, unless they should decide to visit while out of uniform, to watch like any other spectator.[120] It is quite likely that these agreeable Chiefs of the Ten were the same ones that could be expected to turn a sympathetic ear to fellow nobles who came seeking to lessen the punishments that Venetian law, in its impartial ferocity, had imposed on those hapless fighters and *padrini* who had been hauled in by the Captains.

This willingness of at least some of Venice's rulers to let the *battagliole* continue has been taken by both contemporary and modern observers as another indication of the elite's skill at running the Venetian polity. Battles were supposedly staged to give the plebs a chance to let off steam (*sfogare le loro anime*), to provide them with an opportunity to develop martial skills, and, as has already been seen, to get them to pay their taxes. The spectacles made a lively show for the nobility, while spreading good propaganda about the aggressiveness of Venetians to visiting dignitaries.[121] It was also said, both in the seventeenth century and by later historians, that the *battagliole*, despite all their chaos, were yet another proof of the Venetian state's talents for self-preservation. The authorities encouraged factionalism, according to this view, with the aim of keeping the populace perpetually divided in two, such that "[i]f one part plotted against the fatherland or made assertions to rule it, the other would defend and sustain the government and established authority with its own blood."[122]

It was also likely, however, that some seventeenth-century Chiefs of the Ten felt compelled to let the *pugni* continue in order to divert the public—and indeed themselves—from the apparently unstoppable decline of the Republic's diplomatic and economic fortunes.[123] Certainly, Venetian commoners, once keenly interested in imperial and political affairs, showed every sign of wanting to forget the kind of steady social hemorrhaging that accompanied such endless rearguard struggles as the quarter-century long War of Candia. By the last days of the war, both workers and their betters had become so demoralized by the seemingly inexorable advance of the Turks that "one did not hear anybody talk about *battagliole* nor even come close to the bridges, since the whole city was full of bitterness and affliction from the continuous news of Candia, so unhappy and endangered." As soon as the war had concluded, however, Venetians of all classes, including the recently defeated veterans of Crete, appear to have desired nothing more than to go back to their familiar fighting bridges, seeking the glory that had eluded them abroad and "desiring that peace would never be made between the Nicolotti and Castellani factions but rather that the *pugni* should continually arouse and drive them to battle and to restlessness."[124]

That individual Chiefs of the Ten could enforce or suspend state edicts against the *battagliole* more or less on their own whim says at least as much about these laws themselves as about the skills of a ruling elite that manipulated popular recreations for civic ends. The long series of edicts against the *pugni*—from the Ten's initial *proclama* of 1505 to its most ferocious pronouncement in 1644—should in fact be seen more as temporary injunctions than as permanent bans. Their effective power seems to have lapsed after a certain length of time, perhaps at the end of the *battagliole* season in January or even at the end of every month, with the regular changing of one of the Chiefs. The newly installed heads of the Ten—or the beginning of a new battle season in August—would once again invariably find the status quo ante in force, as youths resumed their dueling at the fighting bridges and neighborhood leaders proceeded with their training and recruiting of new pugilists. Only the aggressive imposition of the anti-*pugni* statutes by hostile Chiefs of the Ten could give these

bans real effect: it was this implicitly temporary nature of the edicts themselves (despite their ferocious language), as much as any difficulties posed
by their enforcement, that required them to be reissued virtually on a yearly
basis throughout the sixteenth and seventeenth centuries.[125]

The tentative character of the Ten's bans against the *pugni* only serves
to highlight how complex was the interplay between what was a highly
ordered state's most absolute of magistracies and its ostensibly powerless
people. The Ten, the Collegio, and the Senate in fact all maintained an
acute sensitivity toward the "talk in the streets" (*mormoratione della città*).
Girolamo Priuli and Marino Sanuto recognized this indistinct and unpre-
dictable "will of the people" as a political fact of life at the beginning of
the sixteenth century; 150 years later—in a context of weakened economic
and social vitality—elite awareness of popular grumblings was if anything
more discerning, despite the state's ever more insistent absolutist posturings.[126]
Indeed, in 1675, at what might be considered the height of the cult of the
pugni, the opposition of the plebs was still taken so seriously that "merely
the rumblings of a few boatmen" were enough to convince the nervous
Senate to unmake a newly elected doge and substitute another more to the
popular liking.[127]

By the seventeenth century to *montar sui ponti* had become a powerful popular tradition in Venice, one not easily rescinded by government
edicts. Like the Carnival in late winter, the *battagliole* were expected to
occur in their proper season: beginning at the time "when the sun customarily heats the blood of the two factions." Either of these traditional
celebrations could be abrogated, but the general understanding remained
that such outlawing was the act of specific individuals—generally the Chiefs
of the Ten—in response to particular situations; as such, these were not
treated as a permanent ban. Rather, the people's "right" to go to the
bridges, like their "right" to turn the public world upside-down for the
Carnival, would merely be put in abeyance for a time, to reemerge later
under more sympathetic authorities on a more propitious day. The Chronicler of the *pugni* called this the "liberty of the people," based both on
"the *Jus comune*, as noted in the glosses of the Doctors [of law]" and on
"immemorial custom, that is conserved and validated with the possessive
act and the maintenance of so many hundreds of years."[128]

Faced as they were with a popular celebration that they were unable and
sometimes probably unwilling to suppress permanently, the Chiefs of the
Ten appear to have taken a middle course in dealing with the *pugni*. Since
allowing the *battagliole* to get completely out of hand meant public
embarrassment not only for the Venetian state but also (and perhaps just
as important) for the proud and sensitive Chiefs themselves, the Ten evidently decided at least to keep these factional encounters from dissolving
into open riot.[129] Increasingly, as the seventeenth century wore on, the
Chiefs would order their Captains to the bridges more to keep order during the *battagliole* than to suppress the encounters completely. Whereas re-

garding the 1630s the Chronicler of the *pugni* often wrote of the Captains trying *a viva forza* to pull combatants apart, of the Ten's *sbiraglie* charging at the massed factions, and of their firing muskets over the heads of the crowd, the police actions he reports for the 1660s and 70s, though not without their moments of violence, were on the whole more conciliatory and cautionary. Fearsomely authoritarian as they may have been in the city at large, in the context of the *battagliole* the Captains of the Ten acted less in their normal policing role and more as the state's referees between the factions.[130]

Although the Ten was never too explicit about the aims of this policy, it was apparently intended to encourage those aspects of the *pugni* that the nobles themselves would no doubt have found most appealing: factional loyalty, martial skill, and the quest for glory. At the same time, the state would, if anything, show even more hostility toward the sort of egregious violence that so often marred the event. In practice, this meant having the Captains urge fighters to favor the *mostre*—where the combat was limited to just two participants at a time—over the potentially riotous *frotte*. As much as they could, the Captains would therefore keep the bridge clear and the two factions arrayed on opposite quays ("devouring each other with their eyes"), while allowing only one fighter and one *padrino* from each side to mount the bridge at a time. Their assumption appears to have been that, with enough *mostre*, the energies and antagonisms of the two factions would eventually wear themselves out, if darkness did not fall first. It was a strategy that required a delicate sense of balance, for as already seen, most ordinary fighters and a good many spectators found the *frotte* more exciting and personally satisfying than the one-on-one duels. As a rule, it was only by commandeering the assistance of any available *padrini* or noble partisans that the Captains could expect to squelch the objections of ardent youth and calm the factions to the point where the *mostre* could actually begin, using threats and cajolery to keep the center of the bridge clear and new challengers steadily advancing into the arena.[131] Since the Captains worked so closely with the *mostre*, it was not surprising that before long their function had moved beyond simple crowd control to assisting the *padrini* with their refereeing activities: helping to decide the winners and preventing the kind of unfair fighting that could provoke a knife fight or *sassata*. Once they had decided that the crowd had seen enough combat and had to some measure spent its factional passions, the Captains could then start clearing the area, and generally they might expect to have to deal with a manageably small number of fighters and onlookers who were still excited enough to raise serious objections at being deprived of a *frotta*.[132]

Such an approach seems to have worked, at least in keeping the factions busy enough staging *mostre* that they were diverted from their usual uncontrolled brawling and stone throwing. Whereas in the 1630s the Castellani and Nicolotti often found it difficult to stage even two or three *mostre* before some dispute set off the *frotta*, by the 1660s it was commonplace for thirty, fifty, or even a hundred duelists to present themselves at the *arengo*, filling Sunday afternoons with a continuous and, for many participants, satisfying display of factional combat. When group passions were such that a *frotta* appeared unavoidable, the Captains tried at least to keep the encounter focused on the bridge and not spilling out into nearby *campi* and *fondamente*, where knife fights and stone-throwing melees were more likely. To this end, they encouraged the *capi* of both sides to keep the squads in such tight and orderly formations along the approaches to the bridge that fighters would virtually move in lockstep, and thereby be less likely to break ranks and provoke a riot on their way to the battle site (Figure 4.1, p. 133).[133]

At the same time that orderly combat was being encouraged, a more concerted effort was being made to single out and make an example of those who "went beyond the *pugni* to commit scandals and confusion": the rowdy delinquents who tried at all costs to keep the *battagliole* as violent as possible, coming to the bridges desiring nothing more than a chance to turn the factional clashes into all-out riots. For this reason, three Captains might be sent to police the Castellani while only one was assigned to the Nicolotti, in the knowledge that the former "as more riotous and insolent, have more need of severity and restraint." Their target could be any miscreant who was too quick to draw his knife or who brawled out of turn, but they particularly retaliated against those who launched roof tiles from the tops of nearby houses. Sometimes in the company of concerned nobles, the Captains and their *sbiraglie* would lead sorties to roust these offenders from their safe havens: breaking down the doors of the houses on which they perched, charging up the stairs, and chasing them off across the adjoining rooftops.[134] The Ten also sought to isolate such rioters and tile throwers from the more cooperative followers of the *pugni*, evidently in the hope of gaining the latter's support. Instead of responding to a *sassata* with an automatic general crackdown on all factional activity in the city, the Chiefs of the Ten might allow the weekly *battagliole* to continue, while ordering their Captains to identify and arrest those particularly pernicious troublemakers who had been behind the stone throwing and rioting.[135]

These attempts to tame the *pugni* by encouraging as many *mostre* as possible and by weeding out and punishing the most unruly partisans appear to have coincided with and perhaps stimulated changing popular attitudes about the *battagliole*. *Mostre*, which had once seemed to many but a poor substitute for a "real" battle, were increasingly accepted as the way to satisfy factional honor—especially if they were numerous and were staged between *guerrieri famosi*.[136] Still more important, it was becoming steadily less acceptable to use weapons at the bridges. Fighters who resorted to stones or knives in the heat of battle would increasingly be seen as poorly disciplined or unfit soldiers of the *pugni*; their enemies might taunt them as cowards without honor, who were driven to pick up weapons in desperation, having proven themselves unfit to fight with their fists.[137] Such

rowdy participants, along with those who generally behaved "with vile actions contrary to the rules of battle" could rapidly find themselves
marginalized within their own factions—unable to attract the kind of
patrician protection that went to more worthy combatants and much more
likely to be picked up by the Captains and removed from circulation. In
concluding his history of the *pugni*, the Chronicler seems to have thrown
his support to this "civilizing" tendency, calling for an end to "these dis-
turbances that are caused by the rashness, not to say the bestiality, of a few
fighters . . . [so that] the *Battagliole venetiane* [could] continue to provide wonder and amazement for many."[138]

This tacit understanding between state authorities and the fighting
public was always fragile and never assured. *Battagliole* continued to
degenerate into large-scale urban riots, with all the destructive force that
knives, sticks, and paving stones could inflict. The Captains in their turn
might still respond to such popular violence with the open force of the
state, whether with pikes and muskets at the bridge or with midnight raids
and roundups in the days after the battle.[139] Nevertheless, the perceptible
move of the Ten and its Captains away from a confrontational approach
to the factions, coupled with a growing opposition to gratuitous violence
on the part of the Nicolotti and Castellani leadership, did as a rule produce more stable encounters than those often-fatal riots that were the typical
results of battles earlier in the century.[140]

Considering its reputation for impartial law and inflexible order, the
Venetian state turned out to have been far from decisive in dealing with
its own factional violence. By the later seventeenth century, these two traditional antagonists, the Ten and its police on the one side and the factions and their supporters on the other, could do no more than settle into
a period of uneasy coexistence. It was an anomalous state of affairs for an
absolutist age, when both local and foreign observers had no doubt that
"such popular commotions and hatreds were highly contrary to good
government and to the quiet of states and kingdoms." Foreign princes,
even as they flocked to enjoy the *battagliole*, had little sympathy for the
seemingly dilatory way in which Venetian justice handled the disobedient:
" 'In my country,' " grumbled Giovanni Battista Borghese, "we would have
hanged a couple of [these rioters] by the neck.' "[141]

Yet absolutism—especially in a thousand-year-old Republic with strong
popular traditions—was not always so simple as Prince Borghese would
have had it. The Venetian state's circumspect approach to dealing with the
battagliole reveals not only the practical, physical limits to a government's
power in this era but also the lack of any real consistency among the governing elite themselves. Far from tracing any clear dividing line between
rulers and ruled in an absolutist dichotomy, this long and often halting
official campaign against the *pugni* indicates on the contrary just how
unclear this border was, as well as the extent to which popular amusements
and traditions could still sway and disrupt elite policy. Even those select
few who served on the Ten appear to have recognized that their effective

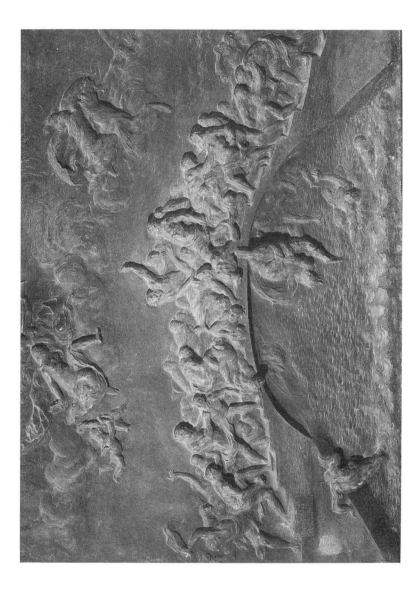

Figure 4.4 Bronze high relief of a *battagliola*, signed "Antonio Bonaci 1683." (Museo Correr, not catalogued)

power was always as much a matter of compromise, cooption, and intimidation as of outright force; but if their subsequent stand-off with the plebeian mob could hardly redound to their credit, it was certainly to the benefit of the *pugni*. By permitting the *battagliole* to continue under calmer conditions, the policies of the Ten effectively allowed ever larger crowds and fighting contingents to congregate without inevitably degenerating into chaotic riot. Along with its new followers, popular factional combat appears to have gained as well a new respectability for its role as the quintessentially Venetian amusement. The result, from the 1660s to the 1680s, was a celebration of the *battagliole* on an unprecedented scale, perhaps best embodied in the rebuilding of the old fighting bridge at San Marziale: finished on 26 May 1670, its *piazza di mezo* boasted the additional ornamentation in each corner of a marble footprint that marked not only the duelists' starting marker but also the state's recognition and consecration, as it were, of a piece of the Venetian cityscape to the factional cult.[142] During these decades the acolytes of the *pugni* seemed to reach for every available medium to express this new enthusiasm: besides the prose accounts of the Chronicler of the *pugni*, Saint Disdier and others, partisans churned out poetry, paintings, popular prints, and even bronzes to represent and immortalize Venice's *battagliole* for both fellow citizens and the interested foreigner (Figure 4.4). For a time even the Ten, satisfied that at least a modicum of order had been established at the bridges, stopped its incessant issuing and reissuing of edicts against those who would *montar sui ponti*: for five months of each year, from August to January, Venetians could enjoy their right to give themselves over to a single passion, the celebration of faction, violence, and the *pugni*.

EPILOGUE

The End of the *Pugni*

*After having described for you, oh Reader, the wars
and the memorable deeds that took place between
these two famous factions of the Castellani and the
Nicolotti, from 1632 to this present year of 1670,
my pen is exhausted and quite worn out . . . [but I]
can imagine how satisfied you have been, to have
seen and heard again, after so many years, all that
which with anxious sighs you would have wished to
have experienced personally.*[1]

Venice's cult of the *pugni* did not long survive the seventeenth century. The great pitched battles of the 1670s and 80s, with all the poetry and artwork that they inspired, may have seemed to contemporaries to be ushering in a golden age for the *battagliole*, but in fact they were marking its final years: the last full-scale encounter was held just a generation later, on 29 September 1705, at San Barnabà. The city's ancient factional hostilities may have remained as pungent as ever, but Venetians would henceforth find other ways of expressing them besides mass fistfights on bridges. Within just a few decades the memory of the once-enormous battles had already started to slip away, surviving only in such placenames as the Ponte dei Pugni at San Barnabà and the Ponte della Guerra at San Zulian. Local artists continued to use the *pugni* as a theme, portraying aging champions *in arnese* or full-fledged *battagliole* at their climactic moment, but the results (while dramatic) no longer commemorated specific encounters but were instead generic: stylized views that could be included in the sort of pictorial surveys of quirky Venetian folklore that were enjoying increasing popularity among foreign tourists.[2] The poets who had once written so enthusiastically of the encounters fell silent, and even the Council of Ten had no more to say on the subject. Indeed, after this final encounter the *pugni* disappeared from the official record altogether, with the single exception (Venetians being what they were) of a case involving one Girolamo Alberti,

165

who in 1711 invoked the battles as part of a petition to reduce the taxes on his house near the Ponte dei Pugni, which "for some time has been empty because the amusement of the *pugni* is no longer staged here."[3]

What was behind this sudden decline of what for centuries had been "the recreation preferred above all others by the Venetian people"? Historians of Venetian social mores who have commented on the *battagliole* have tended to assert that the *pugni* came to an end quite simply because the government finally tired of so disruptive an activity. This conclusion follows quite logically from the assumption—almost an article of faith among Venetianists since at least the eighteenth century—that the Serenissima was a society managed from top to bottom by its ruling class: a society in which the *pugni*, like all other expressions of popular culture in the city, was allowed to continue only for so long as a far-sighted patriciate saw some benefit from it for themselves or the state. When such was no longer the case, it would have sufficed for the Council of Ten to ban the event (with the inevitable threats of the galleys or prison for the disobedient), and for the city's cowed multitudes—indeed, "spineless," according to some—to promptly obey.[4]

Yet such is not exactly the relationship between the Venetian state and its subjects that has emerged in this study of the *pugni*. Aristocratic authorities turn out to have been far more circumspect and much less manipulative in dealing with the citizenry than most Venetianists have assumed. City magistrates were no doubt well aware that the state's powers in controlling the *battagliole* were far from absolute, thanks to uncertain police control of the great factional mobs in the city's narrow streets. While it is true that a concerted police crackdown by the Ten could halt the battles temporarily, nevertheless, within a year, or even a few months, workers would once again be turning up at the bridges, openly asserting their factional enthusiasms. With attempts by the state to stamp out the *battagliole* persistently countered by both stubborn resistence on the part of commoners and by constant meddling in the justice system by patrician fans of the *pugni*, the result was a stand-off between the Venetian government and its citizenry that lasted for centuries. It does not seem that this impasse of centuries could have been finally resolved in 1705 simply by the Ten's issuing yet another edict against the encounters; indeed, there is no indication that the magistrate mounted any special purge of supporters of the *pugni* at this time. Under these circumstances, it is more logical to conclude that at least in part the *battagliole* were ultimately abandoned because the majority of Venetians simply grew tired of them: when the public no longer considered the battles significant or amusing, and when participants no longer found them satisfactory sources of honor and public respect.

Certainly there are signs that by the late 1600s members of Venice's elites—men who a century before might well have thought nothing of whipping off their cloaks and silk blouses and wading into the *frotta* themselves—were beginning to desert the *pugni* for the more refined pleasures of Enlightenment culture. To be sure, in the 1660s and 70s many elites still flocked to the bridges, but these fans increasingly found that their enthusiasm for such rowdy, plebeian amusements evoked the disdain of others in the patriciate. Some of these fans of the *pugni* were apparently embarrassed at finding themselves lagging behind in the changing tastes in patrician amusements and, like the Paduan gentleman Giovanni Antonio Finardo, seem to have been unsure how to proceed:

> Lately, I enjoyed very much the sight of a *battagliola* on the bridge, whence I was left happy beyond words: if my thoughts did not deceive me, I would suppose this to be among the first and the most enjoyable recreations of the city of Venice. But afterward I went drinking with a friend, from whose long discourse on the subject I was informed that the [*battagliole*] are often made damnable, hateful, and open to a thousand scandalous acts; [he] told me that the reason was the perverse doggedness of the factions, which, darkened by [their] excessive tendencies, led them too often, without the slightest regard, into a thousand brawls and disorders, not to mention an incessant hatred, which continuously worked its way between the dearest of friends and relations.[5]

Even the Chronicler of the *pugni*, limitless enthusiast for the bridges though he was, was evidently not altogether unaware of the carping and complaints that circulated about the *battagliole*. In his frequent defenses of the *pugni*, he left little doubt about what critics were beginning to say about the encounters:

> The scope of my History has until now not been other than to tell the world that the battles and wars of the Venetian people are not a simple entertainment of little relevance. . . . [After reading this history] who would then be able to say that these *battagliole* are an insignificant idleness, a simple entertainment of the city, merely a recreation or a popular frivolity, a curiosity of the plebs: that they amount to nothing more than a contest, a pretext for running up and down the bridges, giving rise more to scandal than to admiration?[6]

Yet unquestionably this was precisely what many elites were beginning to think, despite the Chronicler's repeated assurances that the *pugni* were "memorable and worthy of being seen by kings, cardinals, and the first knights of Europe."[7] By the later seventeenth century local patricians had other, more cultivated (and less dangerous) ways of passing their Sunday afternoons than that of watching mobs of artisans pummel each other. And when the city's elite began to abandon the *pugni*, they certainly weakened the event's ability to survive on its own, no matter how great was the popular enthusiasm for it. The departure of upper-class Venetians and foreigners from the bridges not only deprived their factions of essential financing but also lowered the overall prestige of the event. No longer protected by well-connected and powerful patrons, champions and ordinary fighters would increasingly have had to cope with police reprisals by themselves if they wished to keep on showing up at the bridges.

Moreover, it appears that popular support for the *pugni* also weak-ened in these same years, although as the result of different factors. One of these was a steady decline in the numerical strength and thus the battle fortunes of the Castellani faction. The long series of Turkish wars that began in the 1640s and lasted with few breaks until the first decades of the 1700s effectively stripped the Castellani ranks of many of their best fighters: those robust Arsenal workers and sailors who were sent east to fight and die defending the last remnants of the Venetian Empire. As a result, the battle-field relationship between the two sides apparently lost much of its tradi-tional equilibrium, and already by the 1650s the depopulated Castellani had begun to suffer an almost continuous string of defeats. Well aware of their numerical disadvantage, their leaders often tried to change the focus of the encounters from the all-out *frotta* to what would seem to be more equitable one-on-one duels between champions. Yet even restricting the battles to individual *mostre* could not guarantee the Castellani an equal contest. Having many more skilled fighters in their ranks overall, the Nicolotti chiefs could always send forth dozens more champions than their opponents could possibly meet, causing the Castellani an embarrassment as great as any actual defeat: that of having to let such challenges go unanswered.[8]

Of course, a more equitable contest could easily have been arranged for the *battagliole—frotta*, *mostre*, and all—if both sides had been willing to accept rules governing the timing, location, and progression of a battle, and most of all to regulate the number of combatants that each side could bring to the bridge. To treat the *pugni*, in other words, more as sport and spectacle than as war, much as the Medici dukes were successfully doing with their own elaborately staged *Giuoco del ponte* in Pisa. As already noted, many patrician fans of the *pugni* recognized the value of having a "sport-ing" contest at the bridges, where winning could be credited more assur-edly to strength and skill than to deceit, fraud, or illicit violence. It was a trend in the refinement of sport and games that would be followed (admittedly rather slowly) in both prizefighting and in such team activi-ties as cricket in the British Isles during the next 150 years, creating com-petitive conditions that would allow individuals and teams to acquire honor (and sometimes wealth) under circumstances that increasingly would guar-antee "fair play."[9]

Yet, in the end, Venetian workers proved unable to impose any lasting sense of boundaries and limits on the *battagliole*: probably this failure more than any other deficiency ultimately caused the *pugni*'s fall from public favor, among commoners as much as with the patriciate. Dominated by their intense factional antagonisms and the desire to win at any cost, the Castellani and Nicolotti saw no reason not to bring as many men as they could to the encounters, always in the hope that one more squad could tip the balance in their direction. Beforehand each side would travel as far afield as possible to make a general roundup (*rassagne generale*) of every possible supporter: on special occasions the Nicolotti would go as far as

Monselice and Este—70 kilometers away—in their search for able-bodied fighters. Both sides, in fact, appear to have kept up the hope that, given an army sufficiently large and cunning, it might be possible to triumph in a kind of "ultimate battle": an apocalyptical confrontation that would finish off their opponent once and for all. It was this intense desire to (as Saint Disdier put it) "bring about the entire ruin of the [other] party" that also induced both factions to come to the bridges with boats well filled with swords, daggers, pikes, and boat hooks.[10] The result, despite the best efforts of both noble enthusiasts and the police of the Ten, was the constant risk that the sporting pleasures of the *battagliole* would at any moment degenerate into sordid riot. Stonings, knifings, and mass stampedes that may have pleased some onlookers, but that could hardly have provided the sort of sporting conditions in which the more important participants—the *padrini, capi,* and factional champions—could expect to win much personal honor. And if the *pugni* could no longer be counted on to produce reputation for either individuals or their factions, the cult could not long survive. When the heroes of the *battagliole* finally began deserting the bridges for other stages on which to win public glory, the *pugni* were indeed doomed to suppression by the Ten.[11]

Fittingly enough, when the *pugni* went out, it was with a bang. Having attracted an inordinate number of fighters, the encounter of 29 September 1705 soon degenerated into the usual arguments and riot. When the *padrini* disagreed over who had won the final *mostra*, punches were exchanged, followed by a furious *frotta*, a rain of rooftiles, and finally the appearance of daggers and knives. At about the same time word reached the scene that fire had broken out across town, in the convent church of San Girolamo (ironically, considering that 29 September was San Girolamo's Day). In the normal course of things, the task of firefighting in Venice fell to special squads drawn from among porters, longshoremen, and the shipbuilders of the Arsenal; but all these were far too caught up in the melee at the bridge to want to leave the scene. Not until one of the priests of San Barnabà waded into the midst of this "tempest of stones" holding aloft a crucifix did the two sides finally desist from their brawling. Apparently, no one was killed, but thanks to all the delay and confusion the church of San Girolamo was completely gutted. Such lapses and excesses may well have convinced many citizens that partisans of the *pugni* had finally gone too far. In any case, when the Chiefs of the Council of Ten decided to move decisively to suppress the *pugni* once and for all, there seems to have been scant protest raised.[12]

Yet if the *battagliole* were no more, those workers who hungered for personal and factional honor had already long since begun to find other venues for earning reputation. Much of their energy would go to the regatta: those rowing competitions that had already been a feature of the city's unique culture for centuries. Singles, doubles, and group races (involving crews of twenty or more) produced their share of victors and popular champions, while allowing a level of display and public extravagance that could exceed even that of the *pugni*. Racing gondolas and the larger *peote* were often outfitted with whimsical decorations, with the oarsmen (who of course rowed while standing) elaborately clothed in the costumes of Persians, Hussars, or Turks. A least one custom of public recognition that had figured so prominently in the *pugni* appears to have been transferred directly to the regatta: popular portrait painters were soon busying themselves immortalizing the heroes of these races just as they had once done with the champions of the bridges; the only difference being that instead of striking a pugilist's pose for the canvas, winners were portrayed surrounded by the victory flags from the races they had won.

It is not altogether clear, however, that Castellani and Nicolotti contended against each other as factions in the regattas.[13] Such traditional rivalries were more likely to be expressed in the so-called *forze d'ercole*, another form of competition which required both great strength and considerable agility. Here twenty or more costumed participants from each side would attempt to amaze or shame their opponents by building the tallest and most elaborate human pyramid possible. Often starting on the none-too-stable platform of a raft in the Grand Canal, participants would hop and scramble up onto one another (a task made easier since those in the lower levels were linked to each other by yokelike wooden planks on their shoulders) until the final member of the company—generally a small boy holding a flag and a bottle of spumante—would scramble forty or more feet in the air, topping a pyramid composed of seven or eight layers of men.

Two of the essential elements of the *pugni* were thus preserved by these successor amusements: the regattas provided ordinary Venetian men and youths with a continued chance to win personal glory, and the *forze d'ercole* kept in existence a formal arena for factional competition. Both activities would continue for the remaining life of the Republic and beyond, as *la Serenissima* slipped from its role as a Mediterranean great power to one of Europe's first tourist centers. The regatta has endured in Venice, in one form or another, down to the present day. Partly it continues to provide a showcase for the prowess of the city's young men, but at its heart—like so much of what remains of the city—it is put on as an amusement for tourists. The *forze d'ercole* proved less adaptable to the changing times, however. The factionalism that seethed just below the surface of these seemingly innocent displays was bound to attract the attentions of the magistrates of France and then Austria that took over from the Council of Ten after the fall of the Republic in 1797. An especially tumultuous riot that broke out between Castellani and Nicolotti supporters in 1810 marked the beginning of the end of these human pyramids in the city.[14]

In the end, factionalism itself has finally disappeared from the Venetian social fabric. Having lasted by most accounts for a thousand years or more, the rivalry between the Castellani and the Nicolotti faded away, along with most other expressions of Venetian popular culture, under the combined

Figure E.1 Modern factional graffiti, near Campo Santa
Margarita, 1990.

pressure of stricter state controls, economic dislocations, political revolu-
tions, and above all the onslaught of a modern tourist trade that brings
visitors in the tens of millions to crowd a city that sadly is steadily more
depopulated of Venetians. Sly graffiti might occasionally turn up on the
back walls of the city (Figure E.1) but the factionalism that gave life and
identity to an entire populace—the great antagonisms that brought Castellani and Nicolotti to the bridges by the tens of thousands—has dissipated
for good, along with the Venetian people and their once remarkable culture.

NOTES

Abbreviations

ASV Archivio di Stato di Venezia

    ASV:ACP   Avvogaria di comun, penale

    ASV:CDP   Consiglio di Dieci, Proclami

    ASV:PS   Provveditori alla Sanità

    ASV:DSD   Dieci Savii sopra alle Decime

MC Museo Correr di Venezia

    MCAF   Archivio Fotografico,

    MCCC   Codici Cicogna

    MCPD   Miscellanea, provenenze diverse

bu *busta* (bundle)

mv *moreveneziano* (Venetians began the year on 1 March)

Introduction

1. From Caravia, "La verra antiga dei Castellani, Canaruoli, e Gnatti, con la morte de Giurco e Gnagni, in lengua brava" (Venice, 1550), stanza 1; reproduced in Gamba, *Poeti Antichi*, as "La Guerra de' Nicolotti e Castellani dell'anno 1521."

2. Whoever he was, the name of this *anonimo* already seems to have been forgotten by 1750, for in that year Doge Marco Foscarini referred to him in a footnote simply as "a certain writer, who eighty years ago wished to make a story out of [these events]"; see Foscarini, *Della letteratura veneziana*, 233n1.

3. Among the many pamphlets produced in observance of King Henry's visit, see M. Rocco Benedetti, "Le feste e trionfi fatte in onore di Enrico 3zo re di Francia" (Venice, 1574), held in the Museo Correr as MCPD. 11744; also see 11740–43, Sansovino, *Venetia, città nobilissima e singolare*; and Muir, "Images of Power," 44–45.

4. A fair copy of the same manuscript, transcribed onto ruled octavo paper and probably intended as a presentation copy to solicit patrician patronage, is held at the Museo Correr library, as codice Gradenigo 25; see also Emmanuele Cicogna, *Saggio di bibliografia veneziana*, 1:226–27.

5. MCCC 3161, 1574/53, 1635/13, 1639/1, 1668/1, 1673/15.

6. The Chronicler mentions other poets and writers on whose work he evidently drew: "Cornelio Frangipane, Nadal Zamboni, Giacomo Tiepolo, Gasparo de Greci . . . and various poets in Latin, especially Cesare Spinelli, Mario Finetti, and Bernardo Tossitano . . . indeed, the noblewoman Malipiera, being among the most famous poetess of the time could also not fail [the chance] to exalt . . . so great a conflict" (MCCC 3161, 1574/52). Such minor, perhaps amateur poets have left few traces, although Malombra's "Nuova canzone nella felicissima vittoria contro infideli," published in Venice in 1571, and Tiepolo's 1572 work of a similar title have both survived.

7. MCCC 3161, 1574/53. One such redoubtable fighter was Toni d'Alban from Burano, whose appearances in the Chronicle of the *pugni* span forty years: 1633/2, 1673/12.

8. The set of bundles, all written in the same hand, are loosely bound together as a single *busta*, held in the Museo Correr as MCCC 3161. They carry the overall title (in the hand of Emmanuele Cicogna) of "Guerra overo battagliola tra i Nicolotti e Castellani, 1632–1673." The two sections dealing with the background of the *pugni* are titled "Origine dei Castellani e Nicolotti" (not in the hand of the Chronicler and in octavo format) and "Principio delle Guerre tra Castellani e Nicolotti." Yet another bundle, titled "Libro Secondo," tells the story of the War of Candia, from 1645 to 1649. In the Chronicler's hand, it runs to twenty pages and contains brief references to the *pugni*.

9. That is, Antonio de Ville, *Pyctomachia venetia, seu pugna venetorum in ponte annua* (Venice, 1634) and Alexandre Saint Disdier, *La Ville et la République de Venise* (Paris, 1680).

10. Compare MCCC 3161, passim, with ASV: DSD, bu. 424 (1661), parish of San Barnabà: nos. 231–36, 434, 473–80; parish of San Nicolò: nos. 12 and 147; parish of Santa Margherita, nos. 188, 208–9, 296.

11. ASV:CDP, filza 20, 12 Jan., 15 Feb. 1632mv; filza 21, 9 Feb. 1633mv; filza 26, 14 Feb. 1652mv; filza 27, 3 March 1656; filza 34, 2 Sept. 1684; see also MCCC 3231, "La vittoria della Guerra e Mostre de pugni ottentute dalli Nicolotti contro li Castellani, 25 Feb 1687."

12. See ASV: Capi dei Consiglio dei Dieci, busta 1, *ruoli dei capitani*; also see ASV: CDP, filza 18, 12 June 1623; filza 20, 7 Jan. 1631 mv; and filza 34, 13 Nov. 1684. On the policing role of the Council of Ten and its Captains, see Chapter 4.

13. MCCC 3161, 1632/1–2; ASV: CDP, filza 20, 7 Jan. 1631mv.

14. My thanks to Brendan Dooley for pointing out the similarities between the Chronicler's descriptions of certain boxing matches in these early years and Tasso's depiction of the more chivalrous combat between Tancredi and Clorinda in book 12 of his *Gerusalemme Liberata*; also see MCCC 3161, 1632/6-9.

15. Indeed, he has the oarmaker Piero Moro call on "the great god Mars" in his prebattle oration: MCCC 3161, 1632/6–7; also see 1636/21, 1639/20, 1643/7, and 1667/31.

16. In particular, the Chronicler's tales of the theatrical comeuppance of the Ten's police Captains, one of whom has his mustache torn off by a young noble (MCCC 3161, 1638/7), while several others are lured away from the battle site and locked in a storeroom for the duration of the encounter (1635/2, 1637/3).

Both of these anecdotes were in fact recorded in the Ten's records, although at a somewhat earlier date; see ASV: CDP, filza 20, 7 Jan. 1631mv. The Chronicler's story of the patriarch of Venice disguising himself and going to an artisan's shop to beg him to agree to stage a *battagliola* is corroborated by Saint Disdier, *La Ville et la République de Venise*, 449.

17. The accounts of 1635 and 1636 are in a single bundle; that of 1671 amounts to little more than an afterward in the 1670 bundle.

18. MCCC 3161, 1665/3, 1667/21–22, and 38.

19. Darnton, *The Kiss of Lamurette*, 342–43.

20. As the Chronicler himself once put it, "We would expect that reading about these battles would not so easily bring boredom to the reader, [just] because those [of this year] are the same as the ones described earlier, and also like those that will follow, [since] the preparations, motivations, and extravagances of the events, on the part both of the leaders and of the [ordinary] soldiers will in any event always serve to make this history more interesting and indeed more attractive," see MCCC 3161, 1642/1.

21. Davis, *Fiction in the Archives*, 1–35.

22. MCCC 3161, 1637/10, 1641/11, 1673/15.

23. MCCC 3161, 1635/14, 1641/11.

Chapter 1

1. Sorsi, "Descrittione piacevole," stanzas 39 and 41.

2. MCCC 3161, 1136/20–21.

3. On the bridge battles in Pisa; see Heywood, *Palio and Ponte*, 93–137. On the reputation of Venetians for circumspection and sobriety, see Evelyn, *Diary*, 229, and Addison, *Remarks*, 73.

4. The decline in the numbers of bridges in the nineteenth century due to the wholesale filling in of canals has been largely made up for through the subsequent expansion of the city; see Rizzo, *I ponti di Venezia*, 14.

5. As late as 1180, some churches in the city center were still accessible only by water; see Rizzo, *I ponti di Venezia*, 11. For a recent bibliography on Venice's development during these first centuries, see Dennis Romano, *Patricians and Popolani* 162, nn. 4, 7 and 8; see also Dorigo, *Venezia: Origini*, 492–502; and Bellavitis and Romanelli, *La città nella storia d'Italia: Venezia*, 37–39; On the topographic features particular to Venice and their effects on urban life, see Perocco and Salvadori, *Civiltà di Venezia*, I:225–99.

6. MCCC 3276; Gallicciolli, *Delle memorie venete*, 1:97, 122, 2:265.

7. On the earliest Ponte di Rialto, see Bellavitis and Romanelli, *Le città nella storia d'Italia: Venezia*, 39.

8. Rock-throwing battles (*sassaioli*) were popular in medieval Perugia and Rome, while Ravenna, Milan, Modena, Novara, Pavia, and especially Pisa excelled in the so-called *giuocco del mazzascudo*, fighting "with wooden weapons, sometimes all together, sometimes two at a time; [with] a wooden helmet on the head and a padded breastplate of iron." In thirteenth-century Siena such bloody weapons were abandoned in favor of fists alone "as causing less scandal": Muratori, *Dissertazione sopra le antichità italiane*, also Heywood, *Palio and Ponte*, 138–96.

9. It must be noted, however, that knowledge of both these events only comes from much later sources: MCAF, M.24061; Gravembroch, "Partitante Castellano"; MCCC 3161, 1670/40.

10. While noting a battle at the Ponte di San Zulian, Sanudo also records edicts by the Ten "che non fusi più in alcun luogo di venecia le Bataiole come si feva per li campi"; see *I Diarii*, 9:332, 11:409, 13:304.

11. ASV: COP, filza 1, 12 Sept. 1505. Prearranged battles were known as *guerre ordinate*, an early example of which was the *battagliola* staged on the Ponte di Santa Fosca in 1493, for Ercole, duke of Ferrara, and his wife and daughters; see MCCC 3161, 1670/35.

12. For a wooden bridgelike structure that collapsed under the weight of the fighters, see MCCC 3161, 1673/13. One boat-bridge, still bearing the name of Ponte del Batelo, survived in Cannareggio into the nineteenth century. Rizzo, *I ponti di Venezia*, 56–57, 207.

13. Galicciolli, *Delle memorie venete antiche*, 1:246. Another of Venice's large bridges, that over the Cannareggio (the Ponte delle Guglie), had a history similar to that at the Rialto: first built of wood in 1285, it was not converted to stone until 1580; see Tassini, *Curiosità veneziane*, 121.

14. Perocco and Salvadori, *Civiltà di Venezia*, 242–50; Sanudo, *La città di Venezia*, 20; Sansovino, *Venetia città nobilissima*, 3, 456. By 1606 an English guidebook to Venice would write that "amongst eight-hundred bridges there are but two of wood," but this is almost certainly an exaggeration; see "A True Description," in *The Harleian Miscellany*, 80.

15. Some of the many bridges that had enjoyed a certain popularity in the sixteenth century but later fell out of favor include San Zulian, San Basegio, San Zuan Degolà, San Marcuola, the Crosera, the Gesuiti, Soccorso, Gaffaro, Ca' Marcello (Tolentini), and the Frescada; see Tamassia Mazzarotto, *Le feste veneziane*, 42, 50; MCCC 3161, 1632/7, 1633/11, 1665/18.

16. Tassini, *Feste*, 64–87; Tamassia Mazzarotto, *Le feste veneziane*; Padoan Urban, "Feste ufficiali," 592–94, 599; Bromley, *Remarks*, 88–89; Evelyn, *Diary*, 240. Thomas Coryat reported that in 1608 Campo San Polo was still covered in grass, as Campo San Pietro still largely is today: *Coryat's Crudities*, 1:385. For the concentration of shopkeepers around *campi*; see Beltrami, *Popolazione di Venezia*, 54–55.

17. On the development of parish churches and their community space in Venice, see Romano, *Patricians and Popolani*, 14–15; also Muir, *Civic Ritual*, 299–305.

18. Likewise, when Polo Morosini and Bortolo Orsetti decided to put on a "private" *battagliola*, they built a wooden structure to serve as a bridge in the courtyard of Morosini's palace, Ca' Marcello. The Sienese also built such a temporary bridge, when they decided to entertain the visiting emperor Charles V with a *battagliole* in 1536: MCCC 3161, 1633/6, 1668/1, 1670/26.

19. That access to the battle site should be limited was also clearly felt in other towns that staged popular battles in public squares. The Pisan *giuoco del mazzascudo* was held in the city's central Piazza degli Anziani, with entry for the two warring sides controlled by a circle of chains with openings (*bocche*) at either end: Heywood, *Palio and Ponte*, 101.

20. Rizzo, *I ponti di Venezia*, 14, 53, 84–85.

21. MCCC 3161, 1639/6; also 1649/3. On the pervasiveness of a ritualized "theater culture" in Venetian daily life, see Muir, "The Virgin on the Street Corner," 25–29.

22. Lane, *Venice*, 11–17; Tamassia Mazzarotto, *Feste veneziane*, 5. For such a chance encounter that led to blows on the Ponte della Madonetta in 1701, see

ASV:ACP, bu. 372/10. Such refuse heaps were known as *scoazeti*: MCCC 3161, 1667/22.

23. Not exactly matches, of course, but rather *lesca*, a precursor made of sulfur-soaked tinder. Their illicit use of such space, much like the African *vu comprà* in modern Venice, Florence, and Rome, could spark off quarrels and fights with local merchants; for an assault on the Ponte dell'Oglio, involving a woman "che dà la lesca per la città," see ASV:ACP, bu. 284/3. For other vendors who found a space for themselves on bridges, see Zompini, *Le arte che vanno per via.* For "beggars that are lame etc. [and] lie on bridges at church doors and beg," see Skippon, *An Account of a Journey*, 533.

24. Their arguments, brawls, and knifings are scattered through the criminal records: ASV:ACP, bu. 284/6 (Ponte dei Beccari); bu. 373/22 (Ponte di San Canciano); bu. 398/23 (Ponte Storto di San Martino); ASV: Quarantia Criminal, bu. 69 (Ponte Riello); ASV: CDP, filza 17, 9 March 1621 (Ponte di Noal). On bridges as the focus for spontaneous arguments and brawls, see MCCC 3161, 1667/62, 1673/12. For journeymen (*lavoranti*) involving themselves in such brawls: 1637/13, 1668/18, 1669/8, 1670/9.

25. MCCC 3161, 1635/24, 1639/21. Jumping and leaping—*saltando in faccia l'inimico*—was also practiced for provocation: 1669/12.

26. As in 1667, when "a company of youths from San Basegio [parish] came at around 9:00 P.M. with a great quantity of brands as far as the Borgo at San Trovaso, shouting raucously, `Viva! Viva Nicolotti!', sticking the lighted canes inside the doors and balconies;" MCCC 3161, 1667/39; also 1632/6, 1633/1 and 8, 1634/6, 1643/1, 1668/30.

27. Other versions held that the Eracleani came from Malamocco, on the Lido, while their rivals were natives of Jesolo; see Gallicciolli, *Delle memorie venete*, 1:122, 2:265, and *Cronica veneta*, 93.

28. MCCC 3161, "L'Origine dei Castellani e Nicolotti"; MCPD:303/C filza 33, 1–3; MCCC 3276, filza 2.

29. The obvious importance of the Grand Canal in dividing the city has led some scholars of Venetian social history to come to the logical but incorrect conclusion that it also marked the boundary between the Castellani and Nicolotti; see, for example, Paoletti, *Il fiore di Venezia*, 4, 61.

30. Cf Muir, *Civic Ritual*, 103–34, 299–305.

31. The story of Polo's assassination is repeated, with small variations, in MCCC 3161, "Origini," 3–4; MCCC 3278; MCPD, bu. 303/C-33, 3–4; and also in Tamassia Mazzarotto, *Feste veneziane*, 40. Ferdinando Ughelli, the great eighteenth-century chronicler of the Italian ecclesiastical hierarchy, neither confirmed nor exactly denied this legend, noting only that Ramberto (or Alberto) Polo, a Bolognese, was raised from bishop of Castello to succeed Bortolomeo Quirini as patriarch of Venice by Pope Boniface VIII in March 1303. According to Ughelli's sources, Polo's end was uncertain, for although he was clearly dead by 1311, he had ceased to function as bishop as early as 1309; see Ughelli, *Italia Sacra, sive de Episcopis Italiae* 5, 1272–73.

32. On their conflicts with the eel-fishers of Sant' Agnese; see MCCC 3161, 1643/1.

33. The fishermen were known as "the sinew and the defensive wall of all the Nicolotto army": MCCC 3161, 1637/5, 1667/21.

34. The Muranese ambition to be a third faction was asserted without evidence by the nineteenth-century Venetian essayist Alessandro Zanotti, who also

claimed that annoyance at their nickname drove them into the arms of the Castellani; the story is somewhat weakened, however, by the fact that the men of San Nicolò themselves were also referred to as Gnatti; see MCPD, bu. 303/C-33, 7; MCCC 3161, "Origins," 10, and 1670/32–33. The Muranese in any case remained rather inconsistent in their dedication to the *battagliole*, evidently not showing up in any force for years at a time: MCCC 3161, 1665/11.

35. These included the area around the church of Santa Caterina, the Fondamente Nove, and the now-eliminated Campo dell'Erbe, lying in the *contrade* of Santa Sofia and Santissimi Apostoli: MCCC 3161, 1635/6, 1666/29; Tassini, *Curiosità veneziane*, 223–24, 452–53. On the traditional assignment of the Cannareggio *sestiere* to the Nicolotti; see MCPD: 303/C, filza 33, 3.

36. Its location as a Castellani bastion deep in the heart of Nicolotti territory appears to have made the Ponte di San Silvestro a favorite spot for brawls, though for just this reason it was never used for larger *battagliole*: MCCC 3161, 1649/13, 1666/30, 1667/47. For a *scorreria* mounted by the Rialtini against a Nicolotti festival held in Campo San Polo, see 1637/12–13; also see 1632/17, 1633/4, 1643/5, 1667/47.

37. The likelihood that there was a special link between San Canciano and Murano is further supported by the existence of a direct *traghetto*, or ferry, connecting the two communities (still recalled by the Sottoportego del Traghetto behind the church of San Canciano). On the *specchieri*, see MCCC 3161, 1640/7, 1667/30, and 50; ASV:PS, bu. 568 and 570, *San Canciano*; Lane, *Venice: A Maritime Republic*, 310; Rizzo, *Ponti di Venezia*, 224; Tassini, *Curiosità veneziane*, 119.

38. The exact meaning of Bragolini remains unclear. Boerio and others suggested that it may refer to those of the somewhat unsavory Castello *contrada* of San Giovanni in Bragola, but it may also have indicated those who wore the baggy knee breeches (*braghesse* or *bragoni*) favored by arsenalotti and sailors: MCPD 303/C, filza 33, 6–9; MCCC 3161, "L'Origine," 8–11; Tamassia Mazzarotto, *Feste veneziane*, 49n6.

39. By the eighteenth century, after the *battagliole* had been finally suppressed, factional colors had changed: the red beret and jacket had become the distinctive element of the Castellani, while the Nicolotti wore black. Although later writers have assumed that the factional colors that dominated competitions of the 1700s were the same as those of the *battagliole*, the Chronicler of the *pugni* made quite the opposite clear, noting in his report of 1632 the arrival of "all the squads and companies of all the territory from S. Nicolò, dressed in red as is their custom"; likewise, for 1640, he noted how "all the *capi* of the Nicolotti were dressed in red": MCCC 3161, 1632/8, 1630/4; also 1638/4, 1639/6; cf. Tamassia Mazzarotto, *Feste veneziane*, 41, and Padoan Urban, "Feste ufficiali," 583.

40. For such factional confrontations in the Pescaria di San Marco, see ASV: ACP, Penale, bu. 144.22, and MCCC 3161, 1643/1; in the Pescaria di Rialto: 1640/7; on the Grand Canal: 1668/2; along the Mercerie: 1635/11. On the great two *pescarie* of Venice, see Molmenti, *Venice*, 2:2, 136–37.

41. MCCC 3161, 1642/8.

42. MCCC 3161, 1667/44. For a recent overview and bibliography on this Jewish community, see Zorattini, "Gli erbrei a Venezia, Padova e Verona"; on festivities surrounding the cult of the *pugni*, see Chapter 3.

43. The punch was strong enough to knock the captain off the bridge and into the water. Simon was sentenced to a year in the prisons *al scuro*, but

was released after the rather hefty fine of one thousand ducats was paid on his behalf—raised perhaps by other members of his community: MCCC 3161, 1637/4.

44. As with the Pontesello (the "little bridge") of San Barnabà church, which the Nicolotti once proposed for an encounter, but "where never in the memory of men had a war been held, for the bridge was inconvenient [and] even more [because] it was a bridge with parapets." The Ponte di San Silvestro, no doubt along with many others, by contrast was held to be too steep (*precipitoso*); see MCCC 3161, 1642/7, 1667/47.

45. MCCC 3161, 1639/8 and 17. The Ponte dei Gesuati, which lay along the Zattere, was demolished in the 1800s when its canal was filled in. The Ponte di San Basegio, which lay to the west up the Zattere, was avoided by the Castellani because it presented similar dangers, "not only of rocks and stones, but what is worse, of firearms, this being the *contrada* where there live the greater part of the *Officiali da Barca* [state customs officials, also known as *scarafoni*], impetuous people, who only enjoy brawls and other devastations": 1673/7; also see 1633/ 7.

46. For the Muranesi complaining that when at battle in Venice, "they were [too] far from home to change clothes and care for themselves," see MCCC 3161, 1665/12. A leader of the Nicolotti once complained to the Castellani, who wanted to stage a *battagliola* on the Ponte dei Gesuati; "You have a thousand advantages and a thousand conveniences: without traveling, you come out of your houses armed, a privilege that your opponents do not enjoy, because they have to set out very far from your territories, with a thousand discomforts and adversities": 1673/ 10. Local squads were also in a good position change to prepare the battle site to their advantage: 1639/13.

47. An exchange of such sham offers was made in 1638, when the Castellani invited the Nicolotti to come do battle on the Ponte di San Domenico di Castello, and the Nicolotti reciprocated with an invitation to come to the Ponte di San Nicolò. Both bridges were deep within factional territory, and neither offer was taken seriously; see MCCC 3161, 1638/1–2, 1639/14.

48. As some Castellani chiefs once asserted while arguing over which bridge to choose, "We would rather go to the Carmini or to San Basegio and lose—if fate should so rule—in the enemy's house, than in our own territory": MCCC 3161, 1639/11.

49. Much as in the modern Palio of Siena, where horses are assigned to *contrade* by lot. Drawing a superior horse puts the seemingly lucky *contrada* into a difficult position, since winning a victory with such an animal will necessarily lower the accomplishment in the eyes of rivals, while losing will bring far greater shame than a defeat suffered on an inferior mount; see Dundes and Falassi, *La Terra in Piazza*, 62–63.

50. "While the Castellani could not suffer to be conquered *in casa propria*, the Nicolotti ardently presumed to exalt their own audacity, in their [enemy's] own territory": MCCC 3161, 1639/9; also 1638/9, 1673/3.

51. MCCC 3161, 1634/6, 1642/6.

52. Thus, when the Castellani once occupied the *piazza di mezo* of San Barnabà, "it was unpleasing to the people, because they had passed their proper borders": MCCC 3161, 1666/24.

53. MCCC 3161, 1670/10; de Ville, "Pyctomachia venetia," 5. The nearby bridge at the Campo dell'Erba also enjoyed a certain popularity with the factions,

especially in the 1660s: 1667/47, 1668/30–31, 1673/12; but also see 1632/14 and 1641/3.

54. The Castellani generally landed in Cannareggio at the Corte Vecchio and Corte Novo, or at Ca' Lezzo, at the foot of the Fondamenta della Misericordia: MCCC 3161, 1635/4, 1636/17, 1643/3. On the Ponte dei Servi as lying in Nicolotti *casa propria*, see 1638/10.

55. For indications that the Ponte dei Pugni was narrow (*angusto*) and that the site had been *aggiustato* by both factions, see MCCC 3161, 1673/6.

56. The Ponte di San Marziale was evidently the first to be so adorned, on 26 May 1670, after it had been rebuilt; at some later time, however, the four *impronte* were evidently removed and placed on the Ponte di Santa Fosca, where they remain to this day: MCCC 3161, 1670/10; also Nalin, *Pronostici e versi*, 15.

57. MCCC 3161, 1639/7.

58. The Chronicler of the *pugni* may have exaggerated the noise of the crowd, but there is every likelihood that the Venetians, with their tens of thousands of private boats and gondolas and a well-known enthusiasm for the *battagliole*, could easily have filled the Canale della Giudecca to witness a prearranged *querra ordinata*: MCCC 3161, 1639/15–16. On the literary and artistic efforts generated as a result of the *battagliola* for Henry III, see 1574/52.

59. For the collapse of the Fondamenta della Tagliapietra, at San Barnabà, under the weight of "three hundred or more" spectators, see MCCC 3161, 1665/17; also 1666/5.

60. MCCC 3161, 1670/10. On the degradation of the Ponte dei Gesuati, which was missing many of its cut stones and had a number of bricks "broken and out of square," 1673/11; for the bad state of the *fondamenta* at the Ponte dei Pugni of San Barnabà, 1668/24. The so-called "Little Ice Age" and its effects on Venice are surveyed by Jean Georgelin, in "Venise: Le Climat et l'histoire," *Studi veneziani* n.s. 18 (1989): 313–19.

61. "Since on the Nicolotti side the *piazze* [of the bridge] were in some part decayed, [with] missing and broken stones . . . [various Nicolotti leaders] had put down where they were needed some planks, which they had taken with violence from the storeroom at the Ponte Largo": MCCC 3161, 1639/9. For the replacement of *pietre cotte e vive* on the Ponte di Santa Fosca, see 1635/4.

62. On factional arguments breaking out among friars and nuns "even in their own convents," see MCCC 3161, 1673/12.

63. Much like the residents of modern Siena are born into their *contrade*; see Dundes and Falassi, *La Terra in Piazza*, 12–13.

64. It was also said that "those who entered Venice from the side of Chioggia were counted as Castellani, and those who arrived by way of Mestre or by Fusina were known as Nicolotti": Saint Desdier, *La Ville et la République de Venise*, 439. On eminent spectators being "courted and followed" by factional partisans, see MCCC 3161, 1636/19, 1637/6.

65. MCCC 3161, 1649/2.

66. MCCC 3161, 1632/3, 1635/4, 1637/5, 1667/32. At the same time, before a pending *battagliola*, those from outlying areas might also send a delegation to Venice, to inspect the proposed battle site: 1673/12–13.

67. For Bigolo Sanser, a Castellano who kept his loyalties undercover in the Nicolotto parish of San Giacomo dell'Orio, see MCCC 3161, 1642/7.

68. MCCC 3161, 1635/11, 1640/7.

69. Saint Disdier, *La Ville et la République de Venise*, 439. This sort of resis-

tence against crossing factional lines to find a spouse still holds in present-day Siena, where many still see a marriage between residents of rival *contrade* as inappropriate or even offensive: Dundes and Falassi, *La Terra in Piazza*, 70, and note.

70. These marriage figures and the godfather figures presented below were taken from the *libri di matrimoni e battesimi* for the decade 1661–1670 in San Trovaso parish, which now includes the old parish of San Basegio. Endogamy rates (for both marriage and godfathers) in the two parishes ranged from 28 to 45 percent in this decade. On the high rates of artisan endogamy in seventeenth-century Venice; see Davis, *Shipbuilders*, 89–90.

71. MCCC 3161, 1668/1–2. On brothers acting together in affairs or fights related to the *pugni*: 1633/9 and 13, 1641/7, 1666/28, 1673/3. On *compari*, see 1632/7, 1638/7, 1642/6. For a Nicolotto who converted "to the Castellani sect" at the urging of his godfather (and who was promptly beaten up for it), see 1642/7.

72. De Ville, "Pyctomachia venetia," 4. Saint Desdier did assert, however, that the Castellani were "considered *plus honnestes gens* than the Nicolotti, being also more attached to the nobility and more zealous for the government"; see *La Ville et la République de Venise*, 440.

73. No contemporary confirmation is evident for this claim, however, which may have little more foundation than certain other nineteenth-century legends about social life during the Venetian Republic; see Casoni, "Storia civile e politica," 189.

74. MCCC 3161, 1635/13. As happened to "Rizzo the clog maker from the Campo dell'Erbe, one originally of Nicolotti birth who had turned Castellano after a falling out with . . . Giacomo Zavatin [a Nicolotti leader]; whence being recognized mixed in with the Castellani squads, he was by the furor of the Nicolotti with punches and kicks trampled in the middle of the bridge, [such that] he died after the course of three days"; 1637/9. A Castellano who went over to the Nicolotti when his friend was chosen as their policing captain suffered a similar fate; see 1668/35 and 1642/7.

75. Here the Chronicler concluded by indulging in one of his many puns on names: "And so Cenerin was converted into ashes [*cenere*]": MCCC 3161, 1635/14.

76. MCCC 3161, 1635/14, 1673/15. For more on the military spirit in the *battagliole*, see MCCC 3231, "Le Vittorie delle Guerre e Mostre de Pugni Ottenute dalli Nicolotti contro li Castellani, 25 Feb 1687"; and Sorsi, "Discrettione piacevole della Guerra dei Pugni."

77. The enduring importance of the parish and neighborhood in many Italian cities, especially for workers and women of all classes, has recently begun to receive more serious consideration; see Muir and Weissman, "Social and Symbolic places in Renaissance Venice and Florence," 81–103.

78. In most encounters, a certain number of fighters—perhaps as many as 20 percent—were not identified by the Chronicler as coming from any neighborhood or occupational group, but were simply referred to as *gente fra terra*, presumably meaning they came on their own, individually or in twos and threes, with no particular affiliation; see MCCC 3161, 1634/7, 1641/9, 1667/22.

79. MCCC 3161, 1642/2. On the importance of guilds in structuring popular society in Venice, see Romano, *Patricians and Popolani*, esp. 77–90, and Mackenney, *Tradesmen and Traders*, esp. 4–7, 44–65, 133–49.

80. In the end, three died and eleven were badly injured, including some on-

lookers: MCCC 3161, 1670/9. Another time some cobblers brawled in the otherwise factionally peaceful neighborhood of San Filipo Giacomo, leaving two dead: 1641/11.

81. Indeed, it has been suggested that the flowering of the *battagliole* in the first half of the sixteenth century was directly related to the contemporary rise of these two worker communities; see Élisabeth Crouzet-Pavan, *"Soprs le acque salse": Espaces, pouvoir, et société à Venise,* 669–75.

82. MCCC 3161, 1673/4. The *Barche dei Miracoli* are recorded coming back to the city roughly once a month: at Michaelmas (29 Sept.), All Saints Day (1 Nov.), Saint Andrew's Day (30 Nov.), Christmas/Saint Stephen Day (25/26 Dec.), and Candlemas (2 Feb.); 1635/3, 1639/2, 1640/2, 1641/2 and 4, 1642/3. On the Nicolotti fishing community, see Roberto Zago, *I Nicolotti,* esp. 129–43.

83. The overshirts they habitually wore also earned them the nickname "la gente delle camisole." The term Paluani, "the men of the swamp (*paluo*)," evidently was a reference to their residence on the backside of San Nicolò parish; see MCCC 3161, 1635/5, 1637/1, 1640/4, 1641/8, 1642/4, 1665/13, 1667/32.

84. MCCC 3161, 1635/6. Another time, annoyed that a battle had been started without them, the Paluani, "obstinate and stubborn," refused to fight, and went home leaving their comrades to suffer defeat, saying, "Only those who have started it deserve [what they get]": 1643/5.

85. MCCC 3161, 1642/4, 1673/8.

86. On the importance of their naval experience in shaping the *arsenalotti* community, see Davis, *Shipbuilders,* 150–82.

87. MCCC 3161, 1639/5; also see 1638/9 and 1640/4.

88. MCCC 3161, 1634/2, 1635/9, 1637/6.

89. MCCC 3161, 1641/8.

90. MCCC 3161, 1667/22, 1673/2.

91. MCCC 3161, 1637/9, 1639/17; Rizzo, *Ponti di Venezia,* 110; Romano, *Patricians and Popolani,* 148–49.

92. MCCC 3161, 1665/13, 1667/10.

93. Further indicating that Venetian factionalism was founded more on geography than on the workplace, the Gnesotti and the Zuecchini attended their enemy's victory celebrations in San Nicolò parish: "as [their] relatives and companions in the fishing boats"; see MCCC 3161, 1667/42. On the dress of the Gnesotti: 1669/25.

94. MCCC 3161, 1633/4, 1640/7, 1641/8, 1643/7, 1667/22–23. The Chronicler of the *pugni* once identified "the most distinguished territories" of the Castellani as the neighborhoods of "the Giudecca, Saint' Agnese, San Luca, and [San Piero di] Castello": 1667/27; also 1669/9.

95. MCCC 3161, 1643/7, 1666/29.

96. For the Campo delle Gatte; see MCCC 3161, 1634/14, 1641/8. For the Fondamente Nove, Santa Caterina, and Campo dell'Erbe, see 1666/29. For Santa Marta, Fosse Capera, and the Arzere, see 1643/2 and 7, 1665/3 and 20.

97. Also sometimes referred to as the Baresi, they were considered among the "più forti et esperimentati" of the Nicolotti: MCCC 3161, 1637/8, 1640/8. For other possible origins of the name Bari, see Tassini, *Curiosità veneziane,* 59.

98. MCCC 3161, 1667/22–23.

99. MCCC 3161, 1638/5.

100. MCCC 3161, 1639/14–15, 1643/3.

101. MCCC 3161, 1642/6, 1673/3.

102. MCCC 3161, 1634/1.
103. MCCC 3161, 1667/22–23.
104. In his social profile of Venice, Beltrami divided the city into three concentric zones, which might be called "central," "intermediate," and "peripheral." With the exception of fighters from San Luca and the Rialtini, all the fighting squads came from the two outer urban circles; see Beltrami, *Popolazione di Venezia*, 47–48.
105. MCCC 3161, 1667/30.
106. MCCC 3161, 1668/2 and 14.
107. MCCC 3161, 1632/2. Workers could find themselves physically barred even from supposedly "popular" entertainments put on by the state, as in 1782, when those who went to Piazza San Marco hoping to see the bullbaiting staged by the government for visiting Russian nobility were instead kept away from the action by barricades; see Tamassia Mazzarotto, *Feste veneziane*, 3.
108. MCCC 3161, 1641/2.
109. MCCC 3161, 1642/6, 1643/8, 1649/7, 1670/12. On such occasions, the doge proceeded with the patriarch and the entire ruling elite of the regime along a ceremonial route from the Palazzo to San Marco, where he heard high mass, see 1641/2; Casolo, *Viaggio a Gerusalemme*, 108 (English trans., 338). Even on minor saints' days, the doge and the Venetian *Signoria* would make the required procession to the basilica. On the ritual ordering of the Venetian center, see Muir, *Civic Ritual*, 189–211, and map on 9.
110. This ritual agenda, the mainstay of Renaissance and baroque regimes throughout Europe, held sway in both religious and more strictly secular ceremonial occasions; see Muir, *Civic Ritual*, 203–4, 211–12, 250. For a recent overview of the expression of civic harmony in baroque Venice, see Doglio, "La Letteratura ufficiale e l'oratoria celebrativa," 163–87.
111. MCCC 3161, 1642/3. See Chapter 4.
112. When the Russian ambassador, along with the Prince and Princess Collona and *altri Cavallieri d'Italia* were among the spectators, the fighters "punched with insanity, because everyone wanted to make himself be seen [as] excelling and a winner to the Muscovites and to so many *Cavallieri*": MCCC 3161, 1668/5.
113. Crouzet-Pavan has recently asserted that the *battagliole* themselves offer evidence to the contrary: "Moreover, the rapid evolution that, in the 1540's, ties the two factions of the Nicolotti and the Castellani . . . to a strong socio-professional identity [as fishermen and shipbuilders] demonstrates the weakness of the spacial base of the celebration and confirms the contemporary hardening of the urban socio-topography": see Crouzet-Pavan, *Espaces, Pouvoir et Societè à Venise*, 675. She has evidently not taken into account, however, the strong presence of other neighborhood squads that shows up in the Chronicle of the *pugni*. For an up-to-date bibliography on the long-standing debate surrounding the movement of urban Italians from neighborhood to communal center and its resulting impact on the origins of capitalism and civic government, see Muir and Weissman, "Social and Symbolic Places," 101–3.
114. Some have even seen the late Renaissance as the "parochial age" in Venice, as the state actually began returning certain policing and charitable functions to the parishes in the wake of the Tridentine reforms; see Pullan, "The Scuole Grandi of Venice," 272–301. On Venice's "Disenfranchised Masses," see also Muir, "Images of Power," 51; and "The Virgin on the Street Corner," 32.

Chapter 2

1. Sorsi, "Descrittione piacevole," stanza 154.

2. "'Se è da scherzo, è troppo; se è da vero, è poco'": MCCC 3161, 1574/45; Roffaré, *La Repubblica di Venezia e lo sport*, 183.

3. Sorsi, "Descrittione piacevuole," stanza 60.

4. MCCC 3161, 1666/25.

5. Compare with the rules that had already been drawn up for the Sienese Palio and the bridge battle at Pisa by the seventeenth century: Dundes and Falassi, *La Terra in Piazza*, 72 and note, and Heywood, *Palio and Ponte*, 110–31.

6. Saint Disdier, *Le Ville et la République de Venise*, 438–52; see also de Ville, "Pyctomachia venetia." On Venice as a growing tourist attraction by the later seventeenth century, see Burke, *Historical Anthropology*, 188–90.

7. MCCC 3161, 1634/13, 1635/6, 1637/3 and 7, 1639/9, 1640/4, 1641/1, 1643/3, 1665/1. Also see Geertz, "Thick Description: Towards an Interpretive Theory of Culture," in *The Interpretation of Cultures*, 3–30.

8. Such was still the custom years after the *guerre di canne* had been abandoned. Their efficiency could not be better attested to than by a Castellano named Andrea, who was himself a *zacco* maker. Once, when caught in a factional ambush, Andrea "received more than one thrust, but the strength of his extremely fine *zacco* saved his life, though he received such a violent jab in the fabric of the *zacco* that the point of the pike became stuck"; see MCCC 3161, 1640/11; also 1634/8, 10. For two occasions when cheaper *zacco* failed to withstand the thrust of a pike, see 1634/13, 1667/62.

9. Tamassia Mazzarotto, *Feste veneziane*, 41–43.

10. MCPD, 303/C, filza 33, 5–8; Roffaré, *La Repubblica di Venezia e lo sport*, 186–87; Tamassia Mazzarotto, *Feste veneziane*, 44.

11. The Ten were quite specific about their ban, threatening anyone "who dared get up on the *Ponti di Guerra* with sticks or pointed rods (*bacchetti con la punta*)" with five years in the galleys; see ASV: CDP, filza 6, 22 July 1574; also filza 7, 15 Jan. 1575 mv; and MCCC 3161, 1670/32.

12. MCCC 3161, 1670/30 and 37.

13. MCCC 3161, 1634/10, 1637/3, 1642/1.

14. MCCC 3161, 1670/32.

15. By the 1670s the skills for using one's fists against an armed opponent were being taught to Dutchmen as well, by Nicolaas Petter and Robbert Cors in their illustrated manual, *Klare Onderrichtinge der Voortreffelijcke Worstel-Kunst* (Amsterdam, 1674); cited by Schama, in *The Embarrassment of Riches*, 584–86. Schama also links such training to a republican and egalitarian ideology.

16. MCCC 3161, 1637/9, 1670/18. The same apparently held true for visiting sailors and for squads coming from up the Brenta (toward Padua), who, as "people who were not very experienced," were compared unfavorably with "the stronger and more skilled [men] of the [Lista dei] Bari": 1637/8, 1670/6.

17. MCCC 3161, 1670/29. For an account of a *guerra di pugni* staged in Parma by the Nicolotti and Castellani on the occasion of a ducal wedding in 1690, see MCCC 3276, filza 13/5–6.

18. The Ten first indicated their recognition that Venetian workers had changed from *canne* to *pugni* in 1586, although the transition had no doubt been underway for some years; see ASV: CDP, filza 8, 30 Dec. 1586.

19. Not surprisingly, real stick fights between individuals did continue to break

out in the city at large, since so many *popolani* kept up the habit of going about armed with *legni*; see MCCC 3161, 1635/12, 1636/16 (in the Calle del Rimedio), 1638/6 (at the Ponte di San Sebastiano), and 1642/3.

20. Already by the 1630s there appears to have been a sense that wearing a *zacco* at the battle was somehow unsporting, though in the especially heated *battagliola* staged at the Gesuiti in 1639 some *zacchi* were reportedly brought to the site in boats by the Castellani; see MCCC 3161, 1635/12, 1639/19; on the danger of wearing *zacco* and drowning: 1633/8–9.

21. As with the Scalleter, leader of the Castellani: approaching the bridge, he first "took off his *ferrariolo*, and then his red hat, along with his usual black clothes, conspicuous and worthy. [Then] with a small beret on his head, very honorable, he betook himmself to the *piazza* of the bridge, to open discussions with his adversaries": MCCC 3161, 1649/8.

22. As in 1634, when a sudden *frotta* left the canal at San Barnabà littered with floating *cappelli, ferrarioli, e gabbanelle*: MCCC 3161, 1634/10. On factional leaders keeping on their *ferrarioli* as an indication of noncombat status, see 1633/11, 1668/25. By the following century the *ferrariolo* would evolve into the rather more familiar *tabarro*.

23. MCCC 3161, 1668/14, 1670/2. For an accusation by the Ten against a gang of *bravi*, said to have been going about without *ferrarioli* "to be the better disposed to carry out their evil thoughts," see ASV: CDP, filza 17, 18 Dec. 1621.

24. MCCC 3161, 1639/8, 1640/2, 1642/2. The Chronicler once also made a somewhat disparaging reference to "*le persone da Ferrarioli* and [others] unskilled at combat": 1667/35. If their faction's fortunes became truly desperate, however, the *genti dei ferrarioli* might also throw off their overcoats and plunge into the battle: 1638/9, 1641/10, 1667/60. It was considered blameworthy for an overexcited fighter to attack the *ferrarioli* during a battle: 1639/15.

25. As with Toni d'Alban, who came to the bridge "dressed all in white but girdled with a red sash": MCCC 3161, 1649/9; also a certain Ridi who appeared in the *mostre*, "with a naked chest, without corselet and without a cap, since he did not sport a *zazzara*": 1666/12–13. Fighters wore their hair braided (*ingroppati*) for easier control: 1666/23; also 1666/7, 12. On arranging one's clothing to protect the kidneys, see Saint Disdier, *La Ville et la République de Venise*, 444.

26. *Scalfarotti* were slipperlike, without soles; see MCCC 3161, 1666/23, 1667/11, 1670/2. Some fighters might also kick off their shoes beforehand and fight barefoot: 1667/36; on rings: 1670/25.

27. Saint Disdier wrote that for the *guerre ordinate*, fighters would put on "cuirasses of *carte argentée*, with which they covered their seminude bodies as much for the beauty of the show as to ward off the effect of the blows"; see *Le Ville et la République de Venise*, 450; also MCCC 3161, 1634/3, 1635/9, 1643/3, 1668/34. For the complaint of a Nicolotto *capo* that an opponent "who wants to make the *mostra* with me has put on two or three *cassi*, one above the other," see 1667/36.

28. Nor did the Castellani cheer to their usual extent when Bonhomo was nearly killed by his opponent as the result of a single blow to the chin, since "he himself was the portent of his own mortal fall, by appearing dressed in mourning clothes": MCCC 3161, 1668/7. Stramatel's patron was one Alvise Armelini, whose name in Venetian did indeed mean "apricot": 1642/4–5.

29. Saint Disdier, *La Ville et la République de Venise*, 444; MCCC 3161, 1668/ 20; Hendricks, "The Democratization of Sport in Eighteenth-Century England," 12; W. Russell Gray, "For Whom the Bell Tolled: The Decline of British Prize Fighting in the Victorian Era," 54. That both right- and left-handed gloves were made available, see 1633/5: that they were made to measure, see 1670/4.

30. MCCC 3161, 1632/3, 1635/4, 1637/5, 1641/4, 1665/8, 1667/23.

31. The Chronicler wrote at length about the Castellano Vicenzo Tartaro, who was accused of fighting with a glove "sewn with three passes of stitching of lute string, the one above the other between the fingers, such that in hitting it should scratch the face"; see MCCC 3161, 1668/20. For *guanti forti*: 1649/8, 1670/ 33; for long gloves on the right or both hands: 1665/14, 1666/23, 1667/11 and 33.

32. MCCC 3161, 1667/11 and 33; for a similar description of the appearance of a black fighter, "who aroused unusual admiration from everyone," see 1665/14.

33. MCCC 3161, 1636/19, 1640/3, 1667/35, 1668/23, 1673/10. On fighters who battled more enthusiastically near the *pagliazzi montuosi* "because falling they knew they would fall secure, without injury, being protected by the straw," see 1639/5 and 1641/7. On excavating the canal and clearing it of "stones and poles driven in near the bridge," see 1632/3-4. On the use of sawdust, often supplied from the state Arsenal, see 1635/10, 1668/33.

34. Thus some Nicolotti squads once came to the Ponte dei Gesuiti and "quickly filled the convent of the Jesuit Fathers, and for greater convenience they demanded to break [a hole in] the wall of the monastery wall and make a door ... for the advantage of their left flank.... Such damage was stalwartly forbidden by the Fathers, not wanting to ever permit it, although the popular voices thundered resoundingly": MCCC 3161, 1639/15. For a large door (*portone*) that the Nicolotti did manage to break through the external wall of a workshop near San Barnabà, see 1665/1.

35. Although the actual price for a seat was not recorded, Coryat noted that it cost two *soldi* for a similar sitting place to watch a game of *calcio* at Campo Santo Stefano: *Crudities*, 1:385. In the eighteenth century it cost ten to fifteen *soldi* for a place on such *palchi* erected for a bullbaiting; see Tamassia Mazzarotto, *Feste veneziane*, 3. *Palchi* were usually put up in haste the night before a battle, if only to avoid the attentions of the police of the Ten; sometimes they were even thrown up during the fights themselves: MCCC 3161, 1641/5, 1643/2, 1670/ 14. On the collapse of these "towering bleachers occupied by an infinity of spectators": 1635/5-6, 1640/3, 1668/9. On food sellers, see Sorsi, "Descrittione piacevole," stanza 85.

36. For the *battagliola* held at the Ponte di Santa Fosca in 1635, "to have a convenient window it was thought nothing to pay out as much as ten *scudi*"—the equivalent of perhaps two month's income for one of the workers fighting below; see MCCC 3161, 1635/4; also 1670/37. One such house was operated by a certain Signora Venere Mendarossa, perhaps a courtesan, who quarreled with an unnamed Roman gentleman after he refused to pay for his place: 1666/4. The marquis di Fluentes, ambassador of Spain and an habitual supporter of the Nicolotti, watched the battles at Santa Fosca from above a pergola that looked out on the bridge: 1641/10.

37. MCCC 3161, 1632/4. As Sorsi put it: "Tanti, e tanti fu i palchi, e soleretti / Su gondole, su piate, su batelli / Su tressi storti, travi, e trabuchelli / Spende

lirazze, da otto, e grossetti"; see "Descrittione piacevole," stanza 11. Wealthier spectators, if they were not satisfied with the view promised them, might come after the landlord with drawn swords: 1668/28.

38. MCCC 3161, 1637/1, 1643/1.

39. As Philip Skippon noted, "St. Barnaby's bridge is noted for a fight at fisty-cuffs every Sunday in warm weather, between the Castellani and the Nicolotti, two factions maintained among the common people": Skippon, *An Account of a Journey*, 515.

40. As when "Matteo the Barber was inciting the sons [of the *contrade*] to go to the end of the [bridge] steps to provoke the Nicolotti": MCCC 3161, 1635/1; also see 1639/1, 1666/20–21. For a young gang of *Rialtini* led by an elder fighter: 1637/12–13.

41. MCCC 3161, 1669/12; also 1635/24, 1639/21, 1666/1; Saint Disdier, *La Ville et la République de Venise*, 441.

42. At such moments the *piazza di mezo* was considered as "beyond the rightful territories" of either faction; see MCCC 3161, 1666/24; also 1667/35.

43. MCCC 3161, 1634/6. The sign of a particularly successful *scorreria*, as one old Arsenal worker once reminisced, was when "we went right into where . . . they [the Nicolotti] lived and just at our appearance they locked their doors and balconies, not knowing in what hole to hide themselves [*cazzarse*]": 1632/7.

44. Apprentices in particular liked to load up their roomy work aprons (*traverse*) with stones before coming to the bridge; see MCCC 3161, 1634/9, 1642/6, also 1666/2.

45. MCCC 3161, 1666/16.

46. Excellent examples of such escalating conflicts are MCCC 3161, 1666/7–8, 1667/1 and 49, 1669/19. Older fighters might start joining in the groups of youths as early as 24 June, the feast day of Saint John the Baptist: 1669/1.

47. The *capi* of the fighting squads should not be confused with the *Capi*, or Chiefs, of the Council of Ten, the three nobles elected in monthly rotation to head that magistracy (and on whom see Chapter 4); or with *capi di guerra*, a general term used by the Chronicler to describe all factional leaders.

48. As with "Chieppa of Sant' Agnese, of the family of the Chieppi, most famous warriors": MCCC 3161, 1665/17. On the recruiting activities of *capi*; see 1634/11, 1643/2–3. On their disciplining fighters at the bridges: 1639/8–9. That, compared to ordinary fighters, they were known to be "tougher in their hatred and revenge" on behalf of their faction than other fighters: 1667/41.

49. Most *capi* were indeed residents or worked among the contingent they led; see MCCC 3161, 1633/1, 1639/19. An exceptionally large squad, and evidently considered by the Chronicler as worthy of special comment, was that of "Capo Matio Manarin, who came armed and ready at the head of all his company of 150 picked men": 1667/38.

50. de Ville, "Pyctomachia venetia," 5.

51. Toni d'Alban, *caporione* of the contingent of Murano, for example, once decided to inspect the appointed bridge several days before a *guerra ordinata*. In so doing, he appears to have brought his entire squad with him, for he came "in a cutter [*peota*] accompanied by many followers, not only in his boat but in many other small boats": MCCC 3161, 1673/12. The distribution of food and wine to workers and apprentices by *capi* was, of course, essential if fighters were to feel free to take off from their work before a battle: 1632/13, 1635/4.

52. MCCC 3161, 1633/11, 1635/6, 1666/22, 1667/16, 1668/10. It was no doubt largely thanks to the particular skills of their *capi* that some squads could for a time enjoy a superior reputation. One example were the "the Mirror-makers [of San Canciano], who in these days flourish in particular esteem": 1667/58. On the *capi's* customary use of an *insegne*—perhaps a flag—to rally their followers, see 1632/7, 1665/5, 1667/28 and 30.

53. On boats filling the *rio*, see MCCC 3161, 1637/6, 1638/7. On crowd sizes, see 1639/16, 1667/22; also 1632/11.

54. No doubt this was yet another reason why Venetians preferred to stage their *battagliole* on bridges. On the nobility's tendancy toward violence, see MCCC 3161, 1636/22, 1640/6, 1643/2; Ruggiero, *Violence,* 66–70. For occasions of panic among audience members, see 1632/10, 1633/10, 1666/5.

55. MCCC 3161, 1639/3 and 16, 1667/11 and 52, 1669/7, 1670/20.

56. On the spying activities of Heraclito Famagosta, *cipriota,* see MCCC 3161, 1632/8. For a Nicolotto spy discovered in Castellani territory at San Barnabà, see 1667/1. For a Castellano *padrino* boasting about the skills of his faction's *confidanti,* see 1667/32, also 1632/4, 1637/7, 1639/19, 1666/7, 1667/60. On dangers to the *trapassati,* see 1638/8, 1639/9, 1667/10, 20.

57. MCCC 3161, 1666/3 and 29.

58. MCCC 3161, 1667/13. For the example of a battle at the Ponte di Campo dell'Erba, where, thanks to the lack of any factional leadership, control of the bridge shifted "ten or twelve times," see 1667/47.

59. MCCC 3161, 1632/7, 1635/1, 1640/3, 1666/23.

60. MCCC 3161, 1639/2, 1667/22. Older leaders might also prevent their enthusiastic youths from carrying out such symbolically charged acts, however, warning that putting black on the bridge "could portend evil results in the [subsequent] fights": 1639/7. On the *moresca,* see 1635/12.

61. As on 2 Aug. 1665, when the Nicolotti agreed to stage ten *mostre* against fighters from the weaker Castellani contingent, on the condition that a *frotta* would follow; see MCCC 3161, 1665/7.

62. The Castellani once agreed to hold *mostre* only on the condition that, starting completely off the bridge, each side would advance its troops one step every two matches, until, after six *mostre,* they would both arrive at the *piazza di mezo* and then start the *frotta*: MCCC 3161, 1649/8. On being refused a request for *mostre,* see 1666/3. On being forced to admit defeat as a precondition for *mostre,* see 1666/8.

63. Sorsi, "Descrittione piacevole," stanza 28; "Applauso alla vittoria conseguia," stanza 7; Saint Disdier, *La Ville et la République de Venise,* 441–47.

64. MCCC 3161, 1635/1. So successful were the Nicolotti at such posturing that once twenty of their fighters in a row presented themselves without getting a match from the Castellani, with the result that "not only the Nicolotti soldiers but all their supporters sought with offensive and very insulting words to humiliate the enemy, charging him with fear and cowardliness": 1639/2. On a challenger's reputation for scaring off potential opponents, see 1665/12, 1666/18.

65. As when Chieppa, "Castellano famoso" was sent in *mostra,* and "not finding an encounter, loudly challenged Barbuzza of San Nicolò . . . who responded that when it comes to making a *mostra* against him, he would more than happily serve [Chieppa], but that now there was not time enough": MCCC 3161, 1640/8. Also 1669/9, for the example of a challenged fighter who tried to excuse him-

self, but with considerably less honor, on the grounds that a match was impossible since the factional leaders were quarreling among themselves.

66. When the famous Mazzagatte once presented himself in *mostra*, "there appeared a good many brave and valiant [Castellani] youths to meet him, but for some time it was not possible for the padrini to control them, because they kept pushing each other down from the *piazza* with considerable contempt and anger ... since they all fought together for the chance to confront him": MCCC 3161, 1666/21; also see 1634/3, 1665/12, 1667/9, 1668/8.

67. MCCC 3161, 1637/7; the Chronicler took it as normal that one should show off (*faceva pompa di se stesso*): see 1666/13. On selecting fighters to go in *mostra*: 1633/2, 1639/2, 1667/2.

68. In the duels of gentlemen, the term *padrino* was used interchangably (perhaps depending on the region) with *maestro, avvocato,* or *pattino*; see Bryson, *The Sixteenth-Century Italian Duel*, 37. Followers of the *pugni* might also use the term *paregno*, or stepfather, instead of *padrino*: Sorsi, "Descrittione piacevole," stanza 23; "Applauso alla vittoria," stanzas 6 and 8. Saint Disdier used *padrino* (*parin*, or *parrain*), as did the Chronicler of the *pugni*, except on rare occasions, when for some reason he too used *paregno*; see, for example, MCCC 3161, 1632/10 and 13; 1637/2.

69. On *padrini* making tactical decisions during the *frotta*, see MCCC 3161, 1634/13. On their declaring victory or defeat or clearing the bridge, see 1635/9, 1638/10, 1668/11. On their role as active fighters, see 1642/5. For a duelist who refused to fight "without the presence of *padrini*, to assure that they could fight together with equality," see 1668/17.

70. In particular because passions ran higher for these *mostre principali* and could easily lead to battles with knives and rocks without prestigious *padrini* on the scene; see MCCC 3161, 1639/2; also see 1637/2, 1641/1–2, 1667/27. On occasion an unpopular *padrino* could be shouted off the bridge, even by those of the other faction; see 1669/8, 1670/17. For *padrini* choosing themselves, see 1643/2, 1668/10. On their being elected, see 1668/18.

71. MCCC 3161, 1669/3.

72. MCCC 3161, 1670/5. According to Saint Disdier, the *arengo* was "a plain, square area of around four or five paces long, until the steps that descend on either side, and three or four paces wide, paved with bricks and bordered with cut stones without parapets or guardrails"; see *La Ville et la République de Venise*, 432–33. How the term *arengo* made the semantic shift from its medieval sense of a civic assembly to that of a boxing arena is not clear; this usage appears to be restricted to the Chronicle of the *pugni*.

73. Such a gesture was seen as sufficiently threatening that an opposing *padrino* once physically attacked the offender; see MCCC 3161, 1639/4; also 1667/35.

74. MCCC 3161, 1667/35, 1670/2; Saint Disdier, *La Ville et la République de Venise*, 442–43.

75. Sorsi, "Descrittione piacevole," stanza 156; on fighters who sought great initial impact and the importance of their starting each round from their corners, see MCCC 3161, 1632/10, 1642/5.

76. The *padrini* were to see that the two fighters were "arranged at their places in positions of equality," (*agiustati al loro posto di ugual positura*), and that neither tried to start the combat too close to the middle of the *arengo*: MCCC 3161, 1642/5; also 1666/13, 1668/16 and 26, 1669/3. It was to stabilize the starting posi-

tions of fighters and *padrini* that the marble *impronte* were placed on the bridge surfaces of San Marziale and San Barnabà: 1670/11. Despite the tightness of the *arengo*, it was not unknown that two pairs of fighters would box at the same time; see 1670/6.

77. It is possible that the actual duration of the *salti* was open to negotiation; see MCCC 3161, 1643/3. The Chronicler once indicated that sixty matches (specifying that each were of three *salti*) were held in three hours: 1668/34–35. For an occasion when there were more than a hundred *mostre* ("although twenty-five of these did not find an encounter"), see 1669/4.

78. Thus a fighter named Frate was heard to say after three rounds that "[t]hree *salti* were enough, from which it was concluded that he lacked the strength and the wind. Seeing himself at some advantage, [his opponent] Mazzagatte responded that he would want to keep on fighting until one or the other was defeated or broken [*rotto*]": MCCC 3161, 1668/16; also 1669/5. On the *padrini* setting the number of *mostre* beforehand; see 1634/3, 1635/5.

79. On winning by a knockout, see MCCC 3161, 1668/7. On winning by an opponent's voluntarily withdrawing, see 1667/12 and 16, 1668/10.

80. The two or three black fighters who make their appearance in the Chronicle of the *pugni* seem to have enjoyed a certain advantage because when the *padrini* came to check their faces for bleeding, "in so much black one could not clearly see the blood"; see MCCC 3161, 1641/3; also 1668/2 and 16, 1666/9 and 14. Much less honor was to be had from a fight that ended in a draw if both opponents simply gave up at the same time: 1667/14.

81. Although the left-right combination was clearly not unknown: MCCC 3161, 1669/6. "The correct position," according to de Ville, was to hold "the left arm like a shield in front of the mouth, and the right clenched in a fist to strike the adversary"; "Pyctomachia Venetia," 6.

82. Saint Disdier, *La Ville et la République de Venise*, 443. That fighters could be knocked down and still continue the fight, see MCCC 3161, 1667/5. On *fianconi* and fighters' being attacked by spectators, see 1668/2, 1670/13.

83. MCCC 3161, 1637/3; 1642/4; 1667/2; 1668/3, 22, 26; 1670/7. On the public's contempt for fighters who only grappled or pulled each other's hair, see 1642/4, 1666/9.

84. For a Castellano *padrino* stressing that his faction's *capi* and fighters were "especially esteemed for their experience and mature age," see MCCC 3161, 1667/31.

85. *Capi maturi* were necessary if squads were to be disciplined to the peak of *virtù e obbedienza*; see MCCC 3161, 1633/3, 1636/1, 1637/7, 1666/9. On a fighter trying to attack mocking onlookers; 1641/6, 1666/27.

86. MCCC 3161, 1636/15. Manone was apparently still appearing in the *mostre* thirteen years later; 1649/2. Duelists who were distinctly past their prime could be roughly treated by young contenders, however: 1669/7.

87. For such duels fought on workdays, see MCCC 3161, 1649/6; 1668/2, 13, 29; 1670/1, 4, 6. For the continuing rivalry between Manone and Capo Michiele, 1634/3, 1636/15, 1639/1, 1640/9. For the rivalry between Moro Negro and Toni d'Alban: 1641/1, 1649/6.

88. MCCC 3161, 1637/11, 1638/1, 1639/2, 1641/1, 1666/20, 1668/2 and 14, 1669/5, 1670/5.

89. MCCC 3161, 1649/8, 1667/5, 1668/29.

90. MCCC 3161, 1633/6, 1666/18 and 22.

91. MCCC 3161, 1666/11 and 19, 1669/10, 1670/2. The proscription against attacking a rival when he was down was established firmly enough for Saint Disdier to list it as his first rule of the *mostre*, going on to observe that such a man would be considered "a coward, unworthy of fighting"; see *La Ville et la République de Venise*, 443. On fighters who only grappled: 1637/3, 1665/15, 1666/9.

92. MCCC 3161, 1666/22. For two duelists who "certainly gave each other more than thirty-nine heavy punches in the face [without] either moving the other bodily, which made one believe that they had agreed together [beforehand] on such a feeble offense and defense," see 1636/19.

93. For his legalistically minded readers, the Chronicler of the *pugni* explained that the kiss was a sort of contract, to indicate that "the combatants freely, of mutual consent . . . [risk] their own lives, and to such effect renounce every privilege of indemnity"; see MCCC 3161, 1670/26.

94. MCCC 3161, 1670/29. Along with their initial kiss, fighters might also embrace and touch fists; see 1668/8. On *padrini* kissing and embracing to begin the *mostre*, see 1637/7. There was no kiss, of course, if one of the fighters had been knocked unconscious or thrown into the water, but kissing was especially appropriate when a *mostra* ended in a draw: 1635/6, 1641/3, 1669/6.

95. After a *battagliola*, however, the Venetians' comparatively "civilized" outlook could sometimes work to their disadvantage, for less forgiving foreigners might try to revenge themselves on local fighters for insults or injuries suffered during an encounter: MCCC 3161, 1667/2–3.

96. Where matches of three or four hours and over fifty rounds were commonplace in the eighteenth century; see Miles, *Pugilistica*, 1:1–132.

97. MCCC 3161, 1641/3, 1642/4, 1666/25, 1668/9. On a fighter "struck on the chin [*barbuzzo*] with the first punch and falling to the ground as if dead," see 1667/11.

98. "There is no prize for the most valiant other than the glory of it and the reputation that they acquire of being fearsome"; see Saint Disdier, *La Ville et la République de Venise*, 446.

99. Nor is there any indication that renowned duelists would go into business for themselves, opening boxing schools or pubs, as retired prizefighters would later do in Britain; see Gray, "For Whom the Bell Tolled," 54; Miles, *Pugilistica*, 5–6, 29–30, 162–63.

100. On a fighter's leaving his rival *rotto e molto mortificato* with a chance cut after only one round, see MCCC 3161, 1642/4.

101. MCCC 3161, 1668/13. If a fighter refused to admit defeat after falling into the canal and, soaking wet sought to return to the arena and summon his enemy to continue the match, he would most likely be laughed off the bridge: 1670/8. Considered especially amusing was the sight of two duelists falling off the bridge together, still eager to continue the fight in the water, but not knowing how to swim: 1667/2; also see Saint Disdier, *La Ville et la République de Venise*, 447.

102. Saint Disdier, *La Ville et la République de Venise*, 446; MCCC 3161, 1666/48. Thus, the final tally might run something like "Out of sixty *mostre*, twenty-seven turned out in favor of the Castellani, for the Nicolotti seventeen, and the others of equal force"; 1668/34; also 1669/2.

103. On the enduring appeal of the Venetian reputation for social harmony, see Muir, "Images of Power," 16–19 and note 2.

104. MCCC 3161, 1668/33–34.

105. MCCC 3161, 1634/4, 1636/1, 1637/8. Sometimes a *frotta* was touched off by one of the onlookers punching a duelist in the *arengo*: 1642/5.

106. MCCC 3161, 1635/6, 1643/3, 1667/5, 1668/12, 1669/19, 1670/18.

107. MCCC 3161, 1634/3–4, 1637/8, 1639/4, 1641/6, 1668/22. For occasions when the factions were unable even to get the first two duelists into the *arengo* before a *frotta* broke out, see 1640/4, 1643/3.

108. In 1666 Nicolotti partisans found a textile worker who agreed to take on this rather risky task for five ducats: MCCC 3161, 1666/7.

109. MCCC 3161, 1635/5, 1639/8, 1641/5, 1643/4, 1668/24.

110. When the *frotta* first broke out, the *padrini* would have to move quickly to get out of the way, if they were not to be caught in the middle of the ensuing brawl and be forced to jump in the water to save themselves: MCCC 3161, 1636/20; also 1641/6, 1649/11, 1669/13. They were in any case unwilling to risk destroying their clothing, which was generally "honorable, and of [high] price and value": 1667/50.

111. For a Nicolotti scheme "to disperse 150 of the most esteemed soldiers . . . who were to never let themselves be seen [but] to remain hidden in the Convent of the Servi, and to whom was given the order that when they heard the explosion of two firecrackers, they should precipitously come to the bridge well prepared": MCCC 3161, 1637/9.

112. On the role of the *groppo* in a successful *frotta*, see MCCC 3161, 1642/5, 7. For a *groppo* that lasted a full hour: 1638/9, also 1639/4 and 16, 1649/12, 1667/37.

113. The Chronicler often provided such figures, which were clearly highly approximate; see MCCC 3161, 1634/4 and 13 (one hundred falling in the water each time); 1635/9 (two hundred men; the whole Castellano force on the bridge); 1637/10 (three hundred from both sides); 1639/5 (the Nicolotti and all their *padrini*); 1641/9 (at the large Ponte di San Marziale, "more than four hundred people, the largest *groppo* that has ever been seen to fall in our age . . . such that every one believed that the bridge itself had broken"); also 1632/4, 1636/20, 1639/17, 1643/4. On Nicolotti climbing on top of their trapped companions: 1636/21, 1667/54.

114. Well aware of this, *padrini* would sometimes urge their men to concentrate simply on pushing their opponents into the water, "not caring at all about carrying themselves onto the bridge": MCCC 3161, 1668/11 and 24, 1669/15.

115. MCCC 3161, 1667/10–11, 37. On the tendency for superior fighters to end up *trapassati* and unable to get back to the action, see 1667/54.

116. MCCC 3161, 1667/38. Sometimes, indeed, the *frotta* ended in a draw, with both sides too exhausted and depleted to go on fighting: 1667/57. In any case, victories obtained in the dark, even with *canne accese*, were always considered somewhat illicit: 1638/9–10, 1639/11. For the Spanish ambassador holding out a candle to see better from his balcony overlooking the bridge: 1641/10.

117. Although it was considered a sign of *bestialità* when squads were so enraged that they "wanted to contest the impossible" in attacking a heavily defended bridge: MCCC 3161, 1669/12.

118. On the other hand, when fighters came ashore with their faces and hands covered with mud, "having made themselves black, not unlike charcoal burners," it was considered tremendously funny: MCCC 3161, 1666/20; also 1634/13,

1641/6. On various injuries sustained in and out of the water during the *frotte*, see 1632/4, 1633/12, 1634/14, 1638/8, 1639/10, 1668/6.

119. After one such *scioglimento*, "many fell onto the shore, [some] breaking their heads, others [their] arms and legs on the hard stone; [such] laments and tearful voices were heard that everyone was moved to pity"; see MCCC 3161, 1634/5; also see 1639/17 for "30 soldiers half dead in Campo Sant' Angese, trampled in the *frotta*."

120. ASV: PS, *Necrologie*, Buste 842 and 843, 5 Sept. and 1 Oct. 1611; also bu. 865, 29 Oct. 1634 and MCCC 3161, 1634/15. Also see 1665/18 for a similar, fatal panic in 1621 at the Ponte di Ca' Marcello. For deaths from trampling or hitting one's head against the bridge abutments: 1637/8, 1641/11; from drowning: 1639/22; from punches: MCCC 3258, 2 Aug. 1665.

121. MCCC 3161, 1641/11, and the section titled "Libro secondo," dealing with the War of Candia, p. 1.

122. MCCC 3161, 1636/16, 1640/7, 1641/10, 1642/7, 1649/1, 1666/12; also see de Ville, "Pyctomachia venetia," 7–11. On the free availability of wine at the bridges: 1639/20, 1640/3.

123. In particular, see Dunning, "Social Bonding and Violence in Sport," 227–40.

124. On the importance of a fighting reputation for making oneself a *capo*; see MCCC 3161, 1640/5. For a young fighter who first made himself "truly worthy of praise for his actions in battling [in the *frotte*]," before moving on to the *mostre*; see 1666/10, also 1667/18.

125. Among the many factional chiefs who made this sort of progress up the *pugni* hierarchy were: Bastian the Biscuit Maker (or *scaleter*, *capo* 1635–1639, *padrino* 1640–1649), Chieppa of Sant' Agnese (fighter in 1633, *capo* 1635–1649), Coppo of San Nicolò (*capo* 1633–1638, *padrino* 1640–1643), Grinta of San Nicolò (*capo* 1633–1639, *padrino* 1640–1641), Moro Muschier (fighter in 1632, *capo* 1633–1639, *padrino* 1640–1643), and Toni d'Alban of Burano (fighter 1633–1649, *caporione* 1667, *vecchio venerando* 1673).

126. Saint Disdier, *La Ville et la République de Venise*, 442; MCCC 3161, 1649/2, 1666/24. On the rights and prerogatives of the Venetian *cittadini*, see Lane, *Venice: A Maritime Republic*, 151–52, 266; Romano, *Patricians and Popolani* (who also refers to the Venetian nonnoble elite more generally as *popolo grande*), 32, 36–37, 83–89, 145; Pullan, *Rich and Poor in Renaissance Venice*, 99–131.

127. MCCC 3161, 1639/15, 1641/1, 1643/8, 1666/27.

128. MCCC 3161, 1637/5 and 10, 1639/1, 1665/1, 1666/28. The *padrini* might also meet at the neutral island of San Giorgio Maggiore, where "there was prepared a rather considerable lunch for ten, and where, between the [wine] glasses and generous liquors, they determined the time and the means to bring their soldiers together to battle": 1670/17.

129. MCCC 3161, 1632/4 and 6, 1642/3.

130. MCCC 3161, 1667/27, 1669/10 and 13, 1673/4. At the Ponte dei Pugni, the Nicolotti *vecchi* gathered at the Corte of the Tagliapietra, in Santa Margherita parish; the Castellani met in the Corte del Botter, then called the courtyard of the houses of Pietro Balanzan, opening on Campo San Barnabà; see ASV: DSD, bu. 424, San Barnabà, nos. 231, 234–36; also 1639/2. On addressing the factions, see 1632/8, 1639/7. On sending out factional spies, see 1667/1. On receiving visits from enemy "ambassadors," see 1666/22–23. Also, Finlay, "The Venetian Republic as a Gerontocracy," 157–78.

131. As happened in 1639, when it came to the attention of the *vecchi* of San Nicolò that a local fighter named Lorenzo Piva was plotting a "vendetta with all manner of ruin and misfortune" against the opponent who during a *frotta* had squeezed him in the testicles "almost to the point of dying." Three of the *vecchi* went to Piva, who as one of the government's *ufficiali di barche* was well known for being precipitous and belligerent, and persuaded the man to give up his talk of revenge by ambush—on the grounds that such wrongs should better be satisfied in some future battle: MCCC 3161, 1639/10; also 1639/6, 1642/6, 1667/50.

132. On underemployment and the conversion of Venice from a trade and manufacturing to a service economy, see Rapp, *Industry and Economic Decline*, 96–106, 121–26, 164–67; Braudel, *Civilization and Capitalism*, 3:132–35; Grubb, "When Myths Lose Power," 64–65.

133. On the exploitative organization and low status of the city's porters and longshoremen, see Forsellini, "L'Organizzazione economica," 91–95. For a "squad of *piateri* from the Zattera, [fighting] with their usual bravura," MCCC 3161, 1665/19–20.

134. That is: *calegheri, pignateri, scaleteri, barbieri, fruttaroli, gallineri, lasagneri, scortegadori, crivelladori, portadori da vin, sartori, tesseri, fenestreri, pennachieri, stramazzeri, scoazeri,* and *dai lotti.* Venice's host of "street trades" was evocatively portrayed in Gaetano Zompini's *Le arte che vanno per via nella città di Venezia*; many of these hawkers and vendors may well have established their trades in an attempt to evade the city's stringent antibegging laws; see Pullan, *Rich and Poor*, 296–310.

135. For groups of *servitori* battling while their masters watched nearby, see MCCC 3161, 1641/7, 1666/30, 1668/1–2. For servants coming to the support of a master who decided to get personally involved in the fighting: 1667/53.

136. Saint Disdier, *La Ville et la République de Venise*, 441. As Sorsi put it ("Descrittione piacevole," stanza 85):

I servitori abbandona i Paroni
No i s'arecorda d'esser ubligai,
Che con le file al Ponte despoglai
I vien . . .

The servants abandon the masters
Not remembering their obligations,
Except to come with their squads
Stripped down to the bridge.

137. ASV: ACP, bu. 204/7. For edicts of the Ten against Piero Chielelin, Battista Sponzeretto, Paulo "Moro" Muschier, Lazaro "Ballon" of Quintevalle, and Iseppo "Mazzahuomeni" (all *padrini* or *capi* of the Castellani); and Lorenzo Zampa, Nicolotto fighter, as well as both Tonin da San Luca and his son Cesare, for various crimes unrelated to the *battagliole*, ranging from theft to assault to murder, see ASV: CDP, filza 13, 12 Sept. 1611; filza 20, 12 Jan. 1632mv; filza 26, 14 Feb. 1652 mv; filza 27, 27 May 1653 and 15 Aug. 1654; filza 28, 3 March 1656. Also MCCC 3161, 1666/19.

138. At least three hundred of those present were said to have been Giacomo's factional enemies—Castellani shipbuilders from the Arsenal: MCCC 3161, 1637/5 and 10; also 1637/5, 1673/1–2. On worker sodality in funerals, see Davis, *Shipbuilders*, 24–25.

139. See Crouzet-Pavan, "*Sopra Le Acque Salse*," 669–75.

140. On the status (and the profit) which artisans of more prestigious guilds derived from their connections to the city's elite and from state processions and festivals, see Mackenney, *Tradesmen and Traders*, 141–49, 180–81; Romano, *Patricians and Popolani*, 77–90.

141. Geertz, "Deep Play: Notes on the Balinese Cockfight," 432–42.

142. MCCC 3161, 1632/6, 1637/10, 1670/1.

143. Never perhaps more graphically asserted than when a veteran fighter persisted in returning to the bridge "with a bandaged head and his arm in a sling"; see MCCC 3161, 1670/12.

144. MCCC 3161, 1633/6–7.

145. MCCC 3161, 1639/22, 1641/11.

Chapter 3

1. Sorsi, "Descrittione piacevole," stanza 250.

2. MCCC 3161, 1667/41; Saint Disdier, *La Ville et la République de Venise*, 441; MCCC 3257, 20 Sept. 1662.

3. MCCC 3161, 1633/6, 1640/6, 1667/16.

4. The literature on the role of honor in Mediterranean culture has become vast, but its key themes on the links of honor to social status, power, and culture are still to be found in Pitt-Rivers, "Honour and Social Status," 21–77.

5. Political privilege—the right to vote in the Great Council—was reserved for (and indeed played a large part in defining) the nobility alone; see Finlay, *Politics in Renaissance Venice*, 23–24,

6. Beccaria, *An Essay on Crimes and Punishments*, 34; Thamer, "On the Use and Abuse of Handicraft: Journeyman Culture and Enlightened Public Opinion in 18th and 19th Century Germany," 295–96.

7. "Is your stomach feeling queer?"; literally, "Have you eaten a badly cooked omelette?" "Pitch eater" (*magna-pegola*) and "crab catcher" (*pia-granzi*) were derisive terms for *arsenalotti* (who worked with pitch and oakum) and fishermen (who were supposed to catch fish, not crab); see Caravia, "La verra antiga," stanzas 8–10; also stanzas 11–14, 17, 29–31.

8. MCCC 3161, 1667/20; 1668/9, 21, 25; 1670/15.

9. MCCC 3161, 1669/6.

10. Thus, during the preparations for the failed *battagliola* of 1673, wherever the *capi* of the two factions went around the city, they were "followed by a cloud of people . . . a lengthy throng of partisans and followers [who] surrounded and besieged them with exceptional anxiety to know what they had . . . chosen to do"; see MCCC 1673/2, 5, 8; also 1637/7, 1667/31–34.

11. Cf. Pitt-Rivers:

> Honour, therefore, provides a nexus between the ideals of a society and their reproduction in the individual through his aspiration to personify them. As such, it implies not merely an habitual preference for a given mode of conduct, but the entitlement to a certain treatment in return. The right to pride is the right to status . . . and status is established through the recognition of a certain kind of social identity. ("Honour and Social Status," 22).

12. MCCC 3161, 1633/1, 1637/5, 1649/8, 1665/14, 1666/14, 1667/26.

13. MCCC 3161, 1667/21, 31, 35, 55; 1668/21; 1673/8.

14. MCCC 3161, 1667/27, 1669/10, 1673/4. On the largess of the *capi* in

Venice, see 1632/13, 1635/4. On the general importance (and implicit problems) of generosity for gaining honor in Mediterranean culture, see Pitt-Rivers, "Honour and Social Status," 60; Herzfeld, "'As in Your Own House': Hospitality, Ethnography, and the Stereotype of Mediterranean Society," 75–89.

15. MCCC 3161, 1649/8. As the Chronicler rhapsodized, "Who could it be? Who could it be? In whose breast reign deeds [so] *generose* that he does not run hurriedly to the Bridge, like the deer to the longed-for spring?" 1670/26. All public behavior was judged more honorable if it were carried off without obvious effort; see Muir, "The Virgin on the Street Corner," 29.

16. MCCC 3161, 1641/4, 1666/11, 1668/8; Beccaria, *An Essay on Crimes*, 33–37; Pitt-Rivers, "Honour and Social Status," 22–27; Elias, "An Essay on Sports and Violence," 150–60; Brailsford, "Morals and Maulers: The Ethics of Early Pugilism," 126–42.

17. "Tomè" was evidently short for Tomaso; on his brothers, Iseppo (Giuseppe) and Checo (Francesco, also known as "Panchietta"), see MCCC 3161, 1665/12.

18. MCCC 3161, 1666/27, 1673/2. When, during preliminary negotiations, the Castellani leaders once attempted to confuse matters by asserting their desire to fight at an unusual bridge, Tomè "responded with no more than a laugh that was indeed contemptuous and marvelous [to hear]": 1673/7. For an example of his speaking ability: 1667/34.

19. MCCC 3161, 1665/14. Such was Tomè's own self-esteem that he might refuse to serve as *padrino* unless he considered his Castellano colleague to be of equal stature; see MCCC 3161, 1668/22.

20. MCCC 3161, 1667/40; also see 1667/41, 44.

21. MCCC 3161, 1667/32; Tomè was indeed referred to by the Chronicler as the "*capo* esteemed and honored also by the Castellani themselves": 1668/21.

22. MCCC 3161, 1635/12, 1667/21 and 44, 1669/6.

23. MCCC 3161, 1668/19. Similar paintings of champion bullfighters (*tiratori di tori*) were put on view in the *campi* before a bullrunning; see Tamassia Mazzarotto, *Feste veneziane*, 5. The Chronicler of the *pugni* also observed:

> [I]f some private or public festival or observance is made in the city, especially those held for the inauguration of the Procurators of San Marco, at times when the Mercerie are decorated with the most precious objects, [including] pictures and artwork, there are also shown for greater glory portraits of some Castellano or Nicolotto soldier [*bravo*] along with paintings that show battles on the bridges. (MCCC 3161, 1670/40).

24. MCCC 3161, loose inserts at 1667/21 and 22.

25. The Nicolotti of the Lista dei Bari offered a more carnivalesque response to the Castellani provocations, building a cage (*berlina*) outside their local wine tavern and imprisoning inside, not the effigy of an opposition *padrino*, but of Bacchus, evidently as a comment on the considerable drunkenness during the previous disorders. Under the figure, they placed a placard that read:

> Senteve quà, sior Bacco,
> Za che veddo che sè stracco

> Signor Bacco, stay here a while,
> Since we see that you are tired!
> (MCCC 3161, 1639/21, 1667/21).

26. MCCC 3161, 1668/14.

27. The poem was republished in 1603, under the title "La guerra de' Nicolotti e Castellani dell'anno 1521"; under this title it also appeared in Gamba, *Collezione delle migliori opere scritte in dialetto veneziano* (Venice, 1817). For the poem's citations in the Chronicle of the *pugni* (misattributed, however, to a certain Pantalon dei Tresi, in 1585), see MCCC 3161, "Origine delle guerre," 5–6, and 1670/31–35.

28. MCCC 3161, 1635/14, 1637/10; also see 1667/46, 1668/14. Philip Skippon appeared to have once encountered just such a procession:

> We observed one day a funeral passing the streets. First came a cross, then banners, [and] surplice-men singing before the corps, which is laid out on a bier, dress'd up in a monk's habit. . . . Just before it went a mourner in friar's weed, with his face covered . . . and only a lighted taper in his hand; and after it followed a great number of men, two and two together, with lighted tapers in their hands; which tapers were given by the deceased's friends. (*An Account of a Journey*, 510).

According to Fynes Moryson, even the funerals of commoners in Venice could be magnificent and "take up a long way in the streetes"; see *Shakespeare's Europe*, 455–57.

29. Caravia, "La verra antiga," stanzas 185–86.

30. MCCC 3161, 1635/7, 1639/4, 1665/14, 1666/13, 1667/52, 1668/13, 1669/5, 1670/3.

31. As when the Chronicler speculates that a certain Barzaga, when defeated, was "*storno*, I do not know if from the pain of the punches or the loss of his reputation": MCCC 3161, 1670/16, 1666/27; also see 1635/2, 1637/13, 1639/12, 1665/15, 1666/3, 1668/18, 1670/15, 1673/9. For *mortificato* in the sense of a physical wound: see 1665/17.

32. Partisans were quite aware that there could be no honor without shame, as the Nicolotti made clear after losing to their rivals in what they claimed was an irregular battle: "[Since it was] unnecessary to feel the shame of [losing] this war—which was neither provided for nor agreed upon—therefore it should not merit either honors [*corone*] or celebrations"; see MCCC 3161, 1667/21.

33. MCCC 3161, 1670/12. This was, admittedly, an extreme case, and many a fighter's own faction felt compelled "to blame him and indeed to shame him with severe admonishments and scolding for his cruelty"; but see also: 1669/12. For a fighter "unable to bear the ardor and pretension" of his rival and the applause which it attracted: 1666/3; also 1641/3.

34. They rarely were allowed a second match, if only because other duelists were eager to have their turns; see MCCC 3161, 1665/14, 1666/27, 1668/13, 1669/6.

35. MCCC 3161, 1639/21, 1642/4, 1666/27, 1667/12 and 14.

36. On the constantly turning *ruota di fortuna*, see MCCC 3161, 1634/11, 1635/9, 1639/10, 1665/14, 1666/13, 1668/13, 1673/9.

37. De Ville, "Pyctomachia venetia," 16. The contrary, however, was possible. For example, after a number of Nicolotti fighters and spectators were injured by a collapsing wall near San Barnabà, the Castellani were said to have been moved to pity, "because they never wanted to see their rivals mortified by misfortune or the dangers of bad luck, but rather by the [Castellani] on the bridges": MCCC 3161, 1668/27. A fighter might also return to the battle "seeking to avenge the wrongs that fortune had done [him]": 1668/32.

38. As with the Nicolotti butcher Barzaga who, "because he was afflicted by ambition, took heart, hoping that Fortune would help him, but he fooled himself by far. . . .": MCCC 3161, 1670/16; also the Nicolotto Gelmette, "not satisfied with the praise for his name and bravery and wanting to increase it. . . .": 1667/17-18; also 1668/13.

39. MCCC 3161, 1639/11, 1669/6.

40. MCCC 3161, 1670/16. That "victory and the palm" essentially depended on *fortuna* at the bridges: 1649/13, 1667/52.

41. Interestingly, the Chronicler evidently believed that better organization and more supervision would tend to help skill and bravery predominate over blind chance: it was, by contrast, in the melees and *scaramuccie* taking place without *capi* or *padrini* that "everything remained in the hand of Fortune"; see MCCC 3161, 1668/1.

42. MCCC 3161, 1643/3, 1665/3, 1670/2. The Chronicler also wrote of "wrongs and injuries not practiced at the bridges": 1666/11.

43. On disruptive fighters being chased from the bridge, sometimes for good, see MCCC 3161, 1665/2-3, 1670/3.

44. Neither of the two were duelists, nor were they supposed to be in the *arengo*: MCCC 3161, 1668/5; also 1642/5.

45. MCCC 3161, 1649/4 and 11, 1666/11; also 1632/12, 1649/5, 1667/8.

46. The affront could also "be mitigated in some degree" if a *padrini*, *vecchione*, or some other figure of authority (though evidently not a noble) would immediately thrash the offender publicly, on the bridge: MCCC 3161, 1669/10.

47. For fighters or partisans taking offense (and then physically assaulting) *padrini* who had not allowed the agreed-upon number of *mostre* or had otherwise neglected the tacit rules of the *pugni*; see MCCC 3161, 1637/11, 1639/20.

48. MCCC 3161, 1640/10. *Magoghe*, meaning "little old ladies." The Chronicler went on to note that "[t]he people of San Nicolò were sometimes called Magoghe as an insult."

49. On champions who "gnawed within themselves" over their wounded honor, see MCCC 3161, 1636/15, 1667/27, 1668/13. For the gathering *in setta* of men of status, see 1636/15-16.

50. For the custom of seeking revenge with steel for illicit punches; see MCCC 3161, 1638/5, 1649/5. Daggers might have been drawn even more often on the bridges if the sight of them did not so often provoke a barrage of stones: 1666/3. On the prohibition of firearms and the unusual instance of a fighter plotting to revenge himself with one, see 1649/5, 1668/18.

51. The Chronicler wrote of antagonists employing factional traitors, *spie apostate*, to inform on "where the one or the other was to be found, where they were going, and if they were followed by youths armed with stones and rocks or iron balls in their work aprons or even in sacks"; see MCCC 3161, 1632/13; also on spies: 1642/7, 1668/18. For youths with stones, see 1642/6. On seeking out an enemy in his home district, see 1632/11, 1633/12, 1636/15, 1668/13.

52. MCCC 3161, 1667/1. An offended fighter might also call out his rival by means of a written challenge, or *cartello di disfida*, sent by a go-between; 1637/4; also see Crouzet-Pavan, "Violence, Société et Pouvoir à Venise," 920-25.

53. MCCC 3161, 1632/13; also 1635/11. For planned ambushes, see 1637/11-12, 1640/11.

54. MCCC 3161, 1640/11, 1643/1. Here again, champions of the *pugni* appeared to be imitating the behavior of nobles, who could posture without the

intent of meeting in much the same way; see Moryson, *Shakespeare's Europe*, 403, for a very similar account of two gentlemen of Siena quarreling and then marching about *in setta*.

55. For the Ten's bans against those who would *caminar armati in setta*, see ASV: CPD, filza 19, 2 Sept. 1625; filza 21, 9 March 1633; filza 28, 3 March 1656; and MCCC 3161, 1642/3, 1668/13. On go-betweens, see 1642/12, 1665/11.

56. MCCC 3161, 1666/28; also see 1668/13. Although a *padrino* was considered perfectly free to strike or otherwise punish one of his own men, he was not to touch a fighter from the other side unless attacked first.

57. MCCC 3161, 1642/6. On his friends coercing a feuder to make a peace, see 1643/1.

58. MCCC 3161, 1632/10, 1633/12, 1635/13, 1667/62. On brothers pursuing each other's vendettas: 1635/11. In ordinary Venetian brawls, by contrast, the offended parties' friends and relatives were quick to join in: 1669/8.

59. When the Galletto, Castellano *padrino*, "full of disdain, gave a kick to the genitals of [the Nicolotti fighter] Azzalà" in the middle of a *mostra*, the mob of Nicolotti who leapt onto the bridge were apparently more angry with Billora, their own padrino, than with Galletto, because Billora had failed to thrash the Castellano: MCCC 3161, 1670/23.

60. MCCC 3161, 1635/12, 1639/11, 1640/1, 1643/12 and 6, 1665/14, 1667/1, 1670/5. Compare with the use of the *cartello* among elite individuals challenging one another: Bryson, *The Sixteenth-Century Italian Duel*, 7.

61. MCCC 3161, 1649/6, 1668/13.

62. On public *disfide*, to be settled on the bridge, see MCCC 3161, 1640/1 and 3, 1641/1, 1642/4, 1649/2, 1666/8, 1669/5, 1670/3. For long successions of *mostre*: 1668/14, 1669/4, 1670/14–15.

63. MCCC 3161, 1634/7, 1635/5, 1637/7, 1638/3, 1640/7–8, 1649/7.

64. See Rossetti, *I bulli di Roma* 185–210. On the customary seclusion of women and girls and their resulting dominance over the household, Gilmore, *Aggression and Community*, 126–53; Press, *The City as Context*, 117–29; Corbin and Corbin, *Urbane Thought*, 22; Rogers, "Gender in Southwestern France: The Myth of Male Dominance Revisited," 65–86. For this topic in baroque Venice, see Molmenti, *Venice*, 174–79; and Ruggiero, *The Boundaries of Eros*, 154.

65. As Fynes Moryson noted, "The wemen of honour in Italy, I meane the wives and virgins, are . . . locked up at home, and covered with vayles when they goe abroad, and kept from any conversation with men"; see *Shakespeare's Europe*, 409. As if to ensure that they stayed inside, many Venetian women of the period, especially those of the upper classes, were accustomed to go around town on extremely high (up to twenty inches) platform sandals, or *zoccoli*, which made it very hard for them to get about in public (and particularly over bridges) without male support. Coryat noted, "I saw a woman fall a very dangerous fall, as she was going down the staires of one of the little stoney bridges with her high Champineys alone by her selfe: but I did nothing pitty her, because shee wore such frivolous and . . . ridiculous instruments"; *Crudities*, 1:400.

66. Such a "familist" and sex-segregated society was quite strong in Sicily until very recently; see Schneider and Schneider, *Culture and Political Economy in Western Sicily*, 90–95; Gilmore, "The Shame of Dishonor," 8–16.

67. On the tendency of Venetians to identify household and parish (especially the parish church) as particularly female space, see Romano, *Patricians and*

Popolani, 131–42. On the difficulties faced by adolescent boys making this transition, see Trexler, "Ritual in Florence: Adolescents and Salvation in the Renaissance," 244–49.

68. Ruggiero, *The Boundaries of Eros*, 162; Muchembled, *Popular Culture and Elite Culture in France, 1400–1750*, 96–97.

69. For the example of Venice's large community of *facchini*, or porters, many of whom were required by the state not only to work for low wages but also made to sleep together in a dormitory, so that they could be available as firemen; see Davis, *Shipbuilders*, 170–71.

70. Saint Disdier, *La Ville et la République de Venise*, 441; MCPD. 303/C, filza 33, pp. 4–5; MCCC 3161, 1667/28.

71. It was evidently unusual for boys of *età giovanile* to *caminar armati* on their own: MCCC 3161, 1636/1; also 1632/13, 1635/11. If the Captains of the Ten were on active patrol, youth gangs were also quite willing to have brawls and *scaramuccie* just among themselves, on local bridges: 1632/14.

72. Murphy, "Coming of Age in Seville," 376–92; Rossetti, *I bulli di Roma*, 7–16; Ruggiero, *The Boundaries of Eros*, 149–50. For songs "sung against the Nicolotti by the Castellani youth all over the city," see MCCC 3161, 1637/1; also see Dal Medico, *Raccolta di canzoni*, and 1633/1, 1665/1, 1667/25.

73. Cf. youth gangs that mounted the Roman and Perugian *sassaiole*; see Rossetti, *I bulli di Roma*, 174–78, esp. his citation of Pietro Romano, *Roma nelle sue strade e nelle sue piazze* (Rome: 1950).

74. In this, Venetian youths clearly differed from adolescent gangs whose members celebrated their marginal, disruptive status in Carnival and charivari only so long as they were adolescents: see esp. for Venice: Muraro, "Le Feste a Venezia e le sue manifestazzioni rappresentative: Le Compagnie della Calza e *le Momarie*," 318–28. For France: Muchembled, *Popular Culture and Elite Culture*, 167–68, and Davis, *Society and Culture*, 97–128.

75. MCCC 3161, 1633/8, 1634/1, 1667/18; de Ville, "Pychtomachia venetia," 5.

76. As with young Molena ("The Sucker") of the Bari, who knocked the veteran Nane, water carrier of the Giudecca, off into the water in the first round: "His glory was all the greater because [Nane] had never met his match, being held as one of the bravest and most fierce of the soldiers among Castellani": MCCC 3161, 1665/12. On youths quarreling over who got to meet a champion, see 1666/21, 1667/9. For a boy banished from the *mostra* because he was thought too young to compete, see 1636/1.

77. Saint Disdier concluded his discussion of the *pugni* with this account, with the final curse left in Italian: "'via di quà, infami porchi vituperosi!'": *La Ville et la République de Venise*, 452. For a *cartello* presenting defeat at the bridges in emasculating terms, see MCCC 3161, 1667/21.

78. Pitt-Rivers, *The People of the Sierra*, 160–69; Tax Freeman, *Neighbors*, 118–19; Fraser, *The Pueblo*, 134; Menarini, *Uomini e bestie nel dialetto bolognese*, 19–62; also see Morgan, O'Neill, and Harré, *Nicknames*, 46–97, 123–27.

79. It remains unclear just how and when surnames actually replaced the tradition patronymic form among the working population of Venice (for example, Zorzi Panfilo in place of Zorzi di Zuane). Certainly the change was already widespread in the seventeenth century, often with the nickname of a parent becoming the surname of a son or grandson. Nevertheless, the health commissioners of the city were still ordering their census takers in 1670 to record plebeian heads of

household with reference to their given name and occupation only; see also Burke, *Historical Anthropology*, 27–39.

80. Compare the typology of the nicknames of modern English schoolchildren offered by Morgan, O'Neill, and Harré, in *Nicknames*, 36–45. Most of the nearly two hundred nicknames found in the Chronicle of the *pugni* fall into such a category:

Local fish
Pestafumo
Paganello
Gattorusola
Granzo (Crab)
Zirolo

Animals
Gallo (Rooster)
Lumaga (Snail)
Rospo (Toad)
Zazegna (Duck)
Caenazzo (Oystercatcher)

Work/tools
Barcalonga (Long Boat)
Barcagrossa (Big Boat)
Patan (Cobbler's Tool)
Zanchetto (Rudder)
Verigola (Gimlet)

Physical characteristics
Barbuzzetta (Little Chin)
Beimustacchi (Beautiful Mustache)
Boccastorta (Twisted Mouth)
Gobbo (Hunchback)
Mastegabruo (Toothless)
Moro (Dark Skinned)
Mustaffa (Ugly Face)
Naso (Nose)

Pepolo (Dwarf)
Schilato (Skinny)
Scuffia (Forelock)
Zonfo (One Arm)

Behavioral quirk
Bigolo (Lucky)
Buon Ladron (Good Thief)
Capon Lesso (Boiled Capon/Lazy?)
Folla l'uva (Crushes Grapes/Clumsy?)
Marmeo (Stupid)
Mauco (Simpleminded)
Molena (Chump)
Spua Perle (Spits Pearls/Smooth Talker?)
Spua Rospo (Toad Spitter)
Tardina (A Little Late)
Sette Gambe (Seven Legs/Very Fast?)
Tarrabara (Desperate)

Childhood experience? or obscure meaning
Bruolongo (Watered Soup)
Caga nel Orto (Shits in the Garden)
Caga Zalo (Yellow Shit)
Cul de Caldiera (Kettle Bottom)
Cul de Favetta (Tight Ass)
Cul d'Avena (Ass like an Oat)
Malacarne (Bad Meat)
Mastelletto (Chamber Pot)
Mattarello (Rolling Pin)
Pollasfotto (Chicken Teaser)

81. Pitt-Rivers notes, "[In the pueblo], when referring to a person behind his back, he is distinguished by a descriptive nickname. This is never, or virtually never, used as a form of address. To do so would be bad manners, though exactly how bad would depend upon the nickname. Some are obscene and many are uncomplimentary. A person possesses, then, a Christian name . . . his surnames . . . and his nickname, which the pueblo knows him by, but which he is not supposed to know"; see *The People of the Sierra*, 161–62. Also see Pitt-Rivers, "Spiritual Kinship in Andalusia," 60, for the public use of nicknames as a sign that their owners are excluded from the Christian community.

82. Compare the similar uses to which nicknames were put among British boxing professionals a century or more later; see Ford, *Prizefighting: The Age of Regency Boximania* 54–56.

83. MCCC 3161, 1632/17; 1666/7; 1667/13, 19, 61; 1670/3.

84. "La verra antiga," stanzas 18–19, 27, 39, 60, 76, 92; MCCC 2936, stanzas 54, 109; MCCC 3231. The Chronicler also produced such lists of fighters' names and nicknames, sometimes in the plural, as if to underscore that although these champions were real men, they were also archetypal, each of their names standing for the presence and spirit of many fighters:

> To narrate the trials, valor, and extravagances . . . of these *mostre* would make our tale too long and only bring boredom to the reader. Enough to say that on the Castellani side there battled the Bodoli, Rigoni, Tartari, Gotti, Mori, Zighignoli, Fratti, Bobolè, Scarabazzi, Lanotti, Piateri, and Calcinari with other laudable and honored warriors, carrying out deeds worthy of their ancestors, [while] from the Nicolotta side they were bravely met by the Panchi, Pendoli, Gaichi, Mazzagatti, Pei, Balloni, Favri, Stramazzeri, Malduri, Paulazzi, Menegoni, Matareli, Bodoli, Tandini, and by other famous, strong, and audacious soldiers with the highest courage and virtue." (MCCC 3161, 1668/34; also see 1667/32).

Since many of these same names turn up in other sources, including the police records, it is likely that most did indeed belong to real individuals; see ASV: CDP, filza 26, 14 Feb. 1652 mv; filza 27, 27 May 1653; filza 34, 2 and 5 Sept. 1684.

85. And indeed, according to the police files of the Ten, the real name of the Castellano champion Mazzahuomeni was Iseppo (Joseph) and that of the *padrino* Moro Muschier (The Dark Glover) was Paolo (Paul), while the Castellano *capo* Ballon had been baptized Lazaro and the redoubtable Caga in Orto was in reality Matteo the Boatman; see ASV: CDP, filza 26, 14 Feb. 1652 mv; filza 27, 27 May 1653; filza 28, 3 March 1656; filza 34, 2 Sept. 1684.

86. Marvin, *Bullfight*, 109. My thanks to Melvin Adelman for pointing out how other sports have also traditionally used such sobriquets to reinforce a ludic context in which injuries given and received are forgiven after the fact.

87. MCCC 3161, 1641/3, 1665/18, 1666/13, 1668/10 and 12, also see 1633/9, 1638/7, 1667/14 and 16, 1669/4, 7. Later, the Chronicler was able to announce that "Duro ("Tough Guy") the Servant in two rounds badly treated the Ballon, since at his will he could make [Ballon's] face swell up": 1670/2.

88. MCCC 3161, 1666/14, 1668/22; also see 1667/27, 1670/3.

89. MCCC 3161, 1642/4.

90. MCCC 3161, 1667/12.

91. On Frate's earlier experiences as a brawler in the *frotte* and his reputation for never forgiving a slight or insult, see MCCC 3161, 1665/13, 1666/10, 1667/36, 1668/12–13.

92. MCCC 3161, 1666/10, 1667/36, 1668/12 and 15.

93. Specifically, such bad usages included refusing to come freely to the *mostre* or showing off excessively once in the *arengo*, turning away those who offered to fight as unworthy opponents, or treating the proper protests of the *padrini* as if they were a personal insult: MCCC 3161, 1637/7, 1640/8, 1649/11, 1666/27.

94. Davis, *People of the Mediterranean*, 90.

95. MCCC 3161, 1667/30. At other times tambourines were also featured, and weapons might well be loaded into the boats along with the musical instruments; see 1632/5, 1634/2, 1637/6, 1640/9.

96. In the examples recorded in the Chronicle of the *pugni*, this took place at a faction's staging point, rather than at the bridge itself; sometimes the address

was made by one of the factional *vecchione*, rather than an active fighting chief; see MCCC 3161, 1632/6 and 8, 1667/33.

97. There is, admittedly, no other record of any such massacre of Castellani in 1606, although in 1611 mass panic caused twenty-six deaths among fighters and spectators of both sides; see ASV: PS, *Necrologie*, Bu. 842 and 843, 5 Sept. and 1 Oct. 1611.

98. MCCC 3161, 1632/6–9, 1634/11, 1667/31–34, 1669/13–14.

99. Tamassia Mazzarotto, *Feste veneziane*, 2–3; Molmenti, *Venice*, 112–19; MCCC 3161, 1643/6–7.

100. Regarding "the three first evenings after the victory that are permitted to the winning faction to exalt and acclaim itself," see MCCC 3161, 1637/10; also 1632/18, 1634/5 and 14–15, 1649/13.

101. MCCC 3161, 1670/40; compare the guild festivals described by Lane, in *Venice*, 107–9.

102. When neighborhoods held festivals without permission, they ran the risk that the Chiefs of the Ten would send one of their Captains around to make arrests and impound the grandstands, dance platforms, wine casks, and so on: MCCC 3161, 1633/5. On the festivities for a *battagliola* lasting "an entire month," see 1637/11.

103. MCCC 3161, 1638/10, 1639/3.

104. In Venice, boats may have represented symbolic objects for burning, or they may just have been a convenient supply of wood. On making "very high fires of boats, torches, and an immensity of cane," see MCCC 3161, 1637/11; also 1636/22, 1639/20, 1641/11, 1643/6, 1649/13, 1665/9, 1667/20.

105. MCCC 3161, 1667/39; ASV: CDP, filza 20, 12 Jan. 1632 mv. The tocsin (*campana a martello*) was also sometimes illegally rung to attract crowds to the battle site, as well as used legitimately when *battagliole* turned into riots: 1634/10, 1637/13, 1642/2, 1649/5.

106. On the Castellani playing "pipes and castanets of the galleys [*pive e gnacchere alla galea* or *pive ad usanza di galea*]" as well as "sailor's horns [*trombette alla marinaresca*]"; see MCCC 3161, 1634/2 and 11; 1635/4; 1638/2 1639/3 and 19; 1641/5. On dancing the *moresca*, see 1634/5, 1635/12, 1639/21, 1667/43.

107. Three such fetes—held at Cannareggio, San Nicolò, and San Girolamo on the three weekends following the Nicolotti victory of 23 Oct. 1667—are described in detail in MCCC 3161, 1667/39–45. According to the Chronicler of the *pugni*, while these may have been the most splendid affairs put on, there were other celebrations "still more peculiar and exciting" staged at the same time at Santa Margherita, San Polo, and Santi Apostoli parishes.

108. MCCC 3161, 1667/40 and 43. On fireworks (*sbarri, petardi, mortaretti, mascoli, bombe, e fuochi articiali*): 1632/18, 1635/10, 1638/10, 1641/11, 1649/13, 1667/41. For the discharging of cannon "from one of the vessels in the boatyards of San Nicolò," see 1667/43.

109. MCCC 3161, 1667/42–44; also see 1637/6. Such local celebrations would seem to contradict the assertion that in Venice the state kept a virtual monopoly on all forms of festive, artistic expression; see Muir, "Images of Power," 50–52.

110. MCCC 3161, 1667/39–44, also includes descriptions of the decorations on the Ponte delle Guglie, of San Giobbe, the Servi, and San Girolamo. On the sumptuous state triumphs and celebrations given by Venice, see Fortini Brown,

"Measured Friendship, Calculated Pomp: The Ceremonial Welcomes of the Venetian Republic," 136–86; Gay, "Fantasticherie galleggianti," 35–56; Muir, *The Myth of Venice*, 60.

111. Exactly what this music was like remains unclear, although in a city like baroque Venice, where "dancing and singing [outdoors] is the custom of the city," at least it can be assumed that such marches, popular songs, and caprices would have been skillfully played: MCCC 3161, 1632/1. For visitors' descriptions of the more refined Venetian music of the era, see Coryat, *Crudities*, 1:390–92; Moryson, *Shakespeare's Europe*, 425–26; Molmenti, *Venice*, 28–40; Glixon, "A Musicians' Union in Sixteenth-Century Venice," 392–421; and Glixon, "Music at the Scuole in the Age of Andrea Gabrieli," 59–74.

112. The partisans of San Nicolò and San Girolamo would musically organize their festivities in much the same way, although the fishermen of San Nicolò apparently preferred squads blowing small trumpets (*trombette*) to massed drummers; see MCCC 3161, 1667/40, 43, 45; also see 1639/21.

113. No pictorial representation of a crown has so far been turned up, but see Sorsi, "Descrittione piacevole," stanza 250; MCCC 3161, 1637/12. On seeing "crowns hung all over the city, at the *campi* and across the canals," see 1635/10, 1637/11, 1649/13.

114. For descriptions of these *corone*, see MCCC 3161, 1667/39–45.

115. The Chronicler often wrote of "the laurels and crowns of victory" at the bridges: MCCC 3161, 1670/16, 1673/9. Residents of San Nicolò parish also boasted a number of crowns: 1633/10; also 1649/13, 1665/10–11, 1667/40.

116. The Chronicler wrote of processions where the crown was accompanied by "an infinity of brands and torches and sometimes bundles of candles (*torzi di cere*) of sixteen and twenty *lire* in considerable number"; see MCCC 3161, 1637/11; also 1634/14, 1635/10.

117. MCCC 3161, 1667/41 and 43.

118. MCCC 3161, 1667/45. On the custom of ritualized street processions as a means of renewing *Communitas*, see Muir, "The Virgin on the Street Corner," 28.

119. MCCC 3161, 1665/11, 1667/20–21 and 41. The men of San Nicolò, "as the bishops [*metropoli*] of the squads of all the Nicolotti," once also carried a crown "from one community to another, with boats exceptionally decorated with tapestries and liveries ... as has been practiced in similar triumphs after a *guerra ordinata*," see 1637/11.

120. MCCC 3161, 1632/18, 1635/10–11, 1639/21. For placards hung under crowns, see 1634/6, 1639/21, 1667/21–22 (inserts) and 41.

121. MCCC 3161, 1665/11. The encounter followed hard on the heels of another brawl over a crown at the Rialto Novo, see 1665/10-11.

122. MCCC 3161, 1637/12, 1667/41.

123. The crown was hanging in the *campo* of Santa Sofia: MCCC 3161, 1639/21; also 1634/14, 1637/12.

124. MCCC 3161, 1639/22; also see 1637/12 and 1649/13.

125. On factional enemies visiting neighborhood fetes, see MCCC 3161, 1643/7, 1668/1. On bull and bear baitings (*cacce di tori ed orsi*) as both entertainments and provocations in victory celebrations: 1632/18, 1634/15, 1637/11, 1639/21, 1667/40–41, 1668/1. For the provocative implications of similar sports and games in medieval Italy, see Trexler, "Correre la terra: Collective Insults in the Late Middle Ages," 845–902.

126. MCCC 3161, 1635/10, 1636/22, 1643/7. On the rivalry and competition that lay at the foundation of such public festivals, see Muir, "The Virgin on the Street Corner," 39.

127. MCCC 3161, 1637/12, 1668/1-2.

128. Certainly a response that could be termed paternalistic, in that it punished workers for their misbehavior by revoking their amusements: MCCC 3161, 1633/10, 1635/11, 1636/22, 1643/6, 1665/11, 1667/45-6.

129. MCCC 3161, 1667/42-43; also 1634/15, 1635/10, 1667/32. On communities' contending as to which could present the most luxurious crown to another, see 1637/11.

130. Interestingly, the 1665 procession of the Gnesotti to Murano almost caused a rift in the Castellani ranks, for the Zuecchini of the Giudecca angrily claimed that "that honor had belonged to them, as the squad that had sustained the first assaults of the enemy": MCCC 3161, 1665/11; also 1634/15, 1669/18.

131. On the particular efforts of the post-Tridentine Church to insure the doctrinal loyalty of Catholics through establishing its dominant and defining presence at these traditional moments of passage: John Bossy, "The Counter Reformation and the People of Catholic Europe," 51–70.

Chapter 4

1. Caravia,"La verra antiga," stanza 53.

2. That is, at the *campi* of Santa Margherita and San Barnabà, the Carmini, Sant' Agnese, and San Nicolò: ASV: CDP proclami, filza 1, 12 Sept. 1505, filza 2, 15 Nov. 1522. The edict of 1522 was reproclaimed on virtually a yearly basis throughout the 1520s and (in a slightly harsher version) 1530s; see filza 3, 21 Nov. 1536, 26 Jan. 1637 mv, and *passim*.

3. ASV: CDP, filza 23, 29 Nov. 1644. In addition to the locations noted above, this edict was also posted at all the major fighting bridges, the two fish markets, Murano and Burano, and the major *campi* of the city. Further edicts controlling the *battagliole* include: ASV: Compilazione leggi, bu. 85: Baccanali, 23 Oct. 1609; bu. 321: Pugni, 5 Jan. 1546 mv, 15 Nov. 1547, 28 Nov. 1644. On punishments exacted for similar felonies, see Davis, *Shipbuilders*, 126–35.

4. For an overview of the Venetian system of law enforcement with historiography, see Cozzi, "Authority and the Law in Renaissance Venice," 293–345; Cozzi and Knapton, *La Repubblica di Venezia nell'età moderna*, 110–13; Romano, *Patricians and Popolani*, 18–20; Ruggiero, *Violence in Early Renaissance Venice*, 18–39.

5. MCCC 3161, 1641/4-5.

6. This process of taming popular festivals has been called an essential element of Venice's supposed civic peace: Muir, *Civic Ritual*, 135–81. For a recent bibliography of the so-called Myth of Venice, see Romano, *Patricians and Popolani*, 8–9.

7. Saint Disdier, *La Ville et la République de Venise*, 439, 448.

8. Saint Disdier, *La Ville et la République de Venise*, 448, 452; MCCC 3161, 1639/22, 1670/32–33. For patricians "jumping from their boats and stripping off their *ferrarioli* and [their] worthy and honorable clothes, to join the crowd [dressed

only] in silken breeches," see 1636/21; also see 1640/6. On combat between classes, see Baldick, *The Duel: A History of Duelling*, 32–48; Guttmann, "English Sports Spectators," 114–20; Henricks, "The Democratization of Sport in Eighteenth-Century England," 13–14; Becker, *Civility and Society in Western Europe, 1300–1600,* esp. 1–42.

9. MCCC 3161, 1649/20. On the martial traditions (and aspirations) of the Venetian nobility, see Hale, "Military Academies on the Venetian Terraferma, 273–95. For the general argument and a bibliography on the withdrawal of elites from popular culture, see Burke, *Popular Culture in Early Modern Europe*, 244–86.

10. As after a near-riot in 1638, in which "there did not follow any greater disorders because there arrived at the bridge some Castellani nobles, who with their authority made up for the little respect [enjoyed] by the *padrini* and the [police] Captains themselves: MCCC 3161, 1638/5; also 1633/4, 1636/22, 1649/5, 1668/4.

11. Handkerchiefs were also displayed on the bridge itself: "Some gentlemen of the one and the other side, highly feared and respected, carried themselves to the middle of the bridge among the weapons, and with threats and with their authority, waving their handkerchiefs as a sign of peace, they prudently quieted the popular furore": MCCC 3161, 1632/9–11; also 1642/2, 1649/9, 1669/17, 1670/8. On shouted negotiations: 1667/35.

12. By contrast, when plebeian *padrini* wished to ask for peace, they tended to wave their overcloaks (*tabarri*), shirts, or work aprons: MCCC 3161, 1670/8 and 24. On the various symbolic uses of handkerchiefs by nobles, see 1637/9; 1639/9; 1641/2 and 6; 1643/5; 1665/18 and 20; 1666/5, 8, 10, 20, 23; 1667/ 7, 51, 53, 55; 1668/4–5; 1669/4.

13. On the nearly fatal brawl, *per occasione di veder la battagliola a San Barnabà*, between the nobleman Francesco di Domenico Pisani and two commoners who were atop a barrel that blocked his access to one of the better houses near the bridge, see ASV: CDP, filza 26, 23 Dec. 1652; for a similar accusation against Iseppo di Gasparo Diedo, see ASV: CDP, filza 34, 13 Nov. 1684; also MCCC 1649/9, 1666/4.

14. For the prices commanded for balconies and windows overlooking the bridges, see MCCC 3161, 1635/4, 1665/8, 1670/37. For comparison, in 1663, the English visitor Philip Skippon paid around a ducat for a box at the opera and a ducat and a half to hire a gondola and two oarsmen for the day, see Skippon, *An Account of a Journey*, 518–20. On aristocratic display and ostentation in Venice and elsewhere, see Braudel, *Civilization and Capitalism,* 2:489–93.

15. MCCC 3161, 1636/21, 1649/10. It was apparently customary for noble betters to deposit their *grosse scommesse* with third parties before the beginning of a match or *frotta*: 1641/1, 1649/2, 1667/12. On aristocratic gambling in Venice generally, see Tassini, *Feste e spettacoli*, 135–38.

16. MCCC 3161, 1636/21, 1643/2; on nobles fighting in the *broglio*, see 1643/8.

17. On aristocratic promises "to give gifts of great value to the winners", see MCCC 3161, 1649/2; also 1665/8; on the donation of a crown, see 1637/12.

18. MCCC 3161, 1666/1, 1667/28.

19. MCCC 3161, 1649/2 and 9. On patrons giving *calcette di seda, busti e cassi fatti a livrea* to favored fighters, see 1649/2; also 1642/4. On groups of servants fighting together for the amusement of their masters: 1641/7, 1649/4–5, 1665/4, 1668/1–2, 1669/11.

20. Peace was most easily accomplished if the aggrieved parties could be convinced "that since their offenses originated in the *battagliole*, they should be terminated in another [battle]": MCCC 3161, 1643/1–2. Sometimes, however, aristocratic patrons had to work out a convenient fiction that would explain away the insult and allow both sides to claim honor: 1666/28; also 1632/11, 1665/11.

21. On one occasion both sides were so eager to steal a march on the other that squads of Zuecchini and Gnesotti finally decided to go and seize the bridge at 5:00 a.m.—fully ten hours before the scheduled meeting time—only to discover that it had already been taken by the Nicolotti: MCCC 3161, 1667/28–9. On switching or altering bridges to gain the advantage, see 1632/12–13, 16; 1634/7; 1638/3; 1639/13–14.

22. Saint Disdier, *La Ville et la République de Venise*, 448. This connection between gambling and attempts at the imposition of fair play has also been noted in the early history of British boxing: Henricks, "The Democratization of Sport," 11–18.

23. MCCC 3161, 1637/5, 1642/6, 1673/6.

24. MCCC 3161, 1635/6. The Chronicler believed that on most such occasions when the *padrini* could not be brought to an agreement, it was because one of them was afraid his side would lose in a fair battle and thus he made impossible demands: 1673/7.

25. The factional leaders were invited in writing (*con biglietti*) and kept in separate rooms at Ca' Dolfin while the patriarch and his relatives shuttled back and forth between the two contingents: MCCC 3161, 1673/1 and 5. On Giovanni Dolfin, patriarch of Venice and Aquileia, see Ughelli, *Italia sacra* 5, 141–42.

26. In particular the *caporioni* tried to make the patriarch responsible for choosing the bridge. The patriarch was said to have likewise evaded the burden of making this choice, complaining, "My back is not strong enough to support such a weight: I cannot be of service to one without displeasing the other; the side that wins will praise my judgement, but the loser will not only blame but also curse the Dolfin family, since it will seem like the Dolfins were heralds of bad news and portents of unlucky fates": MCCC 3161, 1673/2–15. The curious story of the failed *battagliola* of 1673 is substantially supported by Saint Disdier, *La Ville et la République de Venise*, 449–50.

27. Despite the ambiguity, it is perhaps preferable to refer to such "middle-class" supporters of the *pugni* generally as "merchants" rather than by the somewhat restrictive and legalistic term of *cittadini* ("citizens")—with its implications more of an hereditary caste rather than a socioeconomic class; see Lane, *Venice: A Maritime Republic*, 151–52, 323–24; Romano, *Patricians and Popolani*, 7–8, 29, 156.

28. MCCC 3161, 1634/4, 1636/21, 1649/1, 1667/28, 1668/2 and 14. For middle-class fighters (including goldsmiths, wool merchants, and state officials) presenting themselves in the *mostre*: 1632/13, 1636/15, 1639/10, 1665/17, 1667/50, 1668/7, 1670/2.

29. MCCC 3161, 1632/11, 1643/2. They were also quick to suspect their own *padrini* of throwing a battle, perhaps because they knew about giving bribes themselves: 1635/13, 1667/38. One Venetian noble who was generous with his factional contributions, was Polo di Gerolamo Morosini: 1633/5.

30. MCCC 3161, 1633/6, 1635/14, 1639/11–12, 1641/4, 1649/7, 1665/8. Sometimes the contributions were in the form of materials given directly to the

fighters or their *capi*. For the donation of thirty ducats' worth of *cartoni* and a barrel of wine by Orsetti and Armelini, see 1640/3. The Chronicler also recorded an unnamed *protettore* of the Castellani who claimed to have personally donated two hundred *ongari* (around eight hundred ducats) for a single large battle: 1667/ 23.

31. MCCC 3161, 1649/7, 1666/28.

32. On guards of honor, see MCCC 3161, 1632/13, 1638/6, 1665/22, 1668/13.

33. MCCC 3161, 1642/6 and 8, 1668/18, 1669/18. Sometimes their intervention made matters worse, however, as when "the shopkeepers came out [of their shops] armed with boat hooks and pitchforks, some to put themselves between the fighters [to make a peace] and some to foment their own allies." The result was a brawl that engulfed the Marcerie "from the Ponte dei Baretteri up to [Piazza] San Marco": 1635/11; also 1641/11. For a similar brawl involving the *botteghieri* of the Rialto, see 1665/22.

34. In particular, Filippo Magnone the shoemaker and merchant, whose involvement with the *pugni* extended for at least thirty-five years, until he died "tired and in poor health" in 1667, and whose shop was a constant meeting place of hotheaded young fighters: MCCC 3161, 1632/4; 1639/12; 1640/1; 1649/7; 1667/22, 28, 46.

35. Likewise, Filippo Magnone the cobbler sought the blessing of his community by forgiving 130 ducats of debts that neighbors had run up at his shop. Magnone (and no doubt Martin the Mercer as well) was buried with considerable pomp: dressed in his favorite fighting and festive shirt and accompanied by hundreds of mourners, Nicolotti and Castellani alike: MCCC 3161, 1667/46.

36. MCCC 3161, 1633/10, 1637/12, 1638/5, 1640/10, 1641/10. On foreigners finding themselves under attack by groups of equally hostile Castellani and Nicolotti, see 1668/28 and 31, 1669/1–2. On French and Spanish patricians supporting opposite factions during the *battagliole*, see 1636/14, 1649/2, 1669/ 11.

37. Thus, according to the Chronicler, the Russian ambassador came to Venice knowing all about the *battagliole*, "which had already been described to him back in his most distant country": MCCC 3161, 1668/5.

38. MCCC 3161, 1636/19, 1637/4, 1668/5, 1669/11, 1670/12. The Chronicler also listed other dignitaries who had witnessed such prearranged battles during the preceding century; these included the dukes of Ferrara (1493, 1561, and 1569), the condottiere Bartolomeo d'Alviano (1508), the duke of Milan (1533), the queen of Poland (1555), the archduke of Austria (1569 and 1579), a Turkish diplomatic mission (1582), a Japanese mission (1585), the nephew of Pope Clement VIII (1590s), and the duke of Mantova (1597): 1670/30, 36–38.

39. The cardinal felt that the Castellani would have carried the day "had they not been served by inexperience fighters: that is, by Dalmatians and *Schiavoni*": MCCC 3161, 1637/6, 8, 10.

40. The Chronicler referred to Marshal Charles de Blanchefort, sire de Créqui, as "famoso Gueriere, Monsù Chrichi, Principe Francese": MCCC 3161, 1636/20 and 22; also 1668/5–6. In the years 1634–38 Créqui served both as France's ambassador to Venice and her commander-in-chief against Spanish Lombardy, see Romanin, *Storia documentata di Venezia*, 7:232–34.

41. As with the *battagliola* arranged in 1555 for Bona Sforza, daughter of the duke of Milan and Queen of Poland: MCCC 3161, 1670/36.

42. MCCC 3161, 1668/6, 9–11. "Princess Colonna" would appear to have been the somewhat notorious Maria Mancini, wife of Lorenzo Onofrio Colonna and sister of France's Cardinal Mazarin.

43. MCCC 3161, 1640/5; 1668/6, 11–12. Also see 1667/38: "The passion [of the Nicolotti] grew even greater because this combat was carried out not only in the presence of all the people and nobility of Venice but also before the [papal] nuncio Monseigneur Alessandro Viti, the Ambassador of Spain with his wife, and other great knights and lords, especially the princes of Brandovicchi."

44. The battle of 1557 was staged on a special wooden pontoon bridge erected across the Grand Canal. For Morosini's coronation, the Castellani and Nicolotti repeatedly fought on the Ponte dei Carmini, "with grand decorations, dressed in various uniforms and liveries . . . to the sound of trumpets and drums": MCCC 3161, 1670/36 and 38. On the festivals for these "coronations," see Muir, "Images of Power," 47–48.

45. MCCC 3161, 1632/1–2. During time of plague governments would in any case have rigorously forbidden public assemblies of any kind, see Cipolla, *Faith, Reason, and the Plague,* 6.

46. MCCC 3161, 1649/6. Evidently he conflated the two events into one, asserting that a single *battagliola* was staged on 26 December 1649 to celebrate the two successes that had, in fact, taken place on 18 August 1648 and in July 1650: Setton, *Venice, Austria, and the Turks,* 152–59.

47. MCCC 3161, 1635/4, 1649/6–7. On making fighting gear, see 1639/12, 1640/3.

48. MCCC 3151, 1632/13, 1635/4, 1639/12, 1641/4.

49. MCCC 3161, 1632/3, 1667/32, 1668/6, 1673/12.

50. The Ten were no doubt gratified to hear the French marshal Créqui say that if the Castellani and Nicolotti were trained in the use of arms, they would have the bravura to equal the best French soldiers: MCCC 3161, 1636/21. For the Cardinal de Lion admiring the "natural" leadership qualities commanded by *padrini* of otherwise common and humble appearance, see 1637/6. Similar opinions were expressed by "the colonels and leaders of the Germans that were in the city to embark for the defense of the kingdom of Candia": 1668/24.

51. As when the Ten "permitted the city to mobilize itself [for a battle], perhaps so that the public taxes for the support of the war in Crete would be paid more promptly": MCCC 3161, 1649/6.

52. MCCC 3161, 1637/5.

53. MCCC 3161, 1637/5, 1667/28.

54. Thus, "the militia [squads] that are ignorant or timid or poorly disciplined by their *capi* . . . deserve to be shouted at with offensive words . . . by their *padrini*": MCCC 3161, 1634/7; also 1632/12–13, 1649/11. For *padrini* dragging back fighters *a viva forza,* see 1637/2. On *padrini* promising the Collegio to restrain their men, see 1637/5.

55. For *padrini* persuading their factions not to fear the retribution of the state, see MCCC 3161, 1633/11; also 1635/2, 1636/16. For four *padrini* who were chided by noble supporters when they "withdrew themselves to the wall of the embankment, watching with crossed arms the furor and the carnage that their people were making," see 1634/13; also 1636/20, 1639/7, 1641/6, 1649/11, 1667/4, 1668/22.

56. The trend toward such self-regulation has been considered an essential element in the modernization of such loosely defined "folk" recreations as hunt-

ing, boxing, cricket, and football, see Elias, "An Essay on Sports and Violence," 152–60.

57. For damage to doors, gates, and buildings, see MCCC 3161, 1642/10, 1665/1, 1667/49. For the attendant noise "heard in every corner of the city," see 1639/7. On children and female relatives following the squads, see 1633/3, 1634/6–7, 1637/7.

58. For some Nicolotti "breaking into the house of the nobleman Alessandro Priuli . . . helping themselves to the arms and pikes [they found] in the entryway, see MCCC 3161, 1667/2. On fighters breaking up the spiked garden gate of Ca' Noal to use as weapons, see 1634/8-9; also 1665/18 (from Ca' Soranzo), and 1667/49.

59. MCCC 3161, 1669/14; also see 1632/9.

60. Once amounting to "more than fifty people, [in the water] including two priests of the Carità and some Jews, whose cloaks and red hats drifted away along the canal": MCCC 3161, 1670/23; also 1667/47 and 50.

61. MCCC 3161, 1668/31, 1669/1 and 8. On squads of fighters pushing their way through onlookers "without the least regard for the person, such that many went into the water," see 1643/3. For "the bloody armed attack that took place at the Stretto di Gallipoli [a tight passage near the Frari], as the ebb and flow of people piled up in such a way that nobody could pass, and to make way for themselves, many were moved to pull out their daggers, shields, and *pistolesi* [a sort of machete], such that many were left injured and maltreated," see 1649/3.

62. ASV: CDP, filza 13, 20 Sept. 1611; MCCC 3161, 1668/33; also 1632/17, 1634/2, 1639/19, 1640/2–3, 1641/10, 1649/4, 1665/18, 1667/2. Many types of *arme bianche* were routinely carried by Venetians (and most other Italians as well): knives and daggers (*coltelli* and *pugnali*, or *stochi*); the stiletto (*stillo*); the broad *pistolese* (also known as the *lengua de vaca*, or cow's tongue); and the short halberd (*spontone*: which doubled as a boat hook). All these weapons also regularly found their place in duels of the era, see Bryson, *The Sixteenth-Century Italian Duel*, 51. On the prohibition against carrying firearms in Venice, see 1649/5, 1666/4; Moryson, *Shakespeare's Europe*, 163.

63. As when Castellani partisans, "who could not endure that against every expectation they had lost, and who resolved to impede the glory of the Nicolotti with stones, roof tiles, and weapons; Briseghela Castellano, being on the roof of the houses of the Turchetto, was the first to throw a roof tile . . . ": MCCC 3161, 1669/16.

64. For the Castellani who were "digging up the paving stones from the quays with their daggers," see MCCC 3161, 1634/8; also 1633/8, 1640/9–10, 1667/22. A battle in 1668 provided a typical catalogue of the sort of injuries that could result:

> [B]etween stones and roof tiles and jabbings many ended up wounded and mistreated on both sides: that is, the pharmacist Saleto from a stone in the face; Toni Scarpetto, stabbed by a *spontone* in the thigh; Luccio, woolbeater of the Bari, with his head broken. . . . Andrea Longo, left with an eyebrow cut open by a rock; the captain of the Dalmatian soldiers knocked to the ground by a roof tile in the face; Nane of the Arsenal knocked out; and Faresini left crippled from [the blow of] a stone in the leg: (MCCC 3161, 1668/4)

Also see 1633/14 and 1640/10 (for stones and roof tiles "breaking the heads of more than fifty people").

65. MCCC 3161, 1632/4, 1634/8–10, 1670/24. The poet Pantalon dei Tressi wrote of a similar rock battle in 1585, at the Ponte di San Marziale:

> Dà calle dell'Aseo infin al Ponte
> Verso la Chiesa de San Marcilian
> Le piere de pugnali con la ponte
> Gera tutte cavae da cento man.

> From the Calle dell'Aseo
> Clear up to the Bridge of San Marziale,
> The paving stones were by a hundred hands
> All dug out with the points of daggers (MCCC 3161, 1670/34)

Since the Calle dell'Aseo is about 250 meters from the bridge, and the Fondamenta della Misericordia that connects them averages around five meters in width, this particular fight would have involved something on the order of 100–150,000 paving stones. For a similar reference to fights with paving stones in the poetry of Don Vicenzo Cassantini, see MCCC 861, f. 30r.

66. MCCC 3161, 1633/4, 1668/4. For another full-scale *sassaiola* that lasted over an hour, with repeated sorties and attacks not only along the streets and *campi* but also from roof to roof, see 1636/18; also 1649/4, 1666/20. Stone throwing was considered particularly appropriate (and was indeed evidently approved by some) for Saint Stephen's Day: 1632/11. That the *battagliole* regularly dissolved into knife and rock fights is amply supported by sources other than the Chronicler, see de Ville, "Pyctomachia Venetia," 10–11; and especially MCCC 3257 *Avvisi*, 20 Oct. 1656 ("mercoledì a San Barnabà mentre si faceva Battagliola de pugni, seguì questione d'arme e sassate a causa che molti restono feriti"); also see 29 Aug. 1657, 3 Sept. 1660, 15 Dec. 1663, 10 Aug. 1664.

67. For the most part, the Ten's role in controlling parish banquets, public dances, bull runnings, and other local festivities seems to have amounted to little more than making sure that those who put them on had acquired the necessary license; see Muir, *Civic Ritual*, 162–81, 201–02; also MCCC 3161, 1667/59.

68. There is some indication that the Milizia da Mar, the magistracy whose primary concern was maintaining manpower for the state galleys, was also involved in disciplining excesses at the bridges, perhaps because this was the board that would have handled those condemned to the galleys: MCCC 3161, 1666/28. On the Milizia da Mar, see Rapp, *Industry and Economic Decline*, 49–54.

69. On the Ten's special activities as a court, see Cozzi, "Authority and the Law in Renaissance Venice," 303–9, and his "Considerazioni sull'amministrazione della giustizia nella Repubblica di Venezia (secc. XV–XVI)," 117–26.

70. On the genesis and establishment of the Ten, see Finlay, *Politics in Renaissance Venice*, 20–26; Lane, *Venice: A Maritime Republic*, 116–17; Chojnacki, "Crime, Punishment, and the Trecento Venetian State," 218–28. Some have argued that the Ten's powers, while sometimes arbitrary and uncontrolled, were simply reflecting the absolutist, oligarchic state that lay behind the magistracy; see Giorgio Cracco, "Patriziato e oligarchia a Venezia nel Tre-Quattrocento," 71–90.

71. Originally there was one Captain for each of Venice's six *sestieri*, but on 20 November 1618, during the "Spanish troubles," their number was increased by two more. Their duties were described as including "la Custodia della Piazza, Corte de Palazzo, Cecca, e tutta la Città." At the same time the number of *sbirri* under each Captain was increased from ten to fifteen. See ASV: Consiglio dei Dieci, suppliche, bu. 3, 21 April 1625; Lane, *Venice: A Maritime Republic*, 99, 256.

72. On the dress and arms of the Captains, see MCCC 3161/1638/4, 1670/ 8. On the *barche longhe* "which is customarily without a cabin [*felce*], with a red flag stuck in the thwart [*trasto*], with arms and pikes, indeed . . . with pistols and muskets," see 1635/2, 1638/10; also 1633/11.

73. Thus, the Ten might send their Captains less to forbid an encounter outright than "to prevent with their rigorous presence the ruin and riot of so large a gathering, which in such matches usually happens with great mortality": MCCC 3161, 1632/5; also 1636/19, 1666/4. On their being sent to stop a battle altogether, see 1634/11, 1638/7, 1640/1.

74. Other policing forces in Venice included those of various magistrates, especially the Signori della notte and the Cinque alla pace, as well as the forces of various customs agencies and the Arsenal; see Ruggiero, *Violence in Early Renaissance Venice*, 10–15, 33–39. Venice possessed a sort of worker militia composed of Arsenal shipbuilders that was responsible for crowd control on ceremonial occasions, but since these artisans were also among the most enthusiastic fighters at the bridges, this force would have been worse than useless in the *battagliole*, see Davis, *Shipbuilders*, 144–49, 156–74.

75. MCPD, 303/C, filza 33; also Lina Padoan Urban, "Feste ufficiali e trattenimenti privati," 591.

76. Basaglia, "Giustizia criminale e organizzazione dell'autorità centrale," 193–220.

77. The Captains appear to have smashed down artisans' doors almost routinely, using a large beam in the form of a battering ram [*ariete*]: MCCC 3161, 1670/23. For their freedom to search and arrest, see 1666/4; ASV: ACP, bu. 372/ 22.

78. MCCC 3161, 1638/7; also 1632/11.

79. "The Captains . . . also [tried] at a hurried pace to get themselves to the bridge, but thanks to the skill of people pretending to be unable to pass ahead they were held back": MCCC 3161, 1638/8. Another time, when four Captains tried to reach the bridge, "they were with pushing and shoving injured by the people, who themselves were pretending to be upset and jostled by the crowd": 1641/6.

80. "The Captains . . . could not so easily arrive at the bridges, [since] the people ran from one bridge to another and the Captains anxiously followed them. . . . It was said that this was done by the factions to make the . . . Captains run here and there": MCCC 3161, 1641/1, 1637/2; also 1633/7, 1635/3, 1642/ 4.

81. MCCC, 1666/16 and 19.

82. MCCC 3161, 1640/3. On the staggered, monthly elections of the Chiefs of the Ten, see Lane, *Venice: A Maritime Republic*, 116, 257.

83. "But because, as it is said, on holidays the Captains infallibly showed up at the bridge and also early, [the fighters] made an agreement to brawl on a workday": MCCC 3161, 1668/2. On the Captains' obligation to attend the doge at San Marco during the Christmas festivities, see 1641/2, and 1667/49; for All Saints' Day, see 1642/3.

84. As they were for the Jubilee declared by Pope Clement IX in August 1667: MCCC 3161, 1667/3; also 1670/1; and for their dispersing on the Day of the Madonna (8 Sept.): 1667/6; also 1634/5. On fighters' being "awakened and aroused by *maggiori e padrini*" to resist the Captains, see 1633/11; also 1640/1.

85. "Captain Colombina, as a beginner in the position, seeing himself obeyed

and in some esteem for having stopped the earlier furor of knives and stones, persuaded himself that he could . . . completely stop all the violence, but . . . receiving his own share of punches [and] not knowing which way to flee . . . he was bodily . . . thrown down from the bridge into the water": MCCC 3161, 1633/8. On the crowd's mocking a Captain, see 1667/48. On the shredding of a Captain's mantle "by half a dozen fists in that scrimmage and confusion": 1641/2; also 1632/12, and 16, 1637/4.

86. MCCC 3161, 1633/8.

87. As when Captain Sordo "seeing the danger of weapons and stones, pulled out a pistol to terrify the people: at the sight of which everyone gave themselves to flight": MCCC 3161, 1632/12; also 1641/2, 1665/19, 1668/31, 1670/22. For the drawing of pistols provoking a *sassata*, see 1633/14, 1640/10, 1643/1, 1649/5, 1667/48, 1670/8.

88. Even if it took the Captains eight months to track down the offender: MCCC 3161, 1633/10. On Captains' "threatening to take note of [*pigliar in nota*] the leaders," at a bridge fight, see 1632/12; also 1640/1. On their "indicating this one and that one by name," see 1668/6. On their "threatening participants *col mordersi le dita*," see 1667/14; also 1637/2, 1640/2. For their unsuccessful attempts to break up fights with brute force, see 1633/8.

89. For such raids "terrifying everyone . . . into totally abandoning their rage, hostilities, and acrimony," see MCCC 1637/2, 1638/10, 1641/2, 1670/24. Sometimes just the arrival of the Captains and their *sbiraglia* was enough to calm the factions: 1633/8.

90. The Chronicler of the *pugni* makes no mention of *capi* or *padrini* assaulting the Captains at the bridges, but he offers a host of examples involving minor fighters, including: Manina ("Small Hand") of San Polo (for knocking down Captain Tiraferro: MCCC 3161, 1632/14); Franco the Greek (for pushing Captain Colombina into the water: 1633/11); Samuel the Jew (for punching Captain Gottin in the face: 1637/4); and Paulin Cavalotto (for knocking a vice-Captain in the water with a single punch: 1638/5).

91. On the diffidence of the *padrini*, see MCCC 3161, 1640/1. On their keeping on their *ferarrioli*, to avoid being recognized, see 1632/12, 1633/12. On hiding their cuirasses under their shirts and cloaks, see 1633/12. On their helping the Captains "at least with some appearance of respect," see 1638/5.

92. MCCC 3161, 1633/5. On the crowd stoning a Captain and his *sbirri*, to free a prisoner mistakenly assumed to be "someone of the bridges," see 1666/4. For similar outbreaks in San Pietro di Castello, see ASV: CDP, filza 25, 15 Dec. 1649; filza 26, 24 July and 5 Sept. 1651; ASV: Consiglio dei Dieci, parti criminali, reg. 55, 22 Feb. 1638mv.

93. MCCC 3161, 1649/5, 1668/4. For an occasion when "more than a hundred people, *capi* of said war, hid in the houses of noble protectors . . . staying there with many other *caporioni* for more than a month," see 1641/11, 1669/18; also 1633/5 and 10, 1637/13, 1638/10. On the habit of the Ten of ordering secret arrests of the *capi*, see 1667/48.

94. MCCC 3161, 1669/18. If rigorously administered, the strappado could be fatal: 1638/6.

95. On the *broglio* as an arena for negotiating the sentences of captured *padrini*, see MCCC 3161, 1666/4. For its place as an institution in Venetian politics, see Finlay, *Politics in Renaissance Venice*, 22–23, 197–98, 204–6; Queller, *The Venetian Patriciate*, 51–84.

96. As when two leaders from each faction were locked up in 1666, "and it

was rumored that they would have three hoists of the strappado apiece; however, the importunities and solicitations of noble partisans had such force that as a favor the punishment was commuted into so many days in jail": MCCC 3161, 1666/6. On *protettori* paying a fine or bail (*cautione*), see 1637/4. On freeing *padrini* from the Ten's prisons, see 1666/4.

97. MCCC 3161, 1632/14, 1633/5. The strappado, or *corda*, was evidently displayed in San Marco as a warning, or as sign that justice was about to be publicly administered. The Chronicler reports that, "It was decided to give him [an arrested Nicolotti leader] the strappado . . . and the rope was put out at San Marco, but because in similar occasions the *protettori auttorevoli* of the factions, especially of the leaders and tough fighters [*huomeni bravi*] of the bridges, work hard on their account, they were mostly freed from the danger of the rope": 1634/2; also 1632/13, 1633/10, 1666/4.

98. ASV: CDP, filza 20, 23 July 1631; Consiglio dei Dieci, parti criminali, reg. 57, 20 March 1640; also see Ruggiero, *Violence*, 140-42; Chojnacki, "Crime, Punishment, and the Trecento Venetian State," 189–202; cf. Brackett, *Criminal Justice and Crime*, 1–7, 97–138.

99. "These Castellani nobles . . . were much angered by the impudent persistence of [Captain] Sordo ["Deaf"], who indeed seemed like he did not hear them, or pretended to not understand. Therefore [to make the point], one angry gentleman tore off of him half [his] moustache. . . .": MCCC 3161, 1638/7; also see 1640/1.

100. "And because this Captain [Pollesina] persisted in impeding the common satisfaction [of staging a *frotta*] some *partiggiani auttorevoli* of the Castellani . . . called said Pollesina to them, and they locked him in a storeroom, keeping the key to themselves, until the battle was over": MCCC 3161, 1637/3; also 1635/2.

101. Later reduced to just six months: ASV: CDP, filza 20, 7 Jan. and 27 Feb. 1631mv; 8 March and 20 July 1632. Rather harsher punishments might be imposed on nobles who abused Captains or other officials of the Ten outside of the context of the *battagliole*—in particular, for committing violence within the offices of the Ten themselves: ASV: Consiglio dei Dieci, parti criminali, reg. 55, 27 March 1638 and 11 Feb. 1638mv.

102. In trying to break up the fighting, the Captains were often "reprimanded, reproved, and vilified with some feeling by the *auttorevoli fattionarij*" on the sidelines: MCCC 3161, 1633/12, 1634/12.

103. "The *Capitanio Grande* was expressly and rigorously ordered . . . to stop this war, with the threat to deprive him of his office and his mantle": MCCC 3161, 1641/4; also 1633/5. In 1632 a Captain was jailed for three months for failing to stop the *battagliola*, and in 1638 two Captains were imprisoned for two months each, see 1632/18, 1638/10; also see 1640/2, 1667/62. On the dangers for Captains caught in a *sassata*, see 1670/22–23.

104. "Everyone reasoned that the next morning [Captain Tiraferro] would relate everything that had happened to the Chiefs [of the Ten] . . . but this did not happen, maybe because making [such] a report there could have resulted in [still] greater evil and misfortune to himself": MCCC 3161, 1634/12. In 1640 Captain Polesina "was put in the cells until the end of the month because he did not report on the disorders that transpired at the Frescada on the Castellani side": 1640/2; also 1641/11, 1667/49. On Captains going into hiding to avoid being deprived of their *mantello*, see 1632/18, 1642/2.

105. Thus, after the *Capitanio grande* Barbanegra was told to stop an encounter on pain of losing his position. "[T]hese threats upset Barbanegra not a little . . . firstly, because he recognized that it was impossible that he could deal with a Venetian people so unrestrained and so resolute in those wars . . . well knowing as he did that it was not prudent to irritate a people that against the whole world wants to satisfy itself. In the second place, it was a question of his own interests, that is, [the possibility] of being deprived of his own office and position, which was his living and his reputation": MCCC 3161, 1641/4–5.

106. His plan had some success—although in the process several of his guards and Captains were abused or thrown in the water—for the two armies ended up placidly staging *mostre* at different bridges: the Nicolotti at the Ponte dei Servi and the Castellani at the Ponte di San Marziale: MCCC 3161, 1636/16–18.

107. MCCC 3161, 1641/5–6. The Chronicler called this encounter *Quella delle Barche.*

108. On the Captains' use of spies, see MCCC 3161, 1633/5, 1637/13, 1649/5; also ASV: Avogaria di Comun, penale, bu. 141/8, f. 1r. and 333.10.

109. "Such [news of the impending encounter] being spread . . . about all the neighboring parishes, it gave occasion to everyone to find himself a place: in the balconies, on the roof tiles, and the sun decks [*altane*]; others providing themselves with benches and awnings made at night, others with boats, skiffs, and gondolas in the canal, so that one could not call it canal, but land": MCCC 3161, 1632/3; also 1635/4. On the Captains coming beforehand to haul away the boats and benches, see 1636/18, 1643/8, 1667/48, 1673/14.

110. When the "Ponte di S. Barnabà was guarded at all the hours by the Captains, such that no one dared to draw near, the people decided to find another bridge that would serve to realize their wicked and scandalous inclinations, and that was [the bridge] of San Marziale": MCCC 3161, 1670/10. In should be noted, however, that officially the stands were ordered knocked down as much to protect as to frustrate spectators; when *battagliole* degenerated into rock fights, the flimsy stands often impeded the flight of onlookers trying to get out of the way, or, even worse, collapsed under the sudden, hasty movement of the fleeing audience: 1670/14.

111. Compare with policing forces at the disposal of absolutist regimes elsewhere, see Brackett, *Criminal Justice and Crime,* esp. 30–96; Hughes, "Fear and Loathing in Bologna and Rome," 97–116; Williams, *The Police of Paris,* esp. 42–52, 189–237; Weisser, "Crime and Punishment in Early Modern Spain," 111; Raeff, "The Well-ordered Police State," 1221–43.

112. MCCC 3161, 1666/19; Moryson, *Shakespeare's Europe,* 163–66.

113. MCCC 3161, 1634/12. Another time the Chronicler reported: "At this time, and for the entire month of November, no one dared to approach the usual fighting bridges, because the Captains were everywhere, together with the *barche longhe*; hence everyone feared and everyone obeyed; nor did the plebs risk to gather . . . for the people are quiet, not moving from fear, unless they are aroused and provoked by . . . their betters": 1633/11; also 1632/11, 1638/1, 1640/1, 1667/61.

114. He was known as Biondo, or "Blondie": MCCC 3161, 1668/35. Usually two Captains were assigned per faction: 1632/5, 1638/4, 1640/2.

115. MCCC 3161, 1636/17.

116. The *sbirri* were most likely to join in the battle if their captain had been lured away: "The *sbirri*, seeing themselves without their leader, who was Nicolotto

by birth, profited from this loss themselves, [by] joining up with the Nicolotti squads, some of them following [the squads] into the *frotta*": MCCC 3161, 1635/ 2–3.

117. MCCC 3161, 1632/14, 1635/10, 1638/5. Also, for the state official Lorenzo Piva, who was "in the mob badly bitten and very tightly squeezed in the testicles, such that he was carried [away] from the ground almost dead; from the memory of which insult he asserted the vendetta with every [possible] disorder and misfortune," see 1639/10.

118. Factional arguments at the *broglio* once led "two nobles, one of the Morosini house and the other of the Ca' Magno to fight between themselves . . . about the war; they traded punches, putting a hand to their daggers": MCCC 3161, 1643/8; also 1634/15. On the often extreme age of the Chiefs of the Ten and those who held the highest offices generally in Venice, see Grendler, "The Leaders of the Venetian State, 1540–1609: A Prosopographical Analysis," 35–85; and Finlay, *Politics in Renaissance Venice*, 130–31.

119. "Thus it seemed that in the month of September the same prohibitions [against the *battagliole*] would not be so rigorously enforced by the new Chiefs of the [Ten], whence some small fights were carried out before the Captains would come, and they would only show up late in the day," see MCCC 3161, 1670/11. On some new Chiefs of the month "tacitly giving permission" for *battagliole*, see 1649/6, 1666/16. On others denying it, see 1666/12.

120. On the popular understanding that not sending the Captains to the bridges represented the Ten's tacit permission for *battagliole*, see MCCC 3161, 1668/18, 1666/19, 1667/4. On the Captains "coming there spontaneously, without assignment, only to have a comfortable place to watch the War": 1638/2.

121. As the Chronicler observed, the *battagliole* "permit the mass of youths and the plebs [to receive] military training and allow every sort of grade and status of person, including the private individual, the freedom to give vent with his fist to the arguments and pretensions that typically well up within the people, and that otherwise would end up [decided] by steel, with the effusion of their own blood": MCCC 3161, 1670/25. He also noted that, thanks to a battle (ending in a *sassata*), "the souls of the people had become rather placated": 1670/38; also 1632/14, 1633/5, 1939/21, 1665/13, 1670/13.

122. MCCC 3161, 1670/9; Tassini, *Curiosità veneziane*, 532.

123. MCCC 3161, 1642/3.

124. Unfortunately, the veterans seem to have fared no better at San Barnabà than they did at Candia. As they were forced to retreat yet again, the Nicolotti called out to them, "Hey! Hey! Sailors of the fleet! Let's go, soldiers of Candia!"; MCCC 3161, 1670/3; also 1669/9–10, 19; 1670/18–19.

125. Thus, marginal jottings and formal *proclame* indicate that the edict of 15 November 1522 was reissued at least seven times; that of 21 November 1536 four times; that of 23 August 1555 eight times; and those of 11 September 1611 and 29 November 1644 at least a dozen each, see ASV: CDP, filze 2, 3, 4, 13, 23, and *passim*.

126. Finlay, in *Politics in Renaissance Venice*, 49–59, cites Priuli, Sanudo, and legislation of the Senate and Collegio in this regard.

127. Giovanni Sagredo was removed as doge after less than a day and Alvise Contarini eventually elected in his place, in a drama that had striking similarities to the *battagliole* themselves. The *scalzi* who opposed Sagredo formed a crowd in San Marco and tossed paving stones that they had dug up from the *fondamente* with

their knives, while gentlemen in the crowd showed their support by waving their handkerchiefs. The *sbirraglie* of the Ten fired off their muskets in the air, provoked a *sassata*, and were thrown in the water by the mob. (See Galibert, *Histoire de la République de Venise*, 424; da Mosto *I dogi di Venezia nella vita pubblica e privata*, 414–16.) Some maintained that this opposition to Sagredo was no more than a few boatmen cobbled together by his noble enemies. This explanation may have appealed to both authoritarian aristocrats of the day and to later scholars, but it still fails to account for the wealth of popular and satiric material provoked by the event. For a contemporary account of this poorly studied instance of a popular uprising in Venice, see MCCC miscellanea 104, *Semi della guerra*, cited in Romanin, *Storia documentata di Venezia*, 7:334–36n4.

128. MCCC 3161, 1643/1, 1670/26.

129. Thus, the "*padrini* of both factions feared . . . that they would necessarily incur the indignation of the Chiefs [of the Ten], in having to account for the disobedience and disrespect shown to their officers": MCCC 3161, 1638/5; also see 1633/5.

130. The Chronicle notes that "at that time neither the *mostre* nor the war was prohibited; on the contrary, the factions were free to satisfy themselves: so it had been ordered by Those who Command [the Ten], as long as it was with the presence of the Captains": MCCC 3161, 1670/14.

131. MCCC 3161, 1669/3–4, 8.

132. For the Captains allowing a short-lived *frotta*, followed by twenty-five *mostre*, and then clearing the area, see MCCC 3161, 1667/12; also 1666/16, and 1669/2–3. On their involvement as referees, see 1669/17, 1670/6–8, 12.

133. When they were properly *rollate* the squads could be formed so tightly and under such control that not even factional messengers could push their way through them: MCCC 3161, 1667/23. For long successions of *mostre*, see 1668/14, 22, 34; 1669/2, 4, 7; 1670/6, 14–15, 18.

134. MCCC 3161, 1665/10, 1667/6, 1669/17, 1670/6, 9, 23.

135. For the Captains assiduously seeking out and arresting those who threw stones and roof tiles while allowing the regular Sunday battles to continue, see MCCC 3161, 1666/6; also 1669/18, 1670/9, 24. After at least one *sassata*, however, the Captains made no move at all: 1666/20.

136. MCCC 3161, 1669/8.

137. For example, after one battle some fishermen "began to behave insolently, talking freely around the fishmarket how the Castellani had quaked in the bowels when the Nicolotti had come, and that not being any longer able to resist [the Nicolotti's] fists, they were forced to resort to knives and daggers": MCCC 3161, 1640/3; also see 1673/9. That the use of arms was seen as a sign of poor factional discipline, see 1649/4.

138. MCCC 3161, 1670/24. For a fighter expelled from the bridges by the *padrini* and *protettore* of his own faction, see 1665/21–22. For someone banished by the other faction, see 1666/23, 1670/3.

139. All of which happened during and after the battle on Saint Simon's Day (28 Oct.) in 1669, put on for the Prince and Princess Borghese: MCCC 3161, 1669/17–18.

140. In particular, the disastrous *battagliola* already noted of 4 September 1611, and those said to have occurred in 1606 (recalled in MCCC 3161, 1632/9) and 1621 (1665/18); also see 1634/15, 1639/22, 1641/11.

141. MCCC 3161, 1642/3, 1669/18. On the Venetian state's weakness in

enforcing its laws on the *terraferma* in the face of popular and noble resistence, see Wright, "Venetian Law and Order: A Myth?," 192–202.

142. MCCC 3161, 1670/10–11.

Epilogue

1. MCCC 3161, 1574/53, 1670/19.

2. See especially the views of *battagliole* from the collected views of Venice by D. Lovisa (1720) and Gabriel Bella (1780s), in Tamassia Mazzarotto, *Feste veneziane*, 44–45; and MCAF, M.24062.

3. Tamassia Mazzarotto, *Feste veneziane*, 50n12, citing Tassini, *Curiosità veneziane*, 10.

4. "Spineless": cited in Romano *Patricians and Popolani*, 9; Tamassia Mazzarotto, *Feste veneziane*, 44; Tassini, *Curiosità veneziane*, 594; Tenenti, "The Sense of Space and Time," 19. This notion, that "cynical men stabilized the commune by encouraging private delusions," has already been examined and rejected in the context of popular religion; see Trexler, "Florentine Religious Experience," 9–11.

5. In a letter supposedly written to Basnatio Sorsi, "Descrittione piacevole," 60–61. Finardo went on to ask Sorsi if, "in a few stanzas," he would care to defend the *pugni* from such an attack.

6. MCCC 3161, 1637/10, 1641/11, 1670/9 and 12.

7. MCCC 3161, 1635/13, 1637/10, 1641/11, 1670/8, 1673/15. Muir sees evidence of a "widening cultural separation . . . between the Venetian nobles and the lower classes" already in the later sixteenth century, see *Civic Ritual*, 164.

8. Thus, "The Nicolotti went first and [staged] more than a hundred *mostre*, but twenty-five of these found no response, which gave occasion to the Nicolotto to accuse his enemy of base cowardice, with a thousand insults [coming] from the factional plebes": MCCC 3161, 1669/4.

9. Alderigi and Aliverti, *Il gioco del ponte di Pisa*, 24–26; Heywood, *Palio and Ponte*, 110–31.

10. Saint Disdier, *La Ville et la République de Venise*, 449.

11. The Chronicler of the *pugni* likewise wrote of one or both factions plotting "the ultimate battle" (*la battaglia assoluta*), of the factions wishing to see their opponents "totally extinct," of their "never giving in to [the other's] arrogance and insults," and of an encounter that "should be the decider and arbitrator of all the pretensions asserted by these two factions for so many centuries": MCCC 3161, 1666/25, 1668/8, 1673/13.

12. Biblioteca Marciana, Ms It, classe V, codice 481, no. 7786, p. 98, as interpreted by Tassini, *Curiosità veneziane*, 10; also see MCCC 3643/7. On firefighting in the city of Venice, see Davis, *Shipbuilders*, 169–74. For a similar attempt by a priest to calm a riotous crowd, see Muir, "The Virgin on the Street Corner," 29.

13. See, however, MCPD, 303/C, filza 33, p. 16.

14. MCCC 3643/3, filza 28.

BIBLIOGRAPHY

Archival Sources
Archivio di Stato, Venice

Avogaria di Comun, *processi criminali e civili*
Compilazione leggi
    Baccanali, busta 85
    Pugni, busta 321
Consiglio dei Dieci
    Parti criminali, reg. 55, 57, 61
    Proclami, filze 1–35
    Suppliche, buste 3 and 4
Dieci Savii sopra alle Decime in Rialto, *catastici*, buste 424 and 434
Necrologie, buste 842, 843, 865

Archivio di Stato, Pisa

Il gioco del ponte: origini e attuale ripristino (Pisa, 1935)
"Miscellanea manuscritti"
    100: *Origine del giuoco del ponte in Pisa e sue battaglie numerate*
        Orazione per la benedizione delle bandiere nel giuoco del ponte, 1785

Museo Civico Correr

Codici Cicogna
    861: *Poesia di Don Vicenzo Cassantini*
    1345/3: *Pugni . . . a Venezia*
    1650: *Estratti dalli Diarii di Marino Sanuto*
    2078: Untitled
    2430: *Elenco di tutti li giuochi*
    2936/10: *Poesia di Camillo Nadalin*

3161: *Battagliola ovvero guerra tra Nicolotti e Castellani*
3231/32: *La vittoria della Guerra e Mostre de pugni ottentute dalli Nicolotti contro li Castellani, 25 Feb 1687.*
3235: *Pugni a San Giuliano*
3257–58: *Avvisi*
3276/2: *Pugillatus Venetius*
3278: *Origine delle guerre dei pugni*
3280/6: *Le guerre dei pugni prohibite*
3643/3: *Forza d'ercole*
Codici Gradenigo
 25: *Guerra di canne fatta a 1574*
 155/6: *Castellani e Nicolotti*
Miscellanea MS.
 P.D. 303/C, filza 33
 P.D. 2819
Opuscoli diversi: 11740–44: *Le feste e triomfi fatti*

Other Archives

Biblioteca Marciana: MS. It, classe V, codice 481 (= 7786)
Parish Churches of San Trovaso and S. Pantalon
 libri dei battesimi & matrimoni

Secondary Sources

"A True Description and Direction of What is Most Worthy to Be Seen in All Italy." *The Harleian Miscellany*, 5:1–40. New York, 1965.
Addison, Joseph. *Remarks on Several Parts of Italy . . . in the Years 1701, 1702, 1703*. London, 1718.
Alderigi, Marco, and Maria Ines Aliverti. *Il gioco del ponte di Pisa: Memoria e ricordo in una città*. Pisa, Italy, 1981.
Baldick, Robert. *The Duel: A History of Duelling*. London: 1965.
Basaglia, Enrico. "Giustizia criminale e organizzazione dell'autorità centrale. La Repubblica di Venezia e la questione delle taglie in denaro. Secoli XVI–XVII." In *Stato, società, e giustizia nella Repubblica veneta. Secoli XV–XVIII*, 2 vols., edited by Gaetano Cozzi, Rome, 1985.
Beccaria, Cesare Bonesana. *An Essay on Crimes and Punishments*. English translation, London, 1775.
Becker, Marvin B. "Changing Patterns of Violence and Justice in Fourteenth- and Fifteenth-Century Florence." *Comparative Studies in Society and History* 18 (1976): 281–96.
———. *Civility and Society in Western Europe, 1300–1600*. Bloomington, 1988.
Bellavitis, Giorgio, and Giandomenico Romanelli. *Le città nella storia d'Italia: Venezia*. Bari, Italy, 1985.
Beltrami, Daniele. *Storia della popolazione di Venezia dalla fine del secolo XVI alla caduta della Repubblica*. Padua, Italy, 1954.
Benedetti, M. Rocco. "Le feste e trionfi fatte in onore di Enrico 3zo re di Francia." Venice, 1574.
Bossy, John. "The Counter Reformation and the People of Catholic Europe." *Past and Present* 47 (1970): 51–70.

———. "Godparenthood: The Fortunes of a Social Institution in Early Modern Christianity." In *Religion and Society in Early Modern Europe, 1500–1800*, edited by Kaspar von Greyerz, 194–201. London, 1984.

Brackett, John K. *Criminal Justice and Crime in Late Renaissance Florence, 1537–1609*. Cambridge, England, 1992.

Brailsford, Dennis. "Morals and Maulers: The Ethics of Early Pugilism." *Journal of Sports History* 12 (1985): 126–42.

Braudel, Fernand. *Civilization and Capitalism, 1400–1800*. 3 vols. New York, 1975.

Bryson, Frederick R. *The Point of Honor in Sixteenth-Century Italy*. Chicago, 1935.

———. *The Sixteenth-Century Italian Duel*. Chicago, 1938.

Burke, Peter. *The Historical Anthropology of Early Modern Italy*. Cambridge, Mass., 1987.

———. *Popular Culture in Early Modern Europe*. New York, 1978.

Cameron, Iain A. "The Police of Eighteenth-Century France." *European Studies Review* 7 (1977): 47–75.

Caravia, Alessandro. "La verra antiga dei Castellani, Canaruoli, e Gnatti, con la morte de Giurco e Gnagni, in lengua brava." Venice, 1550. Reprint. Retitled as "La Guerra de' Nicolotti e Castellani dell'anno 1521." In *Poesie di diversi autori antichi*, edited by Bortolommeo Gamba. Venice, 1817.

Casola, Pietro. *Viaggio a Gerusalemme*. Milan, 1855.

Casoni, Giovanni. "Storia civile e politica." In *Venezia e le sue Lagune*, Venice, 1847.

Chojnacki, Stanley. "Crime, Punishment, and the Trecento Venetian State." In *Violence and Civil Disorder in Italian Cities, 1200–1500*, edited by Lauro Martines, 184–228, Berkeley, 1972.

Cicogna, Emmanuele. *Saggio di bibliografia veneziana*, 2 vols. New York, 1967.

Cipolla, Carlo. *Faith, Reason, and the Plague in Seventeenth-Century Tuscany*. New York, 1981.

Corbin, John, and Marie Corbin. *Urbane Thought: Culture and Class in an Andalusian City*. Aldershot, England, 1987.

Coryat, Thomas. *Coryat's Crudities*. Glasgow, 1905.

Cozzi, Gaetano. "Authority and the Law in Renaissance Venice." In *Renaissance Venice*, edited by John Hale, 293–345. London, 1973.

———. "Considerazioni sull'amministrazione della giustizia nella Repubblica di Venezia. secc. XV–XVI. In *Florence and Venice: Comparisons and Relations*. Vol. 2, *Cinquecento*, 117–26.

Cozzi, Gaetano, and Michael Knapton. *La Repubblica di Venezia nell'età moderna*. In *Storia d'Italia*, edited by Giuseppe Galasso, vol. 12. Torino, 1986.

Cracco, Giorgio. "Patriziato e oligarchia a Venezia nel Tre-Quattrocento." In *Florence and Venice: Comparisons and Relations*. Vol. 1, *Quattrocento*. Florence, 1979, 71–90.

Cronica veneta, d'autore incerto, che comincia dall'anno CCCCXXI sino all'anno MCCCCXXXII. Italy, 16th century.

Crouzet-Pavan, Élisabeth, *"Sopra le acque salse": Espaces, pouvoir, et société à Venise, à la fin du Moyen Âge*. Rome, 1992.

———. "Violence, société et pouvoir à Venise. XIV–XV siècles: Forme et évolution de rituels Urbains." *Mélanges de L'École Française de Rome* 96 (1984): 903–36.

da Mosto, Andrea. *I dogi di Venezia nella vita pubblica e privata*. Milan, 1960.

Dal Medico, Antonio. *Raccolta di canzoni*. Venice, 1848.

Darnton, Robert. *The Kiss of Lamurette: Reflections in Cultural History.* New York, 1990.

Davis, John H. *People of the Mediterranean: An Essay in Comparative Anthropology.* London, 1977.

Davis, Natalie Z. *Fiction in the Archives: Pardon Tales and Their Tellers in Sixteenth-Century France.* Stanford, Calif., 1987.

———. *Society and Culture in Early Modern France.* Stanford, Calif., 1975.

Davis, Robert C. *Shipbuilders of the Venetian Arsenal: Workers and Workplace in the Preindustrial City.* Baltimore, 1991.

de Ville, Antonio. "Pyctomachia veneta. Seu pugna venetorum in ponte annua." In *Thesaurus Antiquitatum et Historiarum Italiae,* vol. 5, pp. 368–70. Leuven, 1722.

Doglio, Maria Luisa. "La Letteratura ufficiale e l'oratoria celebrativa." In *Storia della cultura veneta,* vol. 4, no. 1, Vicenza, Italy, 1983. 163–87.

Dorigo, Wladimiro. *Venezia: origini: Fondamenti, ipotesi, metodi.* Milan, 1983.

Dundes, Alan, and Alessandro Falassi. *La Terra in Piazza: An Interpretation of the Palio of Siena.* Berkeley, 1975.

Dunning, Eric. "Social Bonding and Violence in Sport." In *The Quest for Excitement: Sport and Leisure in the Civilizing Process,* edited by Norbert Elias and Eric Dunning, 224–44. Oxford, 1986.

Elias, Norbert. "An Essay on Sports and Violence." In *The Quest for Excitement: Sport and Leisure in the Civilizing Process,* edited by Norbert Elias and Eric Dunning, 150–74. Oxford, 1986.

Evelyn, John. *Diary and Correspondence.* London, 1854.

Finlay, Robert. *Politics in Renaissance Venice.* New Brunswick, N.J., 1985.

———. "The Venetian Republic as a Gerontocracy: Age and Politics in the Renaissance." *Journal of Medieval and Renaissance Studies* 8 (1978): 157–78.

Ford, John. *Prizefighting: The Age of Regency Boximania.* New York, 1972.

Fortini Brown, Patricia. "Measured Friendship, Calculated Pomp: The Ceremonial Welcomes of the Venetian Republic." In *"All the World's a stage . . .": Art and Pageantry in the Renaissance and Baroque. Part 1, Triumphal Celebrations and the Rituals of Statecraft,* ed. Barbara Wisch and Susan Scott Munshower, 136–86. Papers in Art History from the Pennsylvania State University, vol. 6. University Park, Penn., 1990.

Foscarini, Marco. *Della letteratura veneziana ed alti scritti intorno ad essa.* Venice, 1854.

Fraser, Ronald. *The Pueblo.* London, 1973.

Galibert, Léon. *Histoire de la République de Venise.* Paris, 1847.

Galicciolli, Giambattista. *Delle memorie venete antiche profane ed ecclesiastiche.* 8 vols. Venice, 1795.

Gamba, Bartolommeo. *Collezione delle migliori opere scritte in dialetto veneziano.* Venice, 1817.

Gay, Franco. "Fantasticherie galleggianti." *Revista marittima* 115 (1982): 35–56.

Geertz, Clifford. "Deep Play: Notes on the Balinese Cockfight." In *The Interpretation of Cultures: Selected Essays,* 412–453. New York, 1973.

———. "Thick Description: Towards an Interpretive Theory of Culture." In *The Interpretation of Cultures,* 3–30. New York, 1973.

Georgelin, Jean. "Venise: Le Climat et l'histoire." *Studi veneziani* n.s. 18 (1989): 313–19.

Gilmore, David D. *Aggression and Community: Paradoxes of Andalusian Culture.* New Haven, Conn., 1987.

————. *Manhood in the Making: Cultural Concepts of Masculinity.* New Haven, Conn., 1990.

————. "The Shame of Dishonor." In *Honor and Shame and the Unity of the Mediterranean*, edited by David Gilmore, 8–16. Washington, D.C., 1987.

Glixon, Jonathan. "A Musicians' Union in Sixteenth-Century Venice." *Journal of the American Musicological Society* 36 (1983): 392–421.

————. "Music at the Scuole in the Age of Andrea Gabrieli." In *Andrea Gabrieli e il suo tempo,* Atti del convegno internazionale a Venezia, 16–18 Settembre 1985, edited by Francesco Degrada, 59–74.

Gray, W. Russell. "For Whom the Bell Tolled: The Decline of British Prize Fighting in the Victorian Era." *Journal of Popular Culture* 21 (1987): 53–64.

Grendler, Paul F. "The Leaders of the Venetian State, 1540–1609: A Prosopographical Analysis." *Studi veneziani* n.s. 19 (1990): 35–85.

Grubb, James. "When Myths Lose Power: Four Decades of Venetian Historiography." *Journal of Modern History* 58 (1986): 43–94.

Guttmann, Allen. "English Sports Spectators: The Restoration to the Early Nineteenth Century." *Journal of Sports History* 12 (1985): 103–25.

Hale, John. "Military Academies on the Venetian Terraferma in the Early Seventeenth Century." *Studi veneziani* n.s. 16 (1973): 273–95.

Henricks, Thomas S. "The Democratization of Sport in Eighteenth Century England." *Journal of Popular Culture* 18 (1984): 3–20.

Herzfeld, Michael. "'As in Your Own House': Hospitality, Ethnography, and the Stereotype of Mediterranean Society." In *Honor and Shame and the Unity of the Mediterranean*, edited by David D. Gilmore, 75–89. Washington, D.C., 1987.

Heywood, William. *Palio and Ponte: An Account of the Sports of Central Italy from the Age of Dante to the Twentieth Century.* 2d ed. New York, 1969.

Howells, William D. *Venetian Life.* Edinburgh, 1873.

Hughes, Steven. "Fear and Loathing in Bologna and Rome: The Papal Police in Perspective." *Journal of Social History* 21 (1987): 97–116.

Lane, Frederic C. *Venice: A Maritime Republic.* Baltimore, 1973.

Mackenney, Richard. *Tradesmen and Traders: The World of the Guilds in Venice and Europe, c. 1250–c. 1650.* London, 1987.

Malombra, Bartolomeo. "Nuova canzone nella felicissima vittoria contro infideli." Venice, 1571.

Marvin, Garry. *Bullfight.* Oxford, 1988.

Menarini, Alberto. *Uomini e bestie nel dialetto bolognese.* Bologna, 1970.

Miles, Henry Downes. *Pugilistica: The History of British Boxing.* Edinburgh, 1906.

Molmenti, Pompeo. *Venice: Its Individual Growth from the Earliest Beginnings to the Fall of the Republic.* 3 vols. Translated by Horatio Brown. Chicago, 1906.

Morgan, Jane, Christopher O'Neill, and Rom Harré. *Nicknames: Their Origins and Social Consequences.* London, 1979.

Moryson, Fynes. *An Itinerary.* Glasgow, 1907.

————. *Shakespeare's Europe: Unpublished Chapters of Fynes Moryson's "Itinerary."* London, 1903.

Muchembled, Robert. *Popular Culture and Elite Culture in France, 1400–1750.* Baton Rouge, La., 1985.

Muir, Edward. *Civic Ritual in Renaissance Venice.* Princeton, 1981.

————. "Images of Power: Art and Pagentry in Renaissance Venice." *American Historical Review* 84 (1979): 16–52.

————. *Mad Blood Stirring: Vendetta and Factions in Friuli during the Renaissance.* Baltimore, 1993.

————. "Observing Trifles." In *Microhistory and the Lost Peoples of Europe*, edited by Edward Muir and Guido Ruggiero, vii–xxviii. Baltimore, 1991.

————. "The Virgin on the Street Corner: The Place of the Sacred in Italian Cities," in *Religion and Culture in the Renaissance and Reformation*, edited by Steven Ozment. Kirksville, Mo., 1989.

Muir, Edward, and Ronald F. E. Weissman. "Social and Symbolic Places in Renaissance Venice and Florence." In *The Power of Place: Bringing together geographical and sociological imaginations*, edited by John A. Agnew and James S. Duncan, 81–103. Boston, 1989.

Muraro, Maria Teresa. "Le feste a Venezia e le sue manifestazzion rappresentative: Le Compagnie della Calza e *Le Momarie*," in *Storia della cultura Veneta*, vol. 3, no. 3. Vicenza, Italy, 1981, 318–28.

Muratori, Lodovico Antonio. *Dissertazione sopra le antichità italiane.* 3 vols. Milan, 1751.

Murphy, Michael D. "Coming of Age in Seville: The Structuring of a Riteless Passage to Manhood." *Journal of Anthropological Research* 39 (1983): 376–92.

Nalin, Camillo. *Pronostici e versi.* 5th ed. Venice, 1909.

Padoan Urban, Lina. "Feste ufficiali e trattenimenti privati." In *Storia della cultura veneta,* vol. 4, no. 1. Vicenza, Italy, 1983, 475–500.

Paoletti, Ermolao. *Il fiore di Venezia.* Venice, 1840.

Perocco, Guido, and Antonio Salvadori. *Civiltà di Venezia.* 3 vols. Venice: 1973.

Petter, Nicolaas, and Robbert Cors. *Klare Onderrichtinge der Voortreffelijcke Worstel-Kunst.* Amsterdam, 1674.

Pitt-Rivers, Julian. "Honour and Social Status." In *Honour and Shame: The Values of Mediterranean Society*, edited by J. G. Peristiany, 21–77. Chicago: 1966.

————. *The People of the Sierra.* Chicago, 1954.

————. "Spiritual Kinship in Andalusia." In *The Fate of Shechem, or the Politics of Sex: Essays in the Anthropology of the Mediterranean.* Cambridge, England, 1977.

Povolo, Claudio. "Aspetti e problemi dell'amministrazione della giustizia penale nella Repubblica di Venezia. Secoli XVI–XVII." In *Stato, società, e giustizia nella Repubblica veneta. Secoli XV– XVIII*, 2 vols, edited by Gaetano Cozzi, Rome, 1985.

Press, Irwin. *The City as Context: Urbanism and Behavioural Constraints in Sevilla.* Urbana, 1979.

Pullan, Brian. *Rich and Poor in Renaissance Venice: The Social Institutions of a Catholic State.* Cambridge, Mass., 1971.

————. "The Scuole Grandi of Venice: Some Further Thoughts." In *Christianity and the Renaissance: Image and Religious Imagination in the Quattrocento*, edited by Timothy Verdon and John Henderson, Syracuse, N.Y., 1990.

Queller, Donald. *The Venetian Patriciate: Reality versus Myth.* Champagne-Urbana, 1986.

Rapp, Richard. *Industry and Economic Decline in Seventeenth-Century Venice.* Cambridge, Mass., 1976.

Rizzo, Tiziano. *I ponti di Venezia.* Rome, 1983.

Roffaré, Luigi. *La Repubblica di Venezia e lo sport.* Venice, 1931.

Rogers, Susan Carol. "Gender in Southwestern France: The Myth of Male Dominance Revisited." *Anthropology* 9 (1985): 65–86.

Romanin, Samuele. *Storia documentata di Venezia.* 10 vols. Venice, 1972.

Romano, Dennis. *Patricians and Popolani: The Social Foundations of the Venetian Renaissance State.* Baltimore, 1987.

Romano, Pietro. *Roma nelle sue strade e nelle sue piazze.* Rome, 1950.

Rossetti, Bartolomeo. *I bulli di Roma.* Rome, 1979.

Ruggiero, Guido. *The Boundaries of Eros: Sex Crime and Sexuality in Renaissance Venice.* New York, 1985.

———. *Violence in Early Renaissance Venice.* New Brunswick, N.J., 1980.

Saint Disdier, Alexandre. *La Ville et la Republique de Venise.* Paris, 1680.

Sansovino, Francesco. *Venetia, città nobilissima e singolare.* Venice, 1604.

Sanuto, Marino. *I Diarii.* Venice, 1879–1903.

———. *De origine, sitù et magistratibus urbis Venetae, a ouvero, la città di Venetia (1493–1530).* Critical edition by Angela Caracciolo Arico. Milan, 1980.

Schama, Simon. *The Embarrassment of Riches: An Interpretation of Dutch Culture in the Golden Age.* New York, 1988.

Schneider, Jane, and Peter Schneider. *Culture and Political Economy in Western Sicily.* New York, 1976.

Setton, Kenneth. *Venice, Austria, and the Turks in the Seventeenth Century.* Philadelphia, 1991.

Silverman, Sydel. "The Palio of Siena: Game, Ritual, or Politics?" In *Urban Life in the Renaissance,* ed. S. Zimmerman and R. Weissman, 224–39. Newark, Del., 1989.

Skippon, Philip. *An Account of a Journey Made thro' Part of the Low- Countries, Germany, Italy and France.* In *Voyages,* 6 vols. A. Churchill and J. Churchill, eds. London, 1746.

Sorsi, Basnatio. "Scherzi e Descrittione piacevole della Guerra dei Pugni tra Nicolotti, e Castellani. Quaderni in Lingua Venetiana." Venice, 1663.

Tamassia Mazzarotto, Biana. *Le feste veneziane.* Florence, 1961.

Tassini, Giuseppe. *Curiosità veneziane, ovvero origini delle denomiazioni stradali di Venezia.* 2 vols. Venice, 1863.

———. *Feste, spettacoli: Divertimenti e piaceri degli antichi veneziani.* Venice, 1961.

Tax Freeman, Susan. *Neighbors: The Social Contract in a Castilian Hamlet.* Chicago, 1970.

Tenenti, Alberto. "The Sense of Space and Time in the Venetian World of the 15th and 16th Centuries." In *Renaissance Venice,* edited by John Hale. London, 1973.

Thamer, Hans-Ulrich. "On the Use and Abuse of Handicraft: Journeyman Culture and Enlightened Public Opinion in 18th and 19th Century Germany." In *Understanding Popular Culture: Europe from the Middle Ages to the Nineteenth Century,* edited by Steven Kaplan, 275–300. Berlin, 1984.

Trexler, Richard. "Correre la terra: Collective Insults in the Late Middle Ages." In *Mélanges de L'École Française de Rome, Moyen Age–Temps Modernes* 96 (1984): 845–902.

———. "Florentine Religious Experience: The Sacred Image." *Studies in the Renaissance* 19 (1972): 7–41.

———. "Ritual in Florence: Adolescence and Salvation in the Renaissance." In The Pursuit of Holiness in Late Medieval and Renaissance, edited by Charles Trinkaus and Heiko Oberman, 200–64.

Ughelli, Ferdinando. *Italia Sacra, sive de Episcopis Italiae et Insularum Adjacen-tium Rebusque ab iis Praellare Gestis.* Venice, 1717–22.

Weisser, Michael. "Crime and Punishment in Early Modern Spain." In *Crime and the Law: The Social History of Crime in Western Europe since 1500,* ed. V. A. C. Gatrell, Bruce Lenman, and Geoffrey Parker, 76–96. London, 1980.

Williams, Alan. *The Police of Paris, 1718–1789.* Baton Rouge, La., 1979.

Wright, A. D. "Venetian Law and Order: A Myth?" *London University Institute of Historical Research Bulletin* 53 (1982): 192–202.

Zago, Roberto. *I Nicolotti.* Padua, Italy, 1982.

Zompini, Gaetano. *Le arte che vanno per via nella città di Venezia.* Venice: 1968.

Zorattini, Pier Cesare Ioly. "Gli erbrei a Venezia, Padova e Verona," In *Storia della cultura veneta,* vol. 3, no. 1. Vicenza, Italy, 1980.

INDEX